Contemporary Worship M
Everyday Musical Lives

While Contemporary Worship Music arose out of a desire to relate the music of the church to the music of everyday life, this function can quickly be called into question by the diversity of musical lives present in contemporary society. Mark Porter examines the relationship between individuals' musical lives away from a Contemporary Worship Music environment and their diverse experiences of music within it, presenting important insights into the complex and sometimes contradictory relationships between congregants' musical lives within and outside of religious worship. Through detailed ethnographic investigation, Porter challenges common evangelical ideals of musical neutrality, suggesting the importance of considering musical tastes and preferences through an ethical lens. He employs cosmopolitanism as an interpretative framework for understanding the dynamics of diverse musical communities, positioning it as a stronger alternative to common assimilationist and multiculturalist models.

Mark Porter studied at University College, Oxford, and King's College, London, before completing his doctorate in ethnomusicology at City University, London, in 2014. Following this, in 2015, he took up a postdoctoral position at Max-Weber Kolleg, Universität Erfurt in order to investigate concepts of resonance in relation to congregational music. He is co-founder and organizer of the biennial Christian Congregational Music: Local and Global Perspectives conference and his writing has appeared in the *Church Music Quarterly*, *Ecclesial Practices*, the *Journal of Contemporary Religion* and *Christian Congregational Music: Performance, Identity and Experience*.

Ashgate Congregational Music Studies Series

Series Editors
Monique M. Ingalls, Baylor University, US
Martyn Percy, University of Oxford, UK
Zoe C. Sherinian, University of Oklahoma, US

Congregational music-making is a vital and vibrant practice within Christian communities worldwide. Music can both unite and divide: at times, it brings together individuals and communities across geographical and cultural boundaries while, at others, it divides communities by embodying conflicting meanings and symbolizing oppositional identities. Many factors influence congregational music in its contemporary global context, posing theoretical and methodological challenges for the academic study of congregational music-making. Increasingly, coming to a robust understanding of congregational music's meaning, influence and significance requires a mixture of complementary approaches. Including perspectives from musicology, religious and theological studies, anthropology and sociology of religion, media studies, political economy, and popular music studies, this series presents a cluster of landmark titles exploring music-making within contemporary Christianity which will further Congregational Music Studies as an important new academic field of study.

Other titles in this series:

Christian Congregational Music
Performance, Identity and Experience
Edited by Monique Ingalls, Carolyn Landau and Tom Wagner

Congregational Music-Making and Community in a Mediated Age
Edited by Anna Nekola and Tom Wagner

Contemporary Worship Music and Everyday Musical Lives

Mark Porter

Routledge
Taylor & Francis Group

LONDON AND NEW YORK

First published 2017
by Routledge

2 Park Square, Milton Park, Abingdon, Oxfordshire OX14 4RN
711 Third Avenue, New York, NY 10017

Routledge is an imprint of the Taylor & Francis Group, an informa business

First issued in paperback 2018

British Library Cataloguing in Publication Data
A catalogue record for this book is available from the British Library

Library of Congress Cataloging in Publication Data
Names: Porter, Mark James, 1985- author.
Title: Contemporary worship music and everyday musical lives / Mark Porter.
Description: New York, NY ; Abingdon, Oxon : Routledge, 2017. | Series: Ashgate
congregational music studies series | Includes bibliographical references and index.
Identifiers: LCCN 2016018099 | ISBN 9781472472076 (hardback) |
ISBN 9781315451299 (ebook)
Subjects: LCSH: Music in churches--England. | Contemporary Christian
music--England--History and criticism. | Music--Social aspects--England.
Classification: LCC ML3001 .P67 2017 | DDC 781.71--dc23
LC record available at https://lccn.loc.gov/2016018099

ISBN: 978-1-4724-7207-6 (hbk)
ISBN: 978-1-138-61589-2 (pbk)

Typeset in Garamond
by Integra Software Services Pvt. Ltd.

Contents

Acknowledgements   vi

Introduction: The quest to understand diverse musical experiences   1

1   Setting the scene   14

2   Music, attachment, ethics and community   32

3   Bridging worlds through common modes of being in music   59

4   Boundaries: Communal and private, spiritual and secular   82

5   At the edges: Value transfer, judgements, discontent   105

6   Alternative musical spaces   127

Conclusion   151

Appendix A   157
Appendix B   166
Bibliography   168
Index   195

Acknowledgements

I would like to express my gratitude to the many people who have contributed in different ways towards this project. My parents have encouraged me throughout and have helped to make this undertaking possible; their support is something I couldn't have done without. My doctoral supervisor, Laudan Nooshin, allowed me the freedom to explore my ideas, and her gentle encouragement has helped to speed this work along its way. Carolyn Landau encouraged me to pursue this research, and without her prompting I might never have got round to it, while my examiners, Clive Marsh and Stephen Cottrell, are largely to thank for their insistence upon the publication of this work in book form. Monique Ingalls has provided helpful words of advice at almost every stage of this project and I am grateful both for her expertise and for her willingness to share it.

Both Carolyn and Monique, alongside Martyn Percy and Tom Wagner, played an important role in getting this work off the ground through their collaboration in founding Christian Congregational Music: Local and Global Perspectives. Being part of the organization of this event has given me a vivid glimpse of the richness and variety of this field of research and has provided me with an international and interdisciplinary network of like-minded (and not-so-like-minded) researchers, practitioners and friends.

The musicians and congregation at St George's have played an important role in helping me begin to think about many of the issues raised by this research, and I am grateful for their friendship and inspiration. I am equally grateful to the many individuals at St Aldates who have been part of this process, particularly those who were willing to expose the depths of their experience in interview, entrusting me with deeply personal and cherished thoughts and beliefs.

The constant support of friends has helped me to keep going and I want, in particular, to thank Sophie Engel for her generous-hearted encouragement and belief in me and Robert Mitchelmore for sharing in the daily struggles of completing a research project as well as my periodic battles with technology.

The author and publishers would like to thank the following copyright holders for permission to reproduce the following material:

Extract taken from the song 'Praise is Rising' by Brenton Brown & Paul Baloche, copyright © 2005, Thankyou Music*/Integrity's Hosanna! Music. *Adm. By Capitol CMG Publishing worldwide excl. UK & Europe, admin by Integrity Music, part of the David C. Cook family, songs@integritymusic.com.

Extracts from *Marginal Musical Spaces at St Aldates*, Oxford, by M. Porter, *Journal of Contemporary Religion*, published by Taylor & Francis Ltd, http://www.tandfonline.com, reprinted by permission of the publisher.

Introduction

The quest to understand diverse musical experiences

My experiences and motivations

The motivation for this book begins with my own experience. I came up to Oxford in 2002 as an undergraduate student. My principal musical background was in Western art, or 'classical', music, and prior to coming up to study I had spent most of my Sundays acting as an itinerant parish organist for a range of churches at home on the Isle of Wight. Upon coming up to Oxford I quickly became involved with St Aldates church, a city centre Anglican parish in the charismatic evangelical tradition.[1] This provided a continuous engagement with a musical environment which I had previously only encountered on a much more sporadic basis. Contemporary Worship Music and the popular musical styles which formed the basis of St Aldates' music were far from my home territory. Nevertheless, I found the music of the church exciting and compelling and, over time, became used to, and skilled at, participating within it. I learned to play from chordsheets and found, too, that I enjoyed listening to recordings of the music – buying an album which featured electric guitars was initially a somewhat strange activity for me, but I quickly got used to the experience.

Over time my relationship with St Aldates' music slowly evolved and I became increasingly aware of its ambiguous nature. I began to find myself unwilling to own up to any affiliation with the music around people not immersed in that environment and found that there was therefore some kind of split in my musical life and identity. I became aware of the features which I found frustrating or would look down on, while realizing that there were, nevertheless, also a great number of elements that I valued highly. Once or twice I found myself engaged in a conversation with another student in the church in which I would justify my love of classical music over and above pop and rock.

In 2009 I was appointed director of music at St George the Martyr Church in Holborn, London. My initial appointment at the church was on the basis of an advertisement put together largely by members of the PCC (Parochial Church Council). The element of the advertisement which most captured my interest was the diversity of musical backgrounds present within the worship team[2] and the seeming desire on the part of the church to build something fruitful and creative with this diversity. I felt that perhaps here was a place where some of the disjunctures and tensions I had become aware of between the musical environments I inhabited could be addressed, and seemingly disparate musical worlds could be brought together into an integrated whole. I relished the possibility of diversifying St George's musical life away from a relatively uniform soft-rock worship style and, by doing so, of doing better justice not only to the skills, but to the experiences and perspectives of those involved with the musical worship within the church and to the different qualities which I believed different musics were capable of expressing.

Within St George's one of my first priorities was to begin to discover the different skills and backgrounds of the musicians on the team and to begin to think about how these might shape the possibilities present within the church's musical life. I found that the church had, within the congregation, a jazz musician, a film composer, a choral scholar, a session musician, someone who had led gospel choirs, and a classical oboist, amongst others. I found many of the musicians were very welcoming of the opportunity to branch out in different directions – some found the predominant style frustrating or hard to make sense of, others found that within a uniform musical setup there had been little possibility of them contributing their gifts and abilities to the community and worship of the church. I found too that there was a diversity of views within the congregation about musical priorities that the church had adopted. In particular, there were some members who struggled to relate to the focus on expression of divine intimacy which much of the repertoire highlighted – a struggle that I was both often aware of and sometimes sought to challenge. A focus on trying to value the different contributions that could be made by those within the worship team led to a number of people within the congregation feeling they could become part of a musical setup which they had previously not been able to see a place for themselves within. I found different opportunities to push creative boundaries to be exciting – jazz services, classical solos, gospel singing, incorporation of the pipe organ alongside the band, songs in different languages, composition projects and musical experimentation around the communion liturgy. I found too that it was exciting to be able to nurture individual musicians, particularly when they were less confident themselves, and to find ways in which they could contribute their individual gifts to the musical life of the church. Despite this excitement, over time I found that musical departures from the norm weren't ones that were always welcomed. While they were appreciated strongly by many of the musicians and by many of those close to me within the congregation, they were sometimes felt by others to detract from the core musical identity and priorities of the church and thus opportunities to branch out from the norm slowly closed down.[3]

During my time at the church I found that, while I was often most pre-occupied with thinking about those who struggled with assimilating to the predominant music, some individuals found the process of identifying with the church's music to present few problems. For some this seemed to relate in some way to the proximity or distance between the music of the church and the music they would identify with elsewhere, but such a correlation was far from universal. I had little idea why their relationship with the church's musical style and priorities seemed to function productively for some and problematically for others or whether there was any way of moving beyond the way things were and easing some of the tensions and dilemmas. The existence of positive experiences hinted that there might be possible solutions to some of the musical tensions that I had encountered within the life of the church, but didn't leave me with much of an idea as to what these might be.

I felt myself torn between two different sets of priorities without any real understanding of how to mediate between them. On the one hand, I could keep pushing for a diverse musical environment that included the varied musical contributions that different individuals and musical styles could make and try, as best I could, to acknowledge within the musical life of the church the different musical perspectives and attachments that individuals brought. On the other, I could take a firm line on the principles and priorities which had traditionally been felt to represent the core of the St George's style[4] and try to persuade different individuals to adopt and assimilate to this approach. While pressure to conform to a single style came from the rector, the desire to branch out seemed to come from the members of the congregation. I found that I felt a stronger duty to the latter than the former not only in terms of pragmatic loyalty, but on what I felt to be both ethical and theological grounds. In the face of increasing pressure to adopt a strictly assimilationist model in which the different experiences and viewpoints of the musicians would be pushed aside in favour of conformity to a single musical style and approach, I found myself very aware of the injustices it seemed to do to the experiences of some within the congregation and found myself increasingly standing up for diverse musical expression. The situation seemed to present an unresolvable binary polarization between authority and unity on one the hand and individual worshippers and diversity on the other. In the end the rector felt the differences between us to be unproductive and asked me to move on. After a final set of well-received Christmas services I therefore returned to my former church in Oxford.

Returning to Oxford, I believed myself to be in a congregation where the church's musical life contained fewer points of tension. I assumed that St Aldates, as a large church with a strong sense of identity founded upon its long history and strong attendance, lacked a similar diversity of experience and that I was something of an exception within the congregation. A couple of conversations with friends, however, alerted me to the fact that this was, perhaps, not the case and encouraged me that there was a valuable research project that could be undertaken. I wanted to undertake research which would acknowledge the different musical perspectives hidden within the congregation; but more, I wanted to try to understand what it was that made experiences of congregational music productive or problematic for people, and find a way to talk about music within the church which might help to address some of the unfruitful binaries between straightforward conformity or diversity that I had encountered.

Key questions

The research question my encounters and experiences led me to is that of how individuals relate their varied experiences of music outside of a church environment to their experiences within it. This seemed to provide if not the source of many of the problems and questions that I had come into contact with, at least a common way of articulating and encountering them. I am interested in how this experience becomes significant and thus to better understand the issues at stake: what are the factors that give this relationship power and how are they embedded within the lives of individuals? What exactly is lost for those who find the relationship to be problematic; what is gained by those who experience the relationship productively? And what are the mechanisms by which this happens? This points also to questions of ideals: how do lived experiences of congregation members interact with church models of musical community? What new models might they suggest? And how might these situations be negotiated in an ethically satisfactory manner? It is my hope that by asking these questions, the musical dynamics of church communities can be better understood and possible avenues found for grappling with difficult experiences within them.

In asking these questions, this project engages a number of methodological and theoretical concerns (see, in particular, Chapter 2). First and foremost are questions of music and identity (Frith 1996a; Rice 2007, 2010; Turino 2008); in asking how individuals negotiate the regular movement between contrasting musical environments, the manner in which individuals identify with music is raised as a key concern. The interaction of different contexts, both individual and collective, leads to the need to pay particularly close attention to the way in which musical identification and allegiance is understood. Associated with this are questions surrounding the understanding and management of diversity (Berger 1999; Butler 2000; Dueck 2003); by specifically foregrounding the diversity present within a musical group I draw attention to the non-uniform and non-unified nature of collective musical experience, questioning the assumption that simultaneous musical experience is necessarily shared musical experience.

Second, and closely related, are questions of musical style, significance and value (Frith 1996b; DeNora 2000; Rommen 2007b); how do individuals understand and apply these categories and how do they function within the shared ongoing life of a musical community? By bringing the musical style of the congregation into dialogue with other musical styles I highlight the relational and interactive nature of these categories and by focusing on the ongoing life within an established congregation I ask about their communal contestation and regulation.

Third and finally are questions of the function of music in mediating institutional and individual patterns of authority and agency (Rice 2001; Turino 2008). What does the presence of music within such frameworks entail for the relationship between these different levels? Closely related to this are questions of normativity and ethics (Rommen 2007b; Perman 2011; Hesmondhalgh 2013); I draw critical attention to the relationship between institutional norms and individual experience and, by bringing this into dialogue with questions of value and significance, examine the way in which questions of music can become ethically charged.

A developing field of scholarship

My work in this book builds upon a developing field of scholarship. In 2008, Monique Ingalls stated that 'there is no body of scholarly literature that focuses specifically on American evangelical worship music' (2008, p16).[5] While the body of literature connected to Contemporary Worship Music, either in the United States or elsewhere, is still not vast, important contributions have been made in recent years, not least by Ingalls herself, and these recent contributions sit within a growing broader field of scholarship on Christian congregational music.[6] In embarking upon this study I am reliant on important contributions to the literature by a number of scholars. It is their definitions, histories and discussion of debates and issues that provide the foundation for my particular project of ethnographic research and save the need to re-cover ground that has now become well established.

Monique Ingalls and Anna Nekola, both writing from a North American perspective, provide important foundational work in the field from within music scholarship and, as such, are used as important points of reference throughout this book. Thus Ingalls, modifying an earlier definition by Robb Redman (2002, p47) defines Contemporary Worship Music as 'the broad repertory of evangelical congregational song composed from the late 1960s to the late 2000s in mainstream Western popular music styles' (2008, p16). Ingalls traces the history of Contemporary Worship Music beginning with its early days on the West Coast of America, during which there was a large focus on its role as an evangelistic medium 'comprised of Christian lyrics set to popular "secular" styles of the day' (2008, p57). From here she follows its dissemination at charismatic events and conferences and as a commercialized product with increasing influence both in churches and in the wider Christian marketplace. Ingalls draws attention to the enduring influence of key tenets surrounding the music's origins:

> The idea that music was simply a vehicle or tool for promoting the Christian message; that musical style was not an integral part of the evangelical tradition; and that the timeless Christian message not only could, but should, be paired with contemporary cultural styles – each of

these ideas and practices would become increasingly important in the ensuing decade as the contemporary song repertory gained popularity.

Ingalls (2008, p72)

Ingalls charts Contemporary Worship Music's growth as a mainstream form of worship music, not just in the charismatic movement where it originated but in the evangelical church more broadly. She narrates the split between Worship Music and other forms of Contemporary Christian Music, documenting changes in style and focus, in particular a trend towards intimate worship using adult (easy listening) rather than youth styles in the 1980s and 1990s, the battle between contemporary and traditional styles that followed Contemporary Worship Music's adoption in churches and the rise of 'modern worship' music as an 'edgier' rock-derived style heralding from the UK at the beginning of the 21st century. Her work draws attention to important features of discourse surrounding Contemporary Worship Music – in particular, the way in which an imperative to be in some sense 'authentic' is key to the way that the music is understood and practised within contemporary worship spaces. At the same time her tracing of Contemporary Worship Music's history into the present day raises further questions as she highlights the ongoing evolution and negotiation of this musical genre.

Anna Nekola's work focuses specifically on the 'worship wars' in late-twentieth century America, a period of contestation that (as we will see in Chapter 2) has played an important role in shaping Contemporary Worship Music culture. Nekola situates the worship wars firmly within longer Christian traditions of thought and dispute around the role of music; she describes them as:

Public debates over evangelical Christian contemporary music from the 1960s to the beginning of the twenty-first century ... These debates pit contemporary worship songs against 'traditional' Protestant hymns in a struggle over how best to praise God while simultaneously missionizing non-believers. Disputes over worship practice are one of the central areas of contention within contemporary American evangelicalism, eclipsing even discussions of theology as evangelicals struggle to define the 'correct' purpose and style of worship.

Nekola (2009, p1)

Tracing congregational music from Augustine through the period of the Reformation, Nekola emphasizes a number of tensions within evangelical worship manifested particularly strongly in the worship wars – in particular, the political tension between the authority of the individual and the institution that she finds to be at the heart of protestant Christianity. Nekola, while drawing attention to attitudes of ahistoricism within evangelicalism,[7] emphasizes the historical institutionalization of neoplatonic conceptions of music's inherent power through such thinkers as Augustine and Boethius and the way in which these understandings have been deployed in opposition to the use of popular musical styles within churches through an insistence that connotations of worldliness and depravity are inherent and not merely incidental to the music.

Howard and Streck's work on Contemporary Christian Music (1999) focuses largely beyond the realm of the congregation to encompass the Christian music industry as a whole.[8] However, in discussing the relationship between forms of Contemporary Christian Music and the secular 'mainstream', they focus on a relationship with potential parallels to the concerns of this book. Howard and Streck identify a number of different schools of thought, each describing a different approach to the relationship between Christian music and the music of the surrounding culture. They label these 'separational' – which positions Christian music largely as an alternative to the mainstream, 'integrational' – in which Christian artists aim to operate both within the mainstream and the Christian subculture, and 'transformational' – which attempts to grapple with the darker aspects of the world as a whole and to find redemption away from neat categorizations. In describing the tensions between these different schools of thought Howard and Streck's work, drawing on Niebuhr's framework of Christ and culture (1952),[9] helps to situate each of these attitudes as a response to specific questions and pressures, drawing attention to the disputed rather than settled nature of the relationship between Christian music and wider cultural forms.

A few authors have focused specifically on Contemporary Worship in the UK, a form that owes much to the development of Contemporary Worship music in the United States, forming part of the same international scene. Pete Ward provides the most useful and detailed summary of its history and development, charting the music's rise as part of evangelical youth culture in the 1960s and 1970s through movements, events and festivals, groups and publications, and its later association with the charismatic movement, noting that 'charismatic [worship music] has become the default setting in most evangelical churches in Britain' (Ward 2005b, p1). Ward locates the origins of evangelicalism in the early 18th century and traces its 20th-century resurgence in England as conservatives strategically fought back against the spread of liberalism. This strategy, crucially, focused around communicating the gospel to young people, and part of this became the use of popular music in order to communicate with the youth. It was, however, the arrival of the Jesus movement from the United States that moved Christian popular music from the margins to the mainstream. The Jesus movement combined popular music with the compelling power of charismatic experience and revivalist forms of Christianity to enable the spread of Contemporary Worship Music within the English church both through the adoption of American-originated songs and through the work of British artists. In contrast to America, much of this occurred within, rather than outside of, the established Anglican Church with key centres such as Holy Trinity Brompton, St Michael-le-Belfrey and St Andrews, Chorleywood becoming important proponents of charismatic worship, alongside the newly-emerging house church movement.[10]

James Steven (2002), in contrast to Ward, documents the pentecostal rather than evangelical background of charismatic worship in the Church of

England, tracing precursors to the 1960s charismatic renewal back to pentecostal experience in the early 20th century.[11] While Ward focuses primarily on the selling of Contemporary Worship Music, Steven emphasizes instead the importance of the Holy Spirit and spiritual experience and narrates the entry of charismaticism into the Church of England through key figures and events. Steven thus suggests that charismatic worship has 'assimilated aspects of contemporary culture as a means of expressing and heightening an authentic expression of "worship in the Spirit"' (2002, p211), tying the use of contemporary styles of music closely to their associated spirituality over and above their role in evangelism. As Nekola highlights (2009, p127), the alliance between popular music and charismatic experience had been an important one, with a mutual emphasis on personal experience serving to connect the two very closely. As Ward makes clear, Contemporary Worship Music has subsequently circulated beyond simply charismatic circles and Steven thus examines a range of differing environments in his ethnographic work, examining the way in which charismatic worship combines with Anglican structures at different points across the Anglican spectrum.[12] Peter Webster and Ian Jones's work also helps to position Contemporary Worship Music within the Church of England, situating the development of newer musics within longer-standing Anglican traditions, tracing the post-war connection between evangelicalism and popular music and contrasting understandings of newer musical forms with those of more elite[13] pre-existing traditions (Jones and Webster 2006, 2007; Webster and Jones 2008). They help to understand the way in which music and its ideology fits into the existing Anglican establishment and highlight the tensions it can create with older traditions through differing conceptions of musical quality and the nature of authentic worship.

Methodology

While my project is situated in the story that these authors narrate, it is not, primarily, a historical project.[14] The core of this research centres around 42 individual unstructured and semi-structured interviews with members of the congregation, members of the worship team and church staff at St Aldates, through which I interrogate the ways in which individuals frame and articulate their experiences within and outside of a worship context and examine the connections and disjunctures between their experience and evaluation of these different environments. After initially being somewhat uncertain as to the most appropriate strategy for such interview work, I quickly found that the interviews began to settle into a regular format which seemed often to bring out interesting insights and connections which – having hoped for but not dared to expect such useful material – I was often surprised by. After an introductory preamble in which I explained what my research was about I would ask interviewees to tell me about their musical lives, either in their current state or, as most opted for, as a narrative. I would prompt them in order to draw out themes of meaning, significance and value where these seemed worth probing or where their narrative tended to focus on simple description. After this I asked them to describe a similar narrative for their experiences of church music and their thoughts and feelings around this. Having heard the two descriptions I would then ask further questions centring on any interesting points of relationship between the two narratives or musical worlds. This strategy, while carrying the potential weakness of artificially separating two strands of narrative, served well in the task of first building up a picture of a musical life against which the specific facet of church music could then be understood and related.[15] Interviews usually focused on very broad tendencies within individuals' musical experience rather than on specific one-off musical events – I found that this larger-scale focus gave individuals the space to articulate feelings about and attitudes towards music which had been built up over time and which were the results of longer-term reflective thought-processes. This strategy seemed appropriate for the worship context in which a high level of self-involvement is likely to lead to at least some level of reflection and self-examination. I found too that an initial focus away from the music of the church served to open up ways of thinking and talking about the experience of church music that interviewees would have been slow to bring up had the question been approached head-on, preventing the repetition of institutional discourses which can serve to mask the individual and allowing lesser-heard aspects of experience to come to the foreground.

Having been a member of the St Aldates congregation and worship team for the majority of the last ten years, this fieldwork is largely something that has been carried out 'at home' (Amit 2000; Butler 2005; Stock and Chiener 2008). The questions which form the basis of this book arise both from my personal experiences within contemporary worship environments and from past conversations and exchanges within these settings. While this research is, to a large extent, inevitably shaped by my own experiences within a worship environment, in opening up the issues this has raised to others through the posing of questions and engaging in dialogue with them through interviews I both build on my own experiences and observations and subject them to the critique of the worshipping community by which I have been surrounded.[16] Having an existing network of friends and contacts within the congregation meant that the majority of the initial interviews arose from relationships which I had already formed at the church. I intentionally selected those whom I felt would have reason to have particularly strong or significant experiences of moving between musical worlds, and so many of those approached for interview were people I knew either to have strong personal musical or artistic tastes or some level of struggle with the musical aspect of church life. The experiences that I write about are not, therefore, necessarily entirely representative of the congregation as a whole, this is not a goal which I attempt.[17] Instead, they are focused very closely around individuals who have a particularly strong relationship to the research question and offer insights into the musical life of the church on this basis.

While convinced of the utility of such a strategy, I was aware and initially concerned that a deliberate focus on those possessing what I might consider to be a strong musical identity might make the research less applicable to the congregation more generally. Members of the worship team, for example, can often be much more concerned with team politics, band dynamics and the experience of playing, and will often have a much more active interest in observing nuances and changes within the musical life of the church. Musicians, likewise, are often likely to be more attentive to musical details than non-musicians. As I progressed through my research and interviewed a range of people, however, I found that the frameworks which I was beginning to con-struct seemed able to accommodate experiences from a range of perspectives. I found the distinction between musicians and non-musicians to be relatively hard to make in practice, with some people who played instruments in the church not really considering themselves to be musicians, and many non-musicians having a strong sense of musical identity and values. Indeed in some cases musicians would avoid personal musical listening altogether, whilst non-musicians would saturate their waking lives with a constant stream of sound. The structure of congregational singing serves to further weaken this distinction as everyone becomes a participant in the music-making of the church. While I found it might make sense, therefore, to draw a distinction between those who have strong musical values and opinions and those for whom these are a lesser priority and between different kinds of artistic sensibility, there seemed to be a continuity of experience amongst the different congregational groups, with individual variety accounting for a much greater degree of variation in per-spective than levels of musicianship. The sample level of around 40 people represented the point at which I felt that sufficient data had been gathered to see some general patterns emerging and at which I felt that further interviews were likely to serve largely to enrich rather than significantly alter any of the frameworks that I was beginning to construct around the data.

The chapters

In translating this fieldwork into written form I have organized my discussion of the research into six chapters. I begin in Chapter 1 by situating St Aldates church within its broader ecclesiastical context. I introduce some key features of the church before exploring the way in which the church's worship staff reflected upon and explained the musical patterns of the church in interview.

Chapter 2 is largely theoretical in nature, focusing on some of the key issues raised by my research questions and highlighted in the foregoing discussions. I suggest the problematic nature of frequent ascriptions of neutrality to music within the church, alongside associated relegations of musical attachment to the level of personal preference, while suggesting that attention to the ethical has the potential to provide a more-helpful basis for discussion. After a brief discussion of music and identity I examine models of diversity in congregational music, suggesting the applicability of frameworks taken from the 'new cosmopolitanism', and offering this body of social and political theory as an alternative to the shortcomings I find within existing models. I finish by introducing the framework under which I will be discussing material from the interviews.

Chapters 3, 4 and 5 are dedicated to a discussion of the interview data within my chosen framework, the division into three chapters reflecting the framework's tripartite nature detailed at the end of Chapter 2. I discuss in detail individuals' experiences of music both inside and outside the church, paying attention to the way in which they navigate the movement between ecclesiastical and extra-ecclesiastical musical environments and relating this to a variety of concerns in theory and in discourse.

In Chapter 6 I examine two marginal musical spaces within the life of the church: 'Sing O barren woman' – a week long prayer event, and 'Word on the street' – an evangelistic busking group that go out each Saturday onto Oxford's main pedestrianized shopping street. I suggest that these two spaces embody different relationships between individuals' diverse musical back-grounds and the church, offering differently nuanced musical ontologies from that found in the main Sunday worship services. I suggest that these spaces serve both to challenge and to reinforce the musical patterns of the main church services.

Finally, in my concluding chapter, I tie together the previous chapters through a return to the theoretical lens of cosmopolitanism, drawing on a typology of usages set out by Steven Vertovec and Robin Cohen in order to examine the multiple ways in which cosmopolitan thought can be brought to bear on the experiences presented in this book.

Notes

1 I refer to charismatic evangelicals as a tradition rather than as a doctrinal position in order to foreground the collective affinity between churches (Ingalls 2008, p11) and to locate the movement firmly within its late 20th-century, early 21st-century context. See, in particular, Steven (2002) and Ward (1996) for a discussion of the development of this movement in England. Pete Ward (2012, pp58–59) suggests that St Aldates' evangelicalism is characterized by the prominence the church gives to the bible, an emphasis on conversion, an atonement theology focusing on penal substitution and the predominance of 'upbeat' singing. Likewise he locates the church's charismaticism largely in the way in which the Holy Spirit is invoked during services (2012, p60). While Steven (2002, p6) notes the derivation of the charismatic label from its use in 1 Corinthians, referring to the gifts of the Spirit, many writers, Steven included, locate the current significance of the term more firmly in worship-forms and experience. Thus Nekola suggests that 'pentecostals and charismatic Christians center their faith on the mystical and emotional aspects of evangelicalism, focussing on the personal experience and expression of being filled with the Holy Spirit' (2009, p123). Steven emphasizes the way in which charismatics, while sharing beliefs in the importance of the Holy Spirit, are

differentiated from pentecostals through differences in social class, ecumenical vision and differences of opinion as to the significance and role of spiritual gifts and the baptism in the Spirit (Steven 2002, p6).

2   A term which, in this context, refers to the musicians who play or sing during church services. At St George's there were around 20 musicians – a number roughly equivalent to the average morning attendance. A large proportion were young professionals and, while all would play in the Sunday bands, musical leadership for particular services was delegated amongst a subgroup of 'worship leaders'.

3   This was usually expressed to me by the rector and seemed largely reflective of his particular vision and goals for the church. However, at least at times, his views seemed to be representative of others within the congregation who shared this vision.

4   Derived from Holy Trinity Brompton, the church which had, around ten years ago, sent a large number of members over to re-establish a congregation in the St George's building.

5   Throughout this book I will use the terms 'worship music' and 'Contemporary Worship Music' somewhat interchangeably.

6   See Porter (2014) for a detailed overview of this developing field.

7   That is, a tendency to understand current practices without reference to any larger historical context. The ahistorical evangelical emphasis plays an important role in the way in which worship is understood; historical sources are rarely referenced in the framing of Contemporary Worship Music within congregations and, thus, while they assist in understanding the development of this musical form, they are rarely raised in the fieldwork that constitutes the task of this book.

8   While some of this music is devotional in nature there is also a large amount of Contemporary Christian Music in which this is a much less explicit focus.

9   See also Glanzer (2003).

10 House churches are independent of traditional denominations. They are largely charismatic and evangelical in character and often aim to restore aspects of first century Christianity, such as the ministry of apostles, which they believe to have been lost.

11 Pentecostalism largely owes its origins to the 1906 Azusa Street Revival in Los Angeles, bringing with it an emphasis on spiritual experience, speaking in tongues and the gifts of the Spirit.

12 Steven describes the approaches of the different (Anglican) churches he researches as, respectively, modern catholic, 'free' evangelical, Anglican evangelical and 'radical'.

13 In the sense that the music both aimed to, in some sense, elevate worshippers and to be of a particular 'compositional quality' (Jones and Webster 2007, p53).

14 From a methodological perspective a number of projects run, in different ways, parallel to my own: Gordon Adnams, in his phenomenological exploration of experiences of congregational singing (2008), interrogates the way in which individuals frame significant experiences of worship; Jonathan Dueck, in his work on Mennonite singing (2003), examines individual–group relationships, highlighting the multi-layered 'registers' of identity and multiple understandings of musical practices present in congregations; Gerardo Marti (2012) examines questions of music and diversity in relation to race, alongside a consideration of pastoral strategy; Melvin Butler (2000) describes negotiations of musical style and spiritual experience within a Brooklyn pentecostal church, drawing attention to the

spiritually significant role of musical style and to internal congregational diversity; and Timothy Rommen (2007b) develops frameworks for understanding musical style as ethically significant whilst, importantly, relating church musical styles to the broader musical circulations within which they are caught up.

15   Nancy Ammerman connects the telling of multiple narratives very closely to questions of identity: 'We may understand identities as emerging, then, at the everyday intersections of autobiographical and public narratives. We tell stories about ourselves (both literally and through our behavior) that signal both our uniqueness and our membership, that exhibit the consistent themes that characterize us and the unfolding improvization of the given situation. Each situation, in turn, has its own story, a public narrative shaped by the culture and institutions of which it is a part, with powerful persons and prescribed roles establishing the plot, but surprises and dilemmas that may create gaps in the script or cast doubt on the proffered identity narratives of the participants. Both the individual and the collectivity are structured and remade in those everyday interactions' (2003, p215).

16   Within the interviews I was often asked my own opinions on or experiences of a particular matter (see Bithell 2003), and while I was initially reluctant to offer these, as time progressed it often felt somewhat artificial to hold them back. While I was sometimes aware that someone would uncritically assent to what I had said or, somewhat intimidatingly, even suggest that our conversation would shape their future attitudes, on many occasions I was pleasantly surprised by the ways in which my own experiences offered the opportunity for critical reflection. At points during some of the interviews I would try to articulate some of my preliminary thoughts and reflections on what the participants were saying, allowing them space to critique my observations about their experiences if they felt I might be jumping to unwarranted conclusions. This sometimes led to the opportunity for shared reflection and additional insights which would not have been possible had I attempted to keep my research conclusions to myself.

17   See, for example, Robinson (2013) for a discussion of the usefulness of purposive sampling strategies.

1 Setting the scene

I arrive at the church around four in the afternoon, two hours before the service is due to start, ready for the band rehearsal. I am looking forward to playing saxophone again. I have spent the previous couple of terms operating the church visuals system, mixing video loops and projecting song lyrics onto the flat-screen monitors which are suspended from pillars around the church building, but the summer months, where many of the team are away from the city, provide space in the life of the church for more-flexible role taking, offering opportunities to mix up the usual routine of alternating set bands.[1] I am pleasantly surprised to be playing alongside Pete Wigley, someone who has previously had a significant musical leadership role in the church but who has stepped more into the background in recent years.

Lauren, the principal worship pastor is leading worship,[2] and has emailed out the set list ahead of time. Glancing down the email I notice nothing which particularly captures my attention; the list of songs is drawn mainly from a pool of repertoire which is employed fairly consistently across events within St Aldates.[3] The first half hour or so of rehearsal time involves the usual routine of waiting around for everyone to arrive and waiting for the sound technician to finish wiring up the stage before the initial sound check. Pete, with whom I am sharing a music stand, has helpfully drawn up a hand-written sheet containing the chords for each of the songs. As someone who hasn't played in a while I am grateful for this, as the current expectation that repertoire be played from memory doesn't sit entirely well with my own need for some written reassurance of how things should go.

The drums were moved around for the morning service, so the drummer has to spend some time rearranging the kit and reconstructing the drum cage that usually surrounds them. This provides the opportunity for some debate amongst band members: there have been a number of recent complaints to the church leadership about high sound levels within the church so Lauren is keen to ensure that the drum cage is completely closed off; a position which I, as someone standing next to the kit and who isn't a great fan of loud music, am in favour of. Adam, on bass, however, is concerned that this will lead to him losing a proper connection with the drummer as he feels the fold-back system is unable to provide an adequate replacement for the transmission of direct sound through the air. In the end Lauren allows him to open the side of the cage a little, a gesture that seems to satisfy him. A little discussion about Paul's drum setup follows; someone compares the use of a single crash cymbal to a jazz kit, and the tighter sound of the kick and snare this week is also remarked upon by members of the band. Concerns over sound come up again when Adam is asked to turn his bass amp down – he worries that he will no longer be able to properly feel what he is doing, but as the sound is fed back through the fold-back he is reassured.

Upon seeing that I am there to play saxophone, Adam remarks how wonderful it was to play at a wedding gig the night before and to have a horn section inserting funk-stabs into the arrangements. He follows this up later with a comment about how, with the amount of gig playing he's been doing recently and the relatively small amount of worship playing, he's forgotten how to play worship.[4] He nevertheless, after the usual mucking-around during the soundcheck, manages to slip back into the mold fairly effortlessly, at least from the perspective of an onlooker. Later in the evening I think I hear elements of funk coming through in his playing during the bridge of 'You Alone Can Rescue', something I try to encourage and pick up on with my saxophone improvisations. During the soundcheck Paul plays around on the drums, creating patterns which clearly fascinate Adam. This free experimentation is common during soundchecks, but is quickly laid aside when proper rehearsing begins. Later in the rehearsal, however, I notice a similar moment as Adam comments on his enjoyment of some of the acoustic guitar lines which Pete has been introducing into the arrangements.

Lauren is introducing a new song into the repertoire for the first time – 'Beneath the waters/I will rise' from Hillsong.[5] She asks Pete what he thinks of the song and he responds by acknowledging the way in which it fills a gap in the repertoire with its talk of baptism, but suggests that he would have liked it to have a little more focus on the necessity of sharing in Christ's suffering required in order to be raised. I find that I am drawn to some of the imagery of the song, and its connection with aspects of biblical images rarely used in Contemporary Worship Music. Alongside this, however, I find myself slightly disappointed by the predictable way in which the melody lines and chord progressions of the song seem to conform closely to the familiar patterns of the Hillsong repertoire and by the way in which interesting ideas that I feel could have been developed further seem to be hidden within what I find to be a much more generic set of lyrics.

The first song in the set leads to a certain amount of discussion about arrangements. A number of the musicians have been at the New Wine summer conference, where they played and rehearsed an arrangement which Lauren wishes to repeat here.[6] Paul, on drums, doesn't really see the difference between the New Wine arrangement and the regular way in which the piece would be played, but Lauren points out that it is more poppy than the usual way of playing. I'm struck by the way in which everyone seems to have a deep familiarity with the ins and outs of this song in a way that I, as someone who hasn't played in a while, don't.

During the rehearsal there are points where Lauren reflects self-consciously on what she is doing musically within the worship set. When the key of one of the songs requires alteration, she expresses frustration that it is moved into the key of E, not wanting the entire first set within the service to be in this same key – a tendency in her planning that she is aware of and dislikes, wishing for a greater degree of variety.[7] The same frustration emerges when it seems that she will be starting most of the songs in the first set purely on keys and vocals – she doesn't want to become predictable and boring to this extent and so welcomes the opportunity to allow Pete to start 'I will exalt You' on acoustic guitar. At one point I make a comment about something she does which departs from the structure on the set list and she observes that she is much less predictable and structured than fellow worship leader Rich, a comment that leads to a little discussion about whether this should be perceived as a positive or a negative quality. Either way, it clearly seems to be part of her musical self-conception and the way in which she sees her practice of leading musical worship.

As we finish rehearsing and make our way towards the Oak Room for a time of pre-service prayer I am struck by the choice of music put through the sound system by Will on the sound desk. The arrangement seems to break away from the soft-rock of the standard St Aldates sound into a more highly-produced pop sound-world, with greater use of synthe-sised sounds and stand-out melodic figurations. I mentally put this down to his personal tastes and interests and notice that the next song to come through is one which is much more familiar within the regular sound world of St Aldates. Perhaps he had used the period of time when the church was still half empty to demonstrate a little bit of his own tastes before reverting to type as people began to arrive and fill the chairs and aisles of the building.

There is a moment towards the end of the service where Charlie (the Rector) makes it clear that he wants Lauren to continue playing on her own during the prayer ministry time – I share a look with the other musicians questioning whether he really means to exclude us in this way. Adam remarks that Charlie doesn't realise that we're able to play quietly if we want to.

After the service I am pleasantly surprised by the number of people who compliment me on my playing – something which rarely happens when playing keys or mixing visuals. There is something about the rarity of solo instruments within the worshipping environment that seems to lead people to pick up on the elements which they feel they add to the worshipping experience, often expressed in terms of an extra lift, or a sense that the music somehow ministered to them.

Notes on a service, 19 August 2012

This service illustrates well just how much interaction of musical perspectives can occur in connection with a single event at the church.[8] Within this space of time the different concerns of the musicians on the stage come to light in numerous ways, with thoughts and conversations that are prompted by events within the rehearsal referencing much broader issues; issues which I am aware of through interviews and conversations with some of those present. Paul's passing comments on the similarity of different arrangements, for example, connect to a broader sense of the church's music being in some senses too boxed-in and limited. The rehearsal time is both sacred, set apart from the outside world by prayer, location and leadership, and profane, with its focus on aspects of music, technical concerns and the back-and-forth of free conversation. It enacts songs of worship and yet doesn't enter fully into this act.[9] The rehearsal seems in many ways to act as a liminal space, in which musicians can bring their own quirks and favourite ways of playing, particularly in the sound-check and during pre-rehearsal banter (Wood et al 2007, p874). They can employ some of these in the process of negotiating arrangements before the service begins; but at that point they will submit to the decisions that have been made and seek to engage the congregation in worship through the agreed patterns. The space of the rehearsal allows for certain momentary explicit expressions of individuality by the different musicians on the team, but it is also an environment which is largely shaped by the broader structures and discourses of the church and worship ministry. Musicians limit their self-expression to things they know will not cause too much of a disturbance but which may nevertheless reference deeper ongoing debates and conversations held largely outside of the Sunday environment. Much remains implicit, with the scope of dialogue often limited by the particular conversational affordances which individual musical moments allow. In spending time with the team I can slowly begin to work out the deeper concerns behind particular statements or actions – 'his attachment to folk music means that he struggles with the intensity of upbeat rock', 'she has a really eclectic taste so she probably finds it harder to distinguish between songs', 'he always drums like that because he listens to a lot of emo music'. Within the scope of the rehearsal, it is often difficult to grasp the true importance of these various negotiations to the different musicians, to appreciate how much of the discussion reflects deeper ways of being in worship, how much is simply floating on the surface of an overall contentment with and enjoyment of the musical life of the church, and how much of what they say represents an ongoing process of struggle and contestation. Nevertheless, the hints are there that there is something worth exploring.

St Aldates Church

St Aldates is a large Anglican church in the centre of Oxford. It is situated directly opposite the Tom Tower entrance to Christ Church and has a large glass reception area opening onto the busy street outside. The church operates within the charismatic evangelical tradition and would often identify more closely with other churches within this stream than it would with the rest of the Anglican Church. The church building seats between 500 and 600 people and while its origins date back to Saxon times, has been much extended over the years. It was extensively reordered around the turn of the millennium, with the seating orientation turned sidewards in order to provide a state-of-the-art auditorium style environment appropriate to the church's contemporary service style rather than the more traditional east-facing interior that had previously been in existence.

The church parish itself has a relatively small population, mainly encompassing shops, businesses and colleges. Members of the congregation often make a deliberate choice, therefore, to come to the church from further afield, travelling in from different areas of the city as well as the surrounding villages in order to be part of something different from the offerings of their local parish churches. The church's ministry operates on a range of geographical levels, from dispersed local pastorates meetings in members' houses all the way through to international conferences, mission projects and training programmes designed to attract overseas applicants to come and learn from St Aldates. The church, therefore, both welcomes worshippers from a range of backgrounds and includes within itself a diverse range of smaller scale communities. The international element of the congregation is emphasized in the church's tagline 'A house of prayer for all nations at the heart of Oxford', demonstrating an institutionalization of these priorities. The congregation of the church includes a large transient element: students make up a large proportion, and many are present only during term-time and for the duration of their studies. While some, therefore, are committed to making the church their long-term home and settling into the patterns of its life (and music), a large proportion of the congregation do not expect such a lengthy affiliation and will therefore not concern themselves so much with long-term priorities within the community. There is also a regular flow of overseas visitors who are staying in the city for a limited period, some as tourists, some for work and some for study, and the church is very aware of its public face opening out onto a busy Oxford street. There is a strong presence of young families within the congregation, and a large number of professionals of varying ages. While there are a number of older members, and the importance of inter-generational relationships is often spoken of from the platform, this element seems to be one that is less significant than in the past, as many who were part of previous generations of the community move on to other congregations.[10]

There are three regular Sunday services, at 10:30 am, 6 pm and 8:15 pm. The main elements of a service are the time of sung worship, which will last between 20 and 30 minutes, and the sermon, which will last 30 to 40. Extended musical engagement is, therefore, one of the two main components around which services are structured. Communion rotates weekly between the different services, offering the only liturgical element of any length. There is some demographic differentiation between the services which is reflected a little in service style: the morning service is aimed at families, offering a weekly children's church alongside the main service, while the 8:15 pm (late) service operates only during term time and attracts mainly students and youth. The 10:30 am and 6 pm services are largely similar in style, although the morning service is often thought of as the more diverse due to its incorporation of children's songs as well as occasional more traditional elements. The late service offers a very different experience, with the chairs being stripped out of the main church body and house and pillar lights being dimmed, coloured gels being offered in their place. The presentational style is much more informal and the band much louder and rockier. Each service currently has its own dedicated teams of (volunteer) musicians, meaning that a certain degree of distinctiveness is maintained.

Conversations with individuals during my period of attendance at the church have made it clear that people attend St Aldates for a wide range of reasons. Some are drawn in by (or even come to faith through) its musical life and many are drawn in by the large, vibrant church body and the opportunities for becoming part of this community. Some are drawn by particular ministries such as the regular children's church or the international and student work, some are members because they joined in the past and remain loyal and some are drawn to the preaching or particular form of spirituality and theology which the church offers.[11] The prominence of musical worship within the Sunday services doesn't necessarily mean, therefore, that this is always the primary site of identification with the church body. In occupying a large proportion of the service and in being an expected site for divine encounter and spiritual expression in which the deep aspects of a person's life are brought before God, it is, however, an aspect of church life which (as will become clear in later chapters) is inevitably significant within the experiences of congregation members.

The current musical style of the church sits happily within the norms of the Contemporary Worship Music genre, featuring a soft-rock style using acoustic guitar, keyboard, bass, drums and vocalists.[12] Electric guitars will generally be found within the slightly heavier style of the late service and brass instruments (horn, trumpet and occasionally saxophone) are a regular part of the current morning service line-up. Although there is room for occasional departures from these norms, such as the use of organ and a greater range of instruments at Christmas services, such departures are atypical and are generally much remarked upon when they occur. The cultivation of a consistent sound and style has been an important part of the way in which recent musical leaders at St Aldates have shaped its musical life and identity.[13] While recent efforts have been made to encourage a certain degree of diversity among set bands, a broadly uniform musical style still generally prevails.

The musical worship of St Aldates has slowly evolved over the course of the years under the supervision of a number of different worship pastors and musicians. Both repertoire and priorities have gradually evolved in response to broader church trends, in response to the particular concerns of the church leadership and as a result of the changing nature of the congregation and musicians. There is a core repertoire of roughly 70 songs (in addition to just over 20 well-known hymns,[14] children's songs and older archived repertoire) which is in a constant process of evolution as new songs appear and old songs are discarded.[15] Recent repertoire has focused on a number of key song- (and album-) producing sources prominent internationally within the Contemporary Worship industry such as Hillsong, New Wine, Worship Central and Passion.[16] This has been complemented by a growing repertoire of home-grown songs written by members of the worship staff before being recorded and used at national church conferences and summer festivals. As well as providing repertoire, these churches and networks play an important role in shaping worship team culture via conferences, tweets, videos, interviews, albums, blogs, books, sermons and other materials and provide a connection with broader discourses of meaning and significance within a wider international community (Ingalls 2008, pp11–13). While St Aldates represents a particular local form of worship culture, much of it is representative of larger-scale patterns within the charismatic evangelical church (Becker 1999, p10).[17]

The three albums which the church has released over the course of my time at St Aldates (St Aldates Church 2003, 2006, 2010) illustrate some of the ways in which the church sound and focus has evolved. The first album, *Heaven's Door* (on which, as an undergraduate and recent worship-team recruit, I played saxophone and piccolo), was released in 2003 and has a slightly home-produced feel to it. This album was produced mainly for the benefit of the immediate church community, although it was also made available on a wider basis through St Andrew's bookshops.[18] The textures are made up of largely acoustic rather than electric sounds and there is extensive use of wind instruments and some strings. Arrangements are slightly idiosyncratic, drawing from the varied creative imaginations of the musicians on the recording rather than being polished by a producer to conform to a single standardized sound. The album includes liturgical elements such as the Eucharist Prayer and also includes a song designed to represent some of the diversity of the local and world church with its employment of multiple languages. This first album is strongly grounded in the local community of the church and relationships within it, engaging and expressing a degree of diversity both within the congregation and further afield. It reflects a church culture primarily focused on drawing in outside influences rather than one that is necessarily making an attempt to contribute outwards to a wider musical scene and, while a good-quality sound is attempted, this is ultimately something which is held in balance with the skills and abilities that the musicians of the community are capable of offering.

The second album, *Stand in Awe* (on which I played saxophone), was released in 2006 and targeted a broader UK audience through a secondary release on the Kingsway label. For this release an outside producer was brought in, alongside a back-line of (semi-) professional instrumentalists. The album sound is built around a very strong positioning of the electric guitar, with acoustic instruments, where present, tending to fade into the background of the mix. Song arrangements are much more in line with worship industry norms of guitar-driven rock, and song selection is closer to that which might be expected at a major Christian festival. Production quality is higher, although not perfect, and the album is clearly intended for a wider commercial market. This album represents an attempt by the church to professionalize the quality of its music and to bring it into line with the sound and quality of commercial worship music. The church community becomes a lesser focus in and of itself, but is, instead, put firmly into relation to a larger scene, in which it is beginning to find a bigger role.[19] The goal of attaining a certain style and quality of music is prioritized above the varying contributions that members of the community might be able to make. These are welcome and valued, but only insofar as they are able to contribute to larger-scale goals.

The third album, *You*, was released in 2010 and is the first studio album to have been made by the church. The album seems to have been targeted both at the local church community and at the broader New Wine church network in which St Aldates' song-writing is increasingly influential. 'You' was produced by weeksweeksweeks, a production team who have become increasingly ubiquitous within UK Christian music production. The album is much more clearly focussed around creating professional recordings of home-written songs rather than covers of existing repertoire. These songs are likely to circulate more widely around sections of the British church through their use at the main tent meetings at New Wine. The album incorporates tracks of prayer and prophecy reflecting, in part, the growing influence of prayer-room culture within the congregation.[20] While the work of creating the album was done with a team of church musicians, the producers inevitably contributed a great deal of the final sound. Out of the three albums this has by far the highest production values and, with its appearance on the iTunes store, is likely to attract at least some sales beyond the boundaries of the church community. The album, then, represents a church that has an awareness of its now-established role within the broader worship scene and has achieved the confidence to work in a greater degree of partnership with representatives of the industry. The community is once again able to contribute to a greater degree in the activity of arrangement through a process of collaboration, but this is largely because it has, itself, come into greater conformity to broader worship industry norms.

Worship staff, musical values and conceptions

As a relatively large city-centre church, St Aldates employs a team of around 30 staff (which includes six ordained clergy), three of whom, alongside a worship intern, take overall responsibility for the musical life of the church. Lauren, a music graduate in her late 20s, is employed as a full-time worship pastor and has specific responsibility for the 6 pm service and the prayer room. As the one who spends the greatest amount of time working for the church, she tends to be the one who has the greatest role in shaping its musical life. Rich, who studied alongside Lauren before training as a school music teacher, is employed part-time as a worship pastor, with specific responsibility for the morning service, and Jamie, a former intern of the church and of a similar age, is employed partly for his role in worship but also as an administrator for student and youth work. He has particular responsibility for students and for the late service.[21] Prior to Lauren taking over the lead worship role, Martyn Layzell had been employed as worship pastor. Martyn had become a well-known name as a worship leader with the release of his first album, *Lost in Wonder*, and his appearances at the Soul Survivor summer youth festivals and came to St Aldates at the specific request of the rector, Charlie Cleverly. Until departing the post in 2008 he took a strong lead in professionalizing the sound of the Sunday worship bands and in drawing a large number of young musicians to the church by virtue of his established presence on the Christian music scene. All three current leaders, by contrast, were members of the church in some form prior to being appointed to their current posts. They represent, therefore, a certain attempt at continuity in the culture of the church and a sense of stability and capability within it rather than a desire to bring in expertise and ideas from outside the boundaries of the church community.

Within the worship team there are between 30 and 40 regular Sunday musicians, as well as many more involved in other areas of the church. Sunday musicians will generally be scheduled to play on alternate weeks and an audition night is held at the beginning of the university term at which musicians will take turns to play in bands in front of a panel of current leaders and team members. Musicians are expected to perform to a reasonably high level in order to form part of the team, with the expectation on a Sunday being that they will be able to play the arrangements selected by the worship leader without the aid of written music or chord-sheets. The worship staff are responsible to the Rector and work, to some extent, in dialogue with other worship leaders and musicians on the team. While they hold responsibility for regulating this aspect of the life of the church they are also aware that it is not something that they are free to create and define as they wish, being subject both to the weight of expectation imposed by a thousand-strong body of people passing through the church each week[22] and to the limitations of the team which they have at their disposal. This means that, while they articulate and reinforce particular patterns and ways of going about congregational worship, these are as much an expression of the state of the church as a whole as they are the views of the leaders themselves.

It is rare for the details of musical worship to be explicitly spoken about during a Sunday service, the rationale behind many aspects of the church's musical life going largely unexplained. Concepts relating to worship may be touched on in preaching but these often focus on its importance as a spiritual act rather than making explicit connections between this and the particular devotional practices of the church. Instead, the conceptual foundations for worship are laid in other ways within the ongoing life of the church. For the worship team the semi-regular team meetings can be a chance for the worship leaders to express their views and thoughts on the musical worship of the church, and at times this has been a key location for the formation of worship team members. Summer conferences such as New Wine can also be a location in which talk about worship becomes more prominent as seminars are dedicated to topics relating to the worshipping life of the church. It is within the context of Sunday rehearsals, times of prayer and sharing, emails to and from worship leaders, and pastoral chats over coffee that conceptualizations of musical worship are made explicit and the rationales behind particular practices are clarified. For many members of the congregation it will often be in their observations of and participation in musical praxis within the church that they come to understand the church's views on worship. These times will often be framed by prayer and comments by the service leaders as they seek to guide the gathered congregation down particular routes of activity and experience, and can serve to highlight particular spiritual values and attitudes which can serve to make the musical elements of the service meaningful. It is the spiritual purpose of worship that will always be foregrounded, however, with inferences about specific musical practices generally remaining implicit rather than explicit. Song lyrics too can go a long way towards framing the purpose of congregational worship, not only as they help to embody attitudes and actions but in the commentary they can form on the activity of worship.[23] Knowledge about congregational worship music is therefore often primarily formed through experience rather than explicit explanatory discourse, but can nevertheless become subject to the control of discourse, particularly when there is occasion to rationalize particular facets of it or when there is some need to shape and form the experience in a certain manner.

During interviews for this research the worship pastors offered a number of explanations for the musical patterns in place at St Aldates:

> People don't just engage with the musical style, they engage with a community, with an identity ... they're identifying with a certain culture and I think when people join a church ... they're joining a culture ... the style of music reflects the culture, and the culture reflects the style of music.
>
> We have a freedom in our relationship with God ... there's a simplicity to relating to God that we can just come as children ... and we can experience intimacy with God ... and I think that is reflected in the music, that it's quite a fluid style ... it has colour and yet it has simplicity ... and the freedom in the dynamics to reflect the sense of the Holy Spirit leading ... It ... allows for expression that is spontaneous ... there's also a sense of everyone can take part.
>
> Rich – interview with the author, 10 May 2012

Rich, who is largely responsible for the morning service, finds that the music is something that reflects the values of the St Aldates church community, offering a range of important qualities including freedom, fluidity, simplicity, flexibility, the ability to respond to the Spirit, dynamic range, easy participation, accessibility, and easy replicability at home. The musical style adopted by the church is one that is able to fulfil its function well and to serve the purposes to which it is put within the context of the church community through its service to a range of other practical goals. The way in which these goals are embedded in the music connects with the way in which congregation members are expected to identify with the music. If they have already chosen to identify with the congregation, then they are choosing to identify with its values and, since these are embedded in the church's musical practices, should also, as part of that, begin to identify with the music:

> We're not to be selfish ... when we're leading worship ... Our role is to serve the congregation, to lead people in the most helpful, the most universally engaging way possible ... if, on the whole, many in the congregation are finding that they're struggling to engage in worship because the musical style is an issue for them ... that's a different issue ... you have to first of all come to terms with the fact you're never going to please everyone, you're never going to satisfy everyone's personal desires, musical tastes and ... you have to make a decision and commit to it.
>
> It's a bit like a Ferrari ... it fulfils a function of getting you somewhere, but it's also an incredible, incredibly beautiful and awe-inspiring piece of machinery ... the danger is you don't want the music to become more inspiring than the creator to which you're journeying towards and so I think there's a balance to be had, but I think providing the music is inspiring people to look to the creator ...
>
> Rich – interview with the author, 10 May 2012

For Rich, the choice of a single church style necessarily involves a certain degree of compromise in which the preferences and interests of some congregation members may be served to a greater extent than others. However, the making of such a choice is important in order for the musical life of the church to function well. The consistency of the music offers the congregation a safe space within which to worship and provides the musicians with a frame within which to develop specific skills and expertise. As it is impossible to please everybody within the church, choices have to be made and a key priority in the current choice of music is to employ a style that will connect with the youth in the congregation. Older members are expected to have the maturity to set aside their own musical desires whilst youth are, instead, likely to be driven away from the church if not catered to. This, then, is a pragmatic consideration as to how to appeal to a particular demographic by using a style of music familiar to them. The decision is based primarily on the degree to which it allows particular demographics to feel at home but it should not have an impact on the ability of others to worship so long as they are mature enough to lay aside their own preferences and desire to be catered to or appealed to aesthetically in the service of the greater good of the group. There is an assumption that this is a style of music which may carry relatively little value for older members of the congregation; however, as the key locus of its appeal even to the youth is simply that of familiarity and cultural connection, nothing significant is thought to be lost in such a move.

For Rich, musical satisfaction is a secondary priority within the life of the church since music is there principally as a tool. Boredom with the musical style, for example, should not be a regular part of musicians' experiences as that would imply that their focus within the time of worship was on the music rather than on the spiritual goal which they are trying to facilitate. Music should never become more important than God, and should not distract from the core purpose of the services. Likewise, Rich believes that church is not an appropriate place for musicians to bring their personal musical tastes, as the musicians' role in serving the congregation means that the imposition of personal musical preference is generally something which would be considered to be largely selfish in nature. For Rich music does have the potential to carry aesthetic value in the form of beauty, but that beauty remains secondary to the service which the music provides. It is a form of beauty that is fraught with danger – if allowed to become too much of an aesthetic focus then it stops inspiring people to turn to God in worship but instead, itself, becomes the object of attention. There is a clear dichotomy between music's functional service and its presence as an object in its own right:

> I came into this role when it was already pretty much set up in the soft pop rock style ... I think it's a good style for us because in a sense it enables more people to be involved in the journey of worship than perhaps a more traditional setting does ... and I like being part of a community and so the fact that ... this style enables us to have a community of worship leaders, lead worshippers, and musicians is ideal.
>
> Lauren – interview with the author, 6 June 2012

For Lauren, the musical style used in worship is, to some extent, something which was pre-given by the history of St Aldates. However, Lauren also finds that the music enables the opportunity for broad participation, mirroring Rich's emphasis on accessibility. Lauren finds that the chosen church style offers, as a result, the ability to foster a community focussed around a common purpose and church identity, aspects which are also important to her elsewhere in her musical life. Pragmatic considerations play a role in maintaining the current state of the music – a sense of the limitations of the musicians alongside a fear of potential congregational reactions to difference make it important to maintain consistency within the chosen style. The music of the church is one that people are accustomed to, and this accustomization is an important feature in allowing people to be able to engage in the task of worship. Like Rich,

Lauren also emphasizes the importance of music that enables the majority to engage with God in worship, a task for which it provides the medium.

Lauren de-emphasizes personal musical expression in a similar manner to Rich; music in worship is something which is there to serve the majority without distraction and is not a place in which using one's own skills should be a priority. Musicians, in particular, need to maintain a posture of humility and service to others which involves a degree of self-limitation, intentionally refraining from demonstrating their full musical potential. She, nevertheless, expresses openness to the varying contributions that musicians might bring to the bands within which they play, with the move to set bands being something which, for her, provides a greater degree of space to develop a distinctive band identity. Elsewhere in the interview she acknowledges that different musics can inspire people in different ways, although she qualifies this in such a way as to suggest that this isn't a particularly central feature of her thinking. This is, perhaps, mirrored in her choice of word – if music's role is to 'inspire' then it is the activity which it inspires someone towards that is the ultimate aim and, whilst it may be good for music to help with this, it isn't necessarily something at the heart of this activity:

> I sometimes get frustrated with the limitations we have because I feel like we're set in a certain style and that we have certain expectations of this is what church music is, should sound like but, but then I'm constantly reminded and challenged and challenge myself by, you know, who's this for, who's worship for, and you know, I think it's well it's for the Lord, it's not for us, and it's not for our pleasure.
>
> I think I've learnt more and more whenever I go into a church setting, some of which I love going into, and some of which I get to and I'm like urgh, don't really like this ... I think I still feel that I really have to go in with an attitude of I can choose to engage with God at any point that I want to, whether or not I'm really enjoying what's happening around me, and I think of course we know what kind of emotional response we're gonna have, but praying and allowing God to challenge that, and define that and shape that within us I think is possible within any setting.
>
> Lauren – interview with the author, 6 June 2012

Lauren expresses a certain degree of frustration with the way in which the music in the church often ends up all sounding the same, but finds the key to unlocking musical diversity and creativity to be allowing it to flow from intimacy with God, putting spiritual engagement at the heart of any musical change. While acknowledging the difficult pastoral issues that can be thrown up for those who find the church style hard to relate to, something which she believes can arise from deep personal spiritual concerns, she believes that engagement with God is something which can be chosen regardless of the setting within which the worshipper finds themselves. The key element in meaningful participation in worship is therefore dependent on the individual choice of the worshipper and the availability of God to direct encounter rather than on the mediation of the music. Lauren and Rich both emphasize that music has value and that it can fulfil spiritual and communal functions whilst simultaneously positioning many musical concerns as somewhat incidental to the core features of corporate worship:

> There's a lot more to sung worship in church than just the music style, so a lot of people, for example, say oh why can't we just do worship music like Mumford and Sons or why can't we do like I don't know, House or Dubstep or something ... we could do that, but actually I guess there's a pastoral awareness as well to actually if we just suddenly change to doing everything country you know that might be too much of a shift ... People maybe got the wrong end of the stick with thinking oh if we change the sound it's gonna bring revival or change, but, completely aware that actually we need to be engaging with like young people.
>
> I think music can move people and God can move people, and that's the kind of difficult tension ... someone could play the same chord over and over again and I believe I can meet with God as powerfully as if it was an amazingly intricate piece of music, but I also believe that God'll speak to me through, or I can meet God through ... listening to classical music ... so I think music has a massive role to play in that, and I think we wouldn't wanna sort of divorce the two and say well actually you can't meet God if you don't have music ... I think also worship facilitates our response to God.
>
> The youth at these summer conferences ... might catch you round the site and say man, how can I make my church at home like this? and then we sort of spend the whole week diffusing this whole aspect of well actually, cos then people, their spiritual life is just a spiritual high at a summer conference, and then they gradually go into freefall at the local church and so that's, you know teaching the, again like the actual foundational building blocks of what worship is.
>
> Jamie – interview with the author, 29 June 2012

As the person responsible for students, youth and the late service, Jamie is quicker than the other leaders to highlight the frustrations which some feel with the current style. While he sees part of his role on the team as being the one who introduces new sounds and keeps on top of secular musical trends, the pastoral situations within which he finds himself operating also mean that he has a particular concern for helping others to find ways of working with the ecclesiastical and musical situations within which they are placed. For Jamie, musical styles, and therefore music in general, can be thought of as equivalent to 'leaky vessels' which are able to serve their purpose in worship for certain periods of time but should not be relied upon for meaningful encounter with God as they will not last forever. Musical desires and frustrations seem largely to be conceived in terms of people's desire for cultural relevance and connection, a concern Jamie wants to acknowledge while simultaneously putting into perspective.[24] For Jamie, as for Rich and Lauren, the worship experience should be something that relies on God himself rather than on music, and thus God can be encountered regardless of the music being used at any particular time. In this way the youth who find a significant experience of worship in the context of a big Christian summer festival will be able to go home and engage in worship in small parish churches without constantly wishing to completely alter those churches' established musical setups. Pastorally, individuals are affirmed and listened to, whilst church practices need not be engaged or brought into question.

For Jamie, music facilitates a response to an encounter with God but often exists in tension with this, having the potential to become an idol and draw too much attention to itself. Jamie believes that values such as 'excellence' and 'freshness' are still important things to seek within the musical life of the church, primarily in order to maintain the interest of worshippers and to present music of an appropriate standard for divine service, but these seem to be conceived as secondary to the core act of worship rather than sitting at its heart. In highlighting the fact that changing a musical sound is not going to bring about significant change or revival, Jamie questions the assumption that pragmatically adopting certain musical sounds from the world around will have the potential to suddenly bring more people into the church or into a situation where they are better able to engage with God. The implication is that significant changes are things which happen as a result of God's work, and they are on the level of spirituality rather than things which are closely tied up with musical patterns. In a desire to counter potentially troublesome patterns of thinking a dichotomy between music and significant spiritual activity is, once again, reinforced, with music, of itself, able to contribute relatively little to the significance of worship. Jamie makes it clear that God can work through music, and that there can be a connection between this and musical engagement; however, this seems to be the result of God's particular initiative and his freedom to speak through whatever medium he chooses, putting even those things which seem to have some kind of independent and rival power into His service. In suggesting that people's primary reaction to a change in musical style will be that it is 'fun', Jamie demonstrates the same ambivalence, implying that the result is likely to be more a matter of personal enjoyment than something which holds any deeper kind of significance. He nevertheless makes an effort to affirm that this can be a good quality to pursue, thereby affirming rather than denying an aspect of life that many clearly value.

These three perspectives demonstrate common themes while also reflecting the varying challenges and thought processes that the three worship pastors have undergone. Within St Aldates services, music is strongly bound up with its function as a tool for worship. It is there to enable a corporate expression of devotion and, on the whole, is something which is successful in allowing the congregation to engage in this act. Alongside this there is an awareness that music and musical style can sometimes draw other significance to themselves, sometimes in unwelcome ways.[25] The musical leaders offer strategies for handling musical dissatisfaction in line with their conceptualizations of what music is and what it can do and these largely centre on emphasizing spirituality in a way that often seems to deflect talk away from specifically musical questions. Questions of music and of style are not a place where ultimate significance is to be found, and often need to be set to one side. Instead, significance is to be found primarily in the spirituality and heart of the individual and (for musicians in particular) in selfless service to the congregation. The ability for the individual to offer the same act of worship in whatever musical environment they find themselves highlights the degree of independence between the two dimensions and foregrounds, for the purposes of argument, the pragmatic nature of any connections that are made.

The adequacy of these conceptualizations for negotiating the diverse experiences of congregants will be addressed through the interview data in later chapters. However, it is important to note the dependence of pastoral strategies upon these initial conceptualizations. The ability to talk meaningfully about music within the church depends on a certain degree of shared understanding about its purpose and role within the worshipping life of the church. It is this which enables dialogue about the value of certain musical practices and experiences.[26] Experiences that reflect underlying shared understandings within the community are likely to enter relatively smoothly into discussion while experiences which are framed in different terms may find it harder to become part of ongoing conversations, despite forming a regular aspect of personal experience. Nancy Ammerman suggests that:

> Given that members participate in multiple public narratives, from both religious and secular institutional sources, we can ask which religious institutions supply the most robust and portable plot lines. The narratives supplied by religious organizations may be more or less richly nuanced, allowing them to address wider or narrower ranges of human existence. They may also be more or less able to incorporate counter-narratives, making sense of the very events that would seem to challenge their plausibility. Part of the analyst's job is to assess the degree to which any given religious organization is generating, nurturing, and extending the language, grammar, gestures, and stories that are capable of surviving in the everyday practical competition among modern identity narratives.
>
> Ammerman (2003, p218)

Such tasks constitute a key element of my analysis within the remainder of this book. Interrogation of the relationship between church discourse and everyday experience is key to understanding both the way in which individuals feel at home within the community and the tensions that sometimes arise in experience and expectations. As we turn to the next chapter, I begin to examine key discourses relating to musical neutrality, musical tastes and preferences, and individual-group relationships, exploring the work they do in regulating the worshipping community and setting out the understandings of these areas which I will utilize within the later chapters of the book.

Notes

1 'Set bands' at St Aldates are bands in which the same group of people always play together. This contrasts with the model in place when I joined the church in which people from the broader pool of musicians would be placed in different combinations each week.

2 That is, taking the lead role in the band on vocals and, in Lauren's case, keyboard, choosing the repertoire and instructing and leading the band as to how and what they should play.

3 See Appendix A for a list of song titles used in the morning services.

4 A reference both to the style and genre of Contemporary Worship Music and to the particular expectations of playing within a church service.

5 Hillsong are an Australia-based megachurch network well known worldwide for their Platinum-selling worship albums and for the wide circulation and adoption of their songs. See, for example, Evans (2006); Riches and Wagner (2012).

6 New Wine is a network of UK charismatic churches that produces publications and puts on events throughout the year. The summer conference is the main annual event, attracting several thousand people to camp in tents and caravans for a week of meetings and seminars at the Royal Bath and West Showground, Shepton Mallet. There is a large musical element to the conference, including the annual production of an album reflecting the songs sung that year.

7 Worship sets often stay in similar keys for most of the songs in order to allow the set to proceed without any audible gaps and thus smooth its progression. E is a particularly common key as it is easy to play on the guitar.

8 See Berger (1999, pp109–113) for a similar description of musical negotiations between band members and see Bayley (2012) for discussion of conversation within a contrasting rehearsal context.

9 This parallels the general observation in Wood et al (2007, p876) that 'There is music in this recording session, just as there is music in the rehearsal. But both settings are about how to work with snatches of sound – something less than the resulting CD and certainly something less than the concentrated performance event.'

10 The predominance of younger members might be somewhat atypical of Anglican parishes in the UK; however, this balance is far from unusual within the context of a large urban congregation.

11 It is often hard to separate questions of spirituality and theology from questions of musical style – within church culture particular forms of music and spirituality are often tied closely together such that when you find one you tend to also find the other.

12 See Spinks (2010, p91); Ward (2005b, p169); Webster and Jones (2008). Ingalls (2012a) draws a distinction between the soft-rock of earlier worship music and more-recent youth-focussed pop-rock forms. At St Aldates the majority of worship music is led by acoustic-guitar or piano/pad combination and maintains an element of the earlier sentimentality which leads me to favour maintaining the former label.

13 By, for example, limitation of the instruments and keyboard sounds used in bands, culling of song lists to focus on particular sources of repertoire, dissemination of arrangements through CDs and workshops focused on how particular instruments should be played.

14 For example 'How Great Thou Art', 'Crown Him with Many Crowns'.

15 See Appendix A for a list of morning service repertoire from January 2012.

16 And, to a more limited extent, Bethel/Jesus Culture and IHOP (International House of Prayer).

17 See the already mentioned discussion of St Aldates in Ward and Fiddes (2012, pp57–61), although Ward and Fiddes draw stronger distinctions between conservative evangelicalism, charismaticism and revivalism than I would apply.

18 St Andrew's are a UK Christian bookshop chain who, in addition to their high-street shops, carry stalls at the major UK Christian conferences and have an online ordering facility.

19 For an interesting parallel see Riches and Wagner (2012).

20 The prayer room is a space specifically set aside for prayer and worship, much of which incorporates creative and spontaneous declaration of and prayer inspired by scripture. It is influenced in particular by the culture of IHOP (International House of Prayer in Kansas City) which live-streams its ongoing corporate prayer and worship sessions on the internet and the 24–7 prayer movement which serves to network similar spaces. See Chapter 6 for a fuller discussion of some of the life of the prayer room.

21 These descriptions reflect the situation during the period of fieldwork and initial writing-up.

22 This weight is felt and perceived whether or not it is explicitly given voice, largely through the knowledge that the church has a reputation for doing certain kinds of music well.

23 One example of this might be Brenton Brown and Paul Baloche's song 'Hosanna (Praise is Rising)' in which the first verse is largely commentary on the act of worship 'Praise is rising, eyes are turning to You, we turn to You. Hope is stirring, hearts are yearning for You, we long for You. When we see You we find strength to face the day. In Your presence all our fears are washed away, washed away.' (Extract taken from the song 'Praise is Rising' by Brenton Brown & Paul Baloche, copyright © 2005, Thankyou Music*/Integrity's Hosanna! Music).

24 Given Contemporary Worship Music's roots in seeking to engage with broader popular culture, the need to defend it against cultural irrelevance bears with it a certain level of irony.

25 See, for example, Nekola (2009) for a discussion of similar worries in different periods of church history. Rachel Darnley-Smith has made an interesting study of a similar dynamic within music therapy settings, examining the way in which an environment containing significant ambiguity around the functional or artistic nature of the music-making can raise questions surrounding higher-order musical ontologies (2012, p2).

26 See Becker (1999) for a discussion of how different kinds of shared understandings shape the way in which conflict plays out in churches.

2 Music, attachment, ethics and community

Evangelical ontologies of musical neutrality

In order to understand the negotiation and regulation of musical style and experience at St Aldates it is first necessary to discuss musical meaning. What and how does music mean? What kinds of significance is it capable of embodying? Where, in the interaction of sound, text and individual and corporate expression are significance and value to be located? Much recent work in musicology (Small 1998; Chua 1999; Cook 2001; Kramer 2003, 2004; Cross and Tolbert 2008) and ethnomusicology (DeNora 2000, 2003; Clayton 2001; Rice 2001; Nooshin 2011) has sought to conceptualize in a variety of ways the different kinds of meaning that are present within and around music and the activity of music-making. In particular, the ways in which musical meaning can be socially constructed and ascribed have replaced earlier conceptualisations of 'absolute music' which push many forms of musical meaning to the margins in favour of granting music a more autonomous existence.[1] Such an understanding is not, however, one that is immediately at home within the discourses of Contemporary Worship Music; as Monique Ingalls highlights, part of the founding ideology of the movement is that music is a profoundly neutral medium (2008, p248), an understanding that has clear and important historical roots in the worship wars surrounding the introduction of Contemporary Worship Music. Beginning in 1960s America, the (re-)introduction of popular forms of music into the worshipping life of churches initially caused moral outrage, with many arguing that a music associated with so much debased conduct outside of the church was one which had inherently evil qualities which should prevent its use within Christian worship.[2] The response of the supporters of Worship Music was to argue that no music was inherently evil, music simply wasn't that kind of thing – instead music was a neutral medium which was dependent on the messages carried with it to obtain meaning (Ingalls 2008, p110; Nekola 2009, p261). While such debates are, in many places, something which occupy historical rather than contemporary significance within the church, the legacy of musical neutrality is one that has continued to inform and shape discourse within the Contemporary Worship scene.

Lauren, Rich and Jamie's articulations in Chapter 1 seem partially grounded in this understanding; their ambivalent attitude towards musical concerns involves a strategic drawing on an ontology of neutrality at points where it can usefully deflect attention away from music and onto more spiritual concerns and this, to a large extent, governs the way in which the church grapples with individuals' musical attachments and evaluations. The suggestion, for example, that engagement with God can happen regardless of context serves not merely as a description but as a prescription as to the appropriate course of action, should you have issues with the church's musical choices. It achieves this largely through a positioning of music in a neutral realm outside the core concerns of worship. Neutrality has become a model for music which not only denies it inherent moral significance but which, in doing so, sets up a conceptual frame which pushes out other ways in which it might be conceived of as significant. This then goes on to make itself felt in the way that musical preferences are often conceived within the life of the church. If music is neutral, with any meaning existing essentially independently in accompanying words and spiritual practices, then so are musical preferences – they are empty of significant meaning, and if they are neutral then congregation members should be able to set them aside without problem.

Ascriptions of neutrality have also, over the course of time, acquired other significance. As I have already discussed, and as will be shown further in Chapter 5, the fear of distraction from the spiritual aspect of worship is a recurring theme within talk about worship music (Adnams 2008, p115; Marti 2012, p88). Christians worry that talking about music and potentially ascribing power to it in a setting where direct encounter with God is expected risks ascribing power to an aspect of the experience that should not become powerful and potentially confuses the source of encounter. Talk about music, in other words, is talk that has the potential to detract from proper spirituality rather than open up important aspects of spiritual experience, mediation and negotiation. Such concerns seem to stem from a particular conception of what music-talk might be expected to look like – if musical style is neutral and primarily a matter of personal preference, then talk about music will have significance only on a relatively meaningless level and thus will inevitably be a distraction from the true purposes of worship. A certain ontology of music, then, leads to a theological barrier in the way of discussions around music and serves to keep the majority of discussion at St Aldates focused more directly on questions of spirituality. In opening up to discussion the range of meanings and significances which music and musical practice can take on within the context of worship as I am doing in this book, space can be opened up for the music to be discussed in a way that need not feed into evangelical fears by becoming a distraction from the purposes of worship but instead can serve to illumine aspects of such purposes which might otherwise remain hidden. If, for example, someone values the way in which folk music is particularly good at expressing certain models of family and community then this can become directly relevant to questions of how to worship as a church body and how to express biblical models of community. By allowing music to be placed in the same significant realm as worship, rather than on its own separate plane, worries about the rivalry between divine and musical power in the context of worship can be eased a little, as the two are no longer in strict competition with little possibility of relation, but can work within a context of interplay and exchange.

Former Archbishop of Canterbury Rowan Williams, in his reflections on secularist attitudes to the role of *Faith in the Public Square*, uses language that connects the neutralisation of aesthetic judgments with negotiation of religious difference. Williams's discussion of secularization provides an interesting parallel with discourse surrounding the neutrality of music in worship. He suggests that 'by defining ideological and religious difference as if they were simply issues about individual preference, almost of private "style", [secularist] discourse effectively denies the seriousness of difference itself' (2012, p25). Williams maintains that such a situation is undesirable in society and that instead, in order to create a healthy liberal democracy, there is the need for public negotiation of difference in an environment where different voices can be heard and taken seriously without the assumption that in doing so the result would be inevitable animosity, conflict or disloyalty to the larger community.[3] Conversely, he argues that in providing a space for these differences to be taken seriously there is the potential for a more powerful level of social identification to take place. The history of the worship wars has served to embed similar anxieties within the consciousness of those involved in the Contemporary Worship Music scene, a memory of community divisions rooted in musical loyalties being close at hand whenever issues of musical difference are raised. We can, perhaps, see this in Rich's wariness of the potential for musical taste to manifest itself in a selfish way, a wariness which is likely to be rooted in an awareness of this divisive potential. The resultant constraint of meaningful discussion surrounding music, however, can serve to impoverish aspects of the life of the worshipping community just as it can serve to weaken societal bonds. The problems Rowan Williams is quick to see in the privatisation of religious meaning,[4] can, perhaps, serve as a spur to self-examination and reflection around the areas in the common life of the church where it might be complicit in similar problems.

David Hesmondhalgh (2007) examines some of the ways in which discourse around music may have the potential to establish commonality despite differences in perspective and initial dismissals of others and their values. He cautions that initial expressions of difference should not always be taken as irreconcilable. 'What sounds like élitism about "commercial" music, for example, may reflect a yearning for better communication between people' (2007, p524). His work suggests the potential value in investigating musical difference rather than setting it aside as carrying too much potential danger for the community. Such issues cannot remain merely on the level of individual experience; according to Hesmondhalgh 'if aesthetic experience matters, then so does aesthetic discourse' and institutional conditions play an important role in making such discourse possible (2007, p524). It is important, therefore, not only to begin to investigate the concerns behind musical differences but to pursue these in relation to broader institutional conditions that regulate their functioning in community. Monique Ingalls draws attention to the way in which assumptions about the neutrality of style and the emphasis, instead, on the heart and the motives of the individual within the activity of worship can serve to deflect critical reflection away from musical practices (2008, p247). A lack of music-talk provides a means of maintaining authority, allowing the status quo to persist without being open to too much question. Musical deviations from the norm are often critiqued as distracting from this proper emphasis and thus, paradoxically, a discourse which deflects attention from musical style is precisely the discourse which serves to strongly maintain a particular stylistic norm. This suggestion can readily be applied to the way in which Rich, Lauren and Jamie's articulations in the previous chapter largely serve to reinforce existing practices, presenting the church's style as relatively static and given. Ingalls offers critique of the performance medium[5] as one way in which performances of worship music are being critically engaged. However, the opening up of discussion of experience beyond questions of the heart and personal intention through a focus on broader interactions with music seems to offer similar possibilities, enabling us to critically engage questions of musical style rather than have them deflected elsewhere. A specific fore-grounding of the musical also opens up a range of meaningful experiences which have the potential to get concealed behind expected patterns of worship discourse. In a similar way to discussion of the performance medium this focus is able to open up a broad discussion which can reach beyond simple affirmation or rejection of the practices of the church.

The connection between music and ethics

In contrast to ontologies of musical neutrality, the direction of my work is driven in part by a belief that musical practices within a church community have the potential to be a location of ethical significance, and that the inter-action between the musical lives of diverse and different individuals and the church community of which they are a part is a key site for ethical negotia-tion. This belief rests both on theoretical writings (Pickstock 2000; Hauerwas and Wells 2004; Rommen 2007b) and on personal experience of the kind of questions raised when trying to balance the musical priorities of a church. These priorities seem to affect people's relationship with the church community, its worship and its spirituality in wide-ranging and significant ways which, due to the value-laden nature of such relationships, seem to best be thought of in ethical terms (see the Introduction). The particular concerns raised within St Aldates will be discussed during the course of this book; however, we will see in following chapters how questions of music have the potential to draw in matters of spirituality, justice, authority, cultural and contextual engagement, theology and gender, amongst others and how these are negotiated within the life of the church community. The direction of this work is thus bound up with an intuition running in the opposite direction to that of musical neutrality and serves to focus precisely on the significance of music in a community environment. Careful attention to this level of musical engagement has the potential to illuminate worship music in important ways and by examining some of these we will set the tone for much of the rest of this book.

The ethical is something which can be construed in a number of ways – as Nanette Nielsen and Marcel Cobussen point out, the multiplicity of approaches to ethics means that it is often advisable to approach the specifics of a particular context rather than referring to a grand unifying ethical theory (2012, p3). Ethics does not point us to one particular set of concerns, but rather allows a particular mode of attentiveness to the concerns and issues of particular situations, people and things – in the case of this book, those that arise within the St Aldates community. For the purposes of this book, to say that something has ethical significance is to say:

1   that it is not neutral and, instead, is closely bound up with particular goods or evils whether in and of itself or through those things with which it forms some kind of connection.
2   that something matters and it matters for and in relation to particular people or communities.

In the case of music, and within the concerns of this project, this means to say that not only is music a vehicle for a range of meanings but that many of these meanings are in some manner associated with particular values and that, within the context of a community of diverse and different individuals, these will inevitably be subject to negotiation as to their appropriate functioning within that community's ongoing life. This ongoing negotiation can be seen to constitute the practice of ethics. The ethical dimension of music is an inevitable function of its nature as significantly meaningful in the context of shared musicking in community. To the extent to which models of community and the potential for music to connect with a range of meanings vary, so the ethical significance of music as it negotiates these will also vary. Outside of a church context, for example, the musico-ethical questions within a multicultural school music classroom (Green 2005) will differ significantly from those of a gigging band working out how to interact with its audience (Berger 1999, p111) or orchestral musicians negotiating clashes of creative agendas (Cottrell 2004, p117).

In seeking to open up questions of musical ethics relating to the church within the discipline of ethnomusicology, there is an inevitable crossing-over of agendas. While investigation touching on the ethical dimension of church music through an examination of the experiences of congregation members resonates well with academic priorities such as knowledge-seeking and debate, the suggestion that this debate should be opened up beyond the dimensions evident from interview in Chapter 1 is also loaded with goals which inevitably implicate aspects of the church community. My belief that the opening up of such discussion is important for the life of the church, but also important in terms of ethnomusicology, means that it is somewhat difficult to disentangle the two strands. Ethnomusicology is inherently an engaged discipline and this research is by its very nature 'applied' ethnomusicology. By engaging in talk about music within a community where music-talk is often absent, the research by its nature affects, if only temporarily, the life of the community.[6]

Discourse is an important ethical location and the opening up of public discourse is not always an unquestionable ethical good. Matthew Guest, in his study of St Michael-le-Belfrey Church in York – a congregation with which (as Guest notes) St Aldates has historical connections as part of the charismatic renewal – examines the way in which a separation of public and private discourses within the congregation around aspects of doctrine serves to balance differently-held viewpoints on issues such as the nature of evangelicalism, the place of charismatic gifts and the acceptability of homosexuality, thereby preventing them from turning into points of conflict. 'St Michael's is held together by a discourse which accommodates its various schools of belief while also controlling public utterance so that conflict is avoided' (Guest 2004, p77). The lack of certain public discourse, in other words, is precisely what in this situation enables the 'good' which is the communal life of the church.[7]

There is a key distinction to be made, however, between these kinds of debates, which centre on issues which it is often possible to push towards the margins of much of the congregation's shared communal practices, and talk about worship. As Cobussen and Nielsen point out, musical experience is often one that, by its very nature, is unavoidable – if you are present in a setting where there is music you have no option but to encounter it:

> What is often denied in discourses on ethics is the subject's lack of power, its vulnerability and dependence, particularly when it concerns the influence of sonic interventions on the body ... the subject cannot not respond; she cannot not participate – that is, assume a relationship, for before or beyond being the indication of a concept, category, value or desire, the sound of music grips the body, enters the body, solicits the body's participation, the corporeal consense, the e-motion.
>
> Cobussen and Nielsen (2012, p105)

Subjects may have more power to shape the nature of this relationship than this quotation implies; however, it is nevertheless true that music often demands our attention and response in a manner that is hard to avoid. Questions surrounding music will be encountered regularly within the context of the church because musical experience is unavoidable. At St Aldates not only does the service begin with a full 20 minutes of music, but music reappears at later points in the service and is an expected part of almost all church events. Furthermore, in coming into the church environment, a diverse range of individuals with (amongst other things) a diverse range of musical backgrounds not only encounter a pre-given (and well-defined) musical environment, but do so in a space which is spiritually, emotionally and temporally significant and to which they attempt to bring, in worship, an offering which, in theory, sums up and gives meaning to the rest of their lives (Ward 2005a, p34). These questions are not possible to set aside as elements which are of tangential or private relevance to the key activity of the congregation; they are constantly present and public. The decisions that St Aldates makes about music are therefore also unavoidably present for the worshipper to negotiate. The church cannot adopt a neutral position on musical style, as the weekly practice of worshipping together entails choices about what these musical practices are to look and sound like: decisions about such elements as song-choice, the volume of the band, the number of repetitions and the way in which songs are arranged cannot not be made. It may be possible for the dominant discourse of the church to adopt a position on music which is able to accommodate the range of positions and experiences found within the congregation without having to take any of these experiences or positions as in any way authoritative or determinative for the church's actual musical practice.[8] However, such a position will need to have the capacity to acknowledge and in some way deal with the experiences of the congregation, even if doing so requires a relationship of ongoing tension.

Timothy Rommen, in his examination of the Trinidadian Full Gospel community, has sought to draw up a framework within which to think about some of the ethical issues surrounding church music on the island. He proposes an 'ethics of style' which:

> [f]ocuses attention on the discursive spaces between individual and community (self and other) in order to come to a more nuanced understanding of music in its sociocultural contexts ... investigates the process by which musical style informs identity formation for both artists and audience; illustrates how style thus becomes the vehicle for a multifaceted communal discourse about value and meaning; and interrogates the process of personal identification or disidentification with musical style as a moment of ethical significance.
>
> Rommen (2007b, p2)

This broad definition of the ethical serves to open up a range of practices to interrogation while focussing very closely on the process of personal identification with style as the key locus around which they revolve. Rommen's model is, in part, a reflection of the particular situation in Trinidad, in which there is a strong communal discourse surrounding and attributing moral value to particular musical styles.[9] Such discourse is something which is less visibly present within the context of much of the contemporary British church – in a country where liberal and multicultural ideals are a crucial part of predominant social models there is a general (although not universal) wariness of denouncing particular cultural practices and expressions as in any sense immoral.[10] Nevertheless, identification and disidentification with musical style are still significant features of communal life in 21st-century Britain and our sensitivity to identity politics makes us keenly aware of at least one way in which this can still serve as an important ethical juncture. Rommen draws particular attention in his ethical discussion to the 'impossible' choice which can be faced by believers within the Trinidadian churches when positioning themselves in relation to different musical styles:

> On the one hand, choose to identify with this musical offering and you will be changed forever. You yourself will be different in relation to the community of which you are a part. In fact, your identification with this style constitutes, at one level, your disidentification with a portion of the community and its values. On the other hand, reject it and you will pay a different price, asserting in so doing your disidentification with its creator(s).
>
> Rommen (2007b, p37)

Ethics here is, therefore, partly a matter of community relations, but it is also a matter of choosing to identify with the ethical priorities of particular groups, and is bound up closely with the way in which musical practices are associated with and embody particular (potentially good or bad) ideals and beliefs.[11] Rommen's framework seems to suggest two principal foci for questions of musical ethics:

1   ethical priorities embedded within the different musics and their practice;
2   the way in which relationships within the community are affected by relationships with the music.

These aspects, while distinguishable, are not completely separable; the goods embodied within music, for example, can themselves involve particular configurations of community. Indeed, the ability, or mandate, to form particular communal relations is something which is to a large extent enabled by the acceptance of particular goods embodied within the music.[12]

Church ethics is not – as Rommen hints with his mention of 'forever' to reference the eternal and, with it, the transcendent – a question that can be thought of simply on the level of community; the ultimate point of reference for discussion is, by nature, theological. There is a sense that any other ethical priorities are always, to a certain extent, provisional, and able to be called to account by this higher point of reference. Individuals and the community as a whole will sometimes appeal to this point of reference as an appropriate ground for certain beliefs, attitudes or viewpoints – we saw, for example, in Lauren's interview how an emphasis on what the Lord wants takes precedence over issues of style. Such viewpoints are, if valid, positions which demand universal recognition and can therefore provide a strong basis for both unity and division. If, for example, it is important that musical worship enables an element of intimate corporate encounter with God, then it is unlikely that this is an ideal that is supposed to guide some worshippers but not others. A certain degree of ethical (if not musical) consensus is ultimately mandated, even if only in an eschatological sense. This can both empower negotiation in the hope of finding consensus and serve to entrench fixed viewpoints of those who believe they already possess this ultimate justification.[13]

In drawing on the discourse ethics of Jürgen Habermas, Rommen employs a basis for reflection which adopts an attitude of optimism towards the process of negotiation. Habermas's approach to ethics suggests that the validity of the ethical practices of a community are reliant on the consensus of all members of the community via a process of moral argumentation and thus assumes that such a consensus is, at least in theory, possible.[14] Habermas's approach may not match up exactly with the dynamics of a UK Anglican church;[15] however, it serves to highlight the desirability of addressing and listening to the particular perspectives of the range of members within a community and the value of being able to account for these in some manner within communal discourse.[16] Indeed, for Habermas, this seems to be the true heart of discourse ethics:

> Under the pragmatic presuppositions of an inclusive and noncoercive rational discourse among free and equal participants, everyone is required to take the perspective of everyone else, and thus project herself into the understandings of self and world of all others; from this interlocking of perspectives there emerges an ideally extended we-perspective from which all can test in common whether they wish to make a controversial norm the basis of their shared practice.
>
> Habermas (1995, p117)

Habermas and Rommen draw our attention to the fact that the way in which congregation members encounter discourse surrounding music and worship can be highly significant. Within church communities there is a great deal of discourse around the spiritual aspect of worship[17] within sermons, rehearsals, conversations, prayer times, etc., which serves to reinforce common understanding of the significance of worship.[18] This discourse will be encountered in varying ways by the worshippers who assemble to participate. In seeking to understand the perspectives present within a community and to relate these to the publicly articulated models of that community, I can interrogate the gaps that open up between public discourse and individual perspectives while also exploring the possibility of a greater level of mutual understanding.

Ethical questions within these processes and dynamics are very closely bound up with political concerns. The manifestation of certain goods within the community and the balance of perspectives which this entails very quickly becomes bound up with questions surrounding the balance of power. The politics of church music is an area which many churches are much more used to contesting, balancing and considering than the ethics.[19] Conflicts over the nature of the music and about who gets to determine what it should look and sound like will be familiar to most church-goers in some form, and a wariness of such conflict is clearly evident in the way in which Rich, Lauren and Jamie frame questions of musical style in the previous chapter. However, a focus on the politics without simultaneous consideration of underlying ethical issues has led to situations in which power is often contested without the concerns which sit alongside or behind it receiving a great deal of consideration.

Both worshippers and leaders can assume a direct correlation between music and power or a desire to assert the self,[20] an understanding which is incomplete and can potentially also be misleading. If an individual presents a view of what the musical life of the congregation should look like based on the priorities they believe to be important in music but only describes the resultant musical characteristics, then this bid to shape the musical priorities of the congregation will look like a simple and direct claim to power and influence for an individual's musical tastes. The alternative possibility, that such a vision is accompanied by a presentation of the individual's ethical outlook, why they see these particular musical priorities as goods which are important for the community, opens up a mode of negotiation in which self-presentation isn't simply a claim to individual power and influence but in which an individual's position is opened up to contestation and negotiation, providing room for others to object without appearing as if they are simply trying to impose their own desire for control and power in its place.[21] In being attentive to the range of ways in which ethical concerns arise within the community, the relationship of these to ongoing configurations of community life is always close to the surface; the prioritisation of certain concerns or voices within the community, the rationalisations for these prioritizations and the relationship of these to other concerns and voices will naturally be interrogated by such a process.

Nanette Nielsen and Marcel Cobussen suggest a number of key locations through which music can become ethically charged:

> Fundamental to our understanding is music's association with activity ('Interaction'), including contact with music through the act of listening ('Listening' and 'Voice'), music as an immanent critical process that possesses profound cultural and historical significance ('Discourse'), and as an art form that can be world-disclosive, formative of subjectivity, and contributive to intersubjective relations ('Interaction', 'Affect', and 'Voice').
> Cobussen and Nielsen (2012, p4)

It is not simply identification or lack of identification with style that carries ethical weight; a range of processes contribute to forming this significance. Questions of identification, however, can serve as an important location for bringing this broader range of issues into relief and provide a spur to contestation and interrogation of core ethical concerns. According to such a framing it is not simply particular moments that obtain ethical significance; rather, the whole range of musical practice and experience becomes a potential carrier of such meaning. In some senses this is no different from the acknowledgment that music carries and embodies meaning and value and that it does so in relation to the people who participate in it. In addressing such processes as ethical, however, we acknowledge the importance of interrogating their significance in community and the potential to affirm or deny certain aspects of this experience in the ongoing regulation of communal life.

A number of authors have commented on the way in which certain conceptions of both music and ethics have tended to lead to a wide separation between the two realms. Conceptions of music as solely aesthetic in nature combined with an ethics focused narrowly on questions of right and wrong have led to a conceptual gap which offers no easy connection between the two:

> Many twentieth-century philosophers of art have not only neglected th[e] intersection [between aesthetics and ethics], but in fact presented it as irrelevant, or conceptually invalid. This has been due in particular to the Kantian legacy, and to formalism and aestheticism ('art for art's sake'), for which it would make little sense to include discussions of ethics in relation to art.
>
> Cobussen and Nielsen (2012, pp1–2)

> The recent emphasis on game theory in ethics testifies to moral philosophy's lack of concern with either complexity or temporality in our ethical experience. Ethical choice is treated as a game in which clean choices can be made and judged as right or wrong without concern for the particular persons or contexts, except so far as these can be described in terms of 'utility preferences' and 'risk aversion'.
>
> Higgins (2011, pxvii)

> [During the Enlightenment] the realm of the 'aesthetic' emerged as something individual, self-oriented, inward, and autonomous – defined in part by its separation from or exclusion of matters 'social' ... not only did [the Enlightenment project] wrongly separate the musical from the social and the ethical, it actually redefined ethics in a way that foreclosed any possibility of reconciliation ... The outcome of the enlightenment moral philosophers' quest ... was an 'ethics' that was a thoroughly rule-governed affair, concerned with moral uprightness and the avoidance of evil ... (1) The Enlightenment Project deprived music of a claim to moral significance ... (2) The Enlightenment Project conceptualized ethics in a way of which music simply could not partake: for after all, musical people are quite capable of performing morally repugnant acts. If to be ethical is to avoid such acts, music is not a viable candidate for the development of ethical dispositions.
>
> Bowman (2001, pp13–14)

Shusterman (who articulates similar claims) argues that a routine isolation of the aesthetic can even lead to ethically undesirable situations 'provid[ing] an excuse for the powers and institutions that structure our everyday life to be brutally indifferent to natural human needs for the pleasure of beauty and imaginative freedom. These are not to be sought in real life, but in art, whose contrast and escape from the real gives us human sufferers temporary solace and relief' (1992, p20). More recent trends towards a virtue ethics which focuses on the good and the good life (Higgins 2011, pxviii) and a view of music which draws both subjects and social meanings into its very core mean that the conceptual gap has begun to fade to the background. Music can carry with it a range of different *goods* by virtue of the different ways in which it becomes meaningful, and these can thus become part of the process of ethical negotiation as they make themselves felt in different situations and experiences. As we have seen, attention to ethics serves to focus this research on musical value and meaning, encounters with discourse, patterns of authority and community, the relationship between music, subjectivity and the wider world and the negotiation of all of these. Examining these in the course of this book helps to reconnect music with a plane of significance that has both been frequently side-lined, not least within Contemporary Worship Music, and which is deeply meaningful within the life of the church.

The problem of tastes and preferences

In examining the significance of music, both inside and outside the church, one of the major obstacles that is encountered is the language of 'tastes' and 'preferences'.[22] This particular framing of musical opinions, experiences and judgments (illustrated in the previous chapter) means that it can often be hard to justify the need for public debate. They are implied to be purely subjective qualities; something to do with the uniqueness of the individuals experiencing them rather than something which can be opened up in any particularly meaningful way to public contestation or ethical debate. Differences of taste and the specifics of individual attachment are thereby positioned outside the realm of meaningful negotiation and contestation. Psychological studies of music often serve to reinforce this subjectivization of musical judgment, investigating the different traits that lead one person to prefer music with certain characteristics over other kinds of music (Chamorro-Premuzic et al 2010; Schäfer and Sedlmeier 2010; Rentfrow et al 2011) and thereby setting to one side questions of agency, individuality and deeper significance.[23] Antoine Hennion argues for a much more meaningful understanding of taste, something which he prefers to describe in terms of attachment in order to broaden the range of available connotations (2005, 2001).[24] For Hennion 'taste, passion, various forms of attachment are not primary data, amateurs' fixed properties that can simply be deconstructed analytically. People are active and productive; they constantly transform objects and works, performances and tastes' (2005). Taste, for Hennion is something which is bound up in the process of engagement with an object such that the two are inseparable. Hennion, contra Bourdieu (Hennion 2005, p131), wants to move beyond models which conceive musical taste primarily in terms of connoisseurship and beyond sociological accounts which position taste as a product of the social circumstances of the listener

(2005, p135), and thus as something which they are largely passive and ignorant towards.[25]

By conceptualizing taste as a matter of varying modes of attachment and engagement Hennion opens up the discourse around taste in a way that can make it meaningful and productive, able to involve diverse aspects of listener and music and the establishment of different forms of relationship between the two. In formulating broader and more open understandings of both music and taste – indeed, also of ethics and aesthetics – we provide a space in which it is much easier for them to come into dialogue and interrelate. If taste becomes something that can operate in a variety of ways, with modes of attachment taking on their own varieties of significance,[26] then we can start to investigate the ethical significance of some of these modes, not necessarily as a matter of right or wrong, but in the ways they can contribute to or become problematic in relation to particular kinds of good.[27] Likewise, if music and taste both have engagement and interaction at their core, then music is able to become a significant participant in the process of tasting, not merely as a separate object, but as something which can be discussed using a common language. Hennion helps us to move beyond common models which locate taste largely in the internal make-up of the subject, thus subjectivizing it, and instead allows taste to become part of an interaction in which both subject and object (music) have crucial roles to play and in which the relationship between the two stands as the key determining element. This, in turn, opens taste up much more readily to negotiation – the process of tasting and the activity of the relationship is one that can provide room for manoeuvre that is harder to come by in a space where there is a strict dichotomy between a subject's tastes and the properties of a musical object. Such a view is remarkably at home in the situation of congregational worship music, in which worshipers actively engage in the process of singing. Views about preferences in such a situation are hard to frame without addressing individuals' experiences of being present and their modes of engagement within the process of congregational singing.

Negotiating individual and group identities

Questions of musical taste are often closely connected to (perhaps sometimes becoming synonymous with) issues of identity; the nature of the connection between the two is a key determining element behind the kinds of negotiation that are possible. If, for example, taste maintains a close and relatively fixed relationship with individual identity then negotiation in a group context is likely (as the worship staff seem well aware) to present significant challenges, while if it is tied closely, instead, to group identity (as Rich suggested it could become) then individual attachments are likely to become less significant. The fixity or fluidity of connections between taste and identity are an important element in mediating the relationship between individual and group. Gordon Adnams, following Charles Taylor, suggests that one of the church's chief dysfunctions can be an over focus on the self, there being a need to recognise wider horizons of significance (Adnams 2008, p182). However, the opposite problem is also one that I have encountered, with an over concern for the problem of selfishness on the part of musicians and worshippers leading to a failure to take personal views and experiences seriously both by these individuals and by those with pastoral responsibility over them.

Timothy Rice, in his survey of articles in the journal *Ethnomusicology* has noted the somewhat incoherent nature of conceptualisations of identity within the discipline (2007). He observes that while there are a huge variety of approaches to conceptualizing identity and its links with music:

> What is missing in all this variety is the desire to create a coherent, interrelated, unified body of work that connects with the larger literature on identity and works out the potentially fascinating cross-cultural theoretical implications and general tendencies at work whenever music is used to create a sense of individual or social identity.
>
> Rice (2007, p37)

In a later follow-up article, Rice summarizes some of the questions he would ask in order to clarify how the concept of identity is being used.[28] While the responses (in the same issue) to Rice's desire for greater systematisation (as well as to his chosen method of analysis) are mixed, the list provides a helpful overview of some of the diverse ways in which music and identity can be conceptualized:

1   Do we want to argue that music contributes to the psychology of an individual's identity or to some form of collective social identity or to both?
2   If we want to argue that music contributes to the psychology of identity, then are we talking about a sense of 'who am I?' – that is, 'what is my essential nature?' – or are we talking about a person's desire to 'suture' himself or herself to a social group?
3   How many identities does an individual have? Do all individuals have the same possibilities for multiple identities or are the possibilities constrained by social, economic, and political inequalities? Does music contribute in the same way to all of them?
4   If we are arguing that music contributes to the social identity of a group, then how does it do that? Through performativity? Symbolization? Boundary formation?

> Rice (2010, p322)

If we look at some of the influential theoretical models of music and identity over the last 40 years or so we find that they diverge quite widely in their answers to some of these questions. In the 1970s the relationship between popular music and identity was heavily theorized through the concept of subculture (Hebdige 1979; Gelder 2005; Hesmondhalgh 2005; Huq 2006). Subcultural studies drew a strong connection between style, youth culture and alternative (non-mainstream) group identities. Subcultural studies gradually waned in favour as the fluid, fragmented and individual aspect of identity became more prominent (Gelder 2005, p12). Alternative notions such as the neo-tribe (Bennett 2000) and the scene (Straw 2001) aimed to loosen the strict bonds of subcultural studies in favour of looser, more flexible and more inclusive kinds of affiliation. Both neo-tribe and scene have, in turn, been subject to critique. David Hesmondhalgh criticizes both alternatives for failing to offer sufficient power to analyse the way in which distinctions and bonds are formed and made (Hesmondhalgh 2005) and believes that 'the search for an overarching term is likely to be unsatisfactory' (2005, p32).

Tia DeNora, rather than focusing on group identity, takes the individual as a starting point, focusing on the way in which music is present within the regular patterns of daily life (2000, 2003). Music, for DeNora, gains meaning through its ability to 'afford' different meanings depending on context.[29] She uses case studies to show how music can afford different meanings for particular individuals, allowing them to exploit these affordances for identity-formation and meaning. Thomas Turino's work on music and identity is similar to DeNora's in its emphasis on the individual. For Turino 'identity is the representation of selected habits foregrounded in given contexts to define self to oneself and to others by oneself and by others ... Social identities are based on recognized similarities within groups, and differences from others, which in turn serve as the basis of collective feeling and action. Group identities are the foundation of all social and political life' (2004, p8). Turino notes that these identities will tend to play out differently between different groups depending on whether it is helpful to highlight difference or unity. He has a strong the-oretical sense of how he believes individual and group identity to be related, and, as a consequence, also has the confidence to develop an ethical stance on what group music-making should look like.[30]

Stuart Hall questions such neat frameworks as he suggests that 'identities are never unified and, in late modern times, increasingly fragmented and fractured; never singular but multiply constructed across different, often intersecting and antagonistic, discourses, practices and positions. They are subject to a radical historicization, and are constantly in the process of change and transforma-tion' (Du Gay and Hall 1996, p4). On the whole, models of music and identity demonstrate little agreement as to the fixity or fluidity of the way in which people identify with music either individually or socially – indeed the level of divergence here hints precisely at the complexity of this relationship. Hesmondhalgh, DeNora and Turino, while all pursuing their preferred frame-work or methodology, all emphasize that different forms of bonds and expressions can be formed in different circumstances as well as the potential of this diversity as a location for productive research. The manner in which individuals connect music to their identity will affect their ability to move between different musical worlds and the way they relate their selves to the music which they experience. Georgina Born and David Hesmondhalgh interrogate precisely this issue, highlighting the complex range of negotiations required in order to negotiate multiple varieties and levels of identity:

> How, then, can we account for movement across and between identities? Here it becomes critically important to distinguish between individual self-identity and collective identity in relation to music. Because of the ubiquity of music in the mass-mediated world, and individuals' sub-jectification and socialization by a number of different musics, each bearing different dimensions of both their existing and desired, potential identities, rather than musical subjectivity being fixed and unitary, several musical 'identities' may inhabit the same individual. These are expressed in different musical tastes and practices, some of them in tension with each other or in contradiction with other parts of the self. Thus states of both 'authentic,' 'essential' musical identity and more playful, postmodern relations of desire and protoidentification through music coexist in many individuals, producing a state of fragmentary and multiple ima-ginary musical identification ... [W]e should ... develop an awareness of the multiple musical identifications or subject positions to which individuals are susceptible as producers and consumers ... Without such a distinction between individual and collective forms of musical identity ... we cannot address the potential disjunctures and conflicts between individual and collective musical identities, the way that cultural expec-tations and norms, or dominant musical discourses, may be in tension with individual identities and may exert powerful pressures of musical subjectification.
>
> Born and Hesmondhalgh (2000a, pp32–33)

Nancy Ammerman proposes a similar position from the sociology of religion:

> I am unwilling to discard the possibility that persons seek some sense of congruence within the complexity of their lives. Nor do I believe that structured categories exist untouched by the actions and resistance of the actors who inhabit them ... What we need is a way to talk about who we are and how we behave without reducing ourselves either to a single determining structural essence or to complete chaotic indeterminacy ... At its root, differences over fluidity and constraint in the formation of identity grow out of different understandings of agency and structure. ... Agency is located ... not in freedom from patterned constraint but in our ability to invoke those patterns in nonprescribed ways, enabled in large measure by the very multiplicity of solidarities in which we participate ... Acting within and between structures, across time and space, we cumu-latively build up a persona and collectively shape the solidarities of which we are a part.
>
> Ammerman (2003, pp211–212)

Suggestions such as these provide a helpful starting point for my research questions, allowing interrogation of the nuances of individual/communal relationships. The disjunctures and conflicts which these authors reference provide key sites for ethical negotiation. People can form different kinds of ties to particular musics either in relation to a group or simply as individuals with different concerns and constructions taking priority in different circumstances. Richard Jenkins suggests that it is precisely this process of identification and negotiation that is key to identity (2008, p5). In considering music-making within a church community we cannot pre-adopt one particular model of identity as a basis for evaluation – we must, instead, pay attention to the different ways in which individuals articulate this relationship before we can understand how ethical concerns are raised and how they might be addressed.

The inadequacy of assimilation and multiculturalism

Two common frameworks pre-answer questions of individual and group identity in suggesting ways in which a diversity of worshippers are able to make themselves at home within a particular church, and it is the tension between these that served to frame my experience at St George's. The first, assimilation, suggests that whatever ties people may have outside of the worshipping environment, as they spend time in the congregation they will gradually internalize the different elements of a church's culture such that they become a content and well-adjusted part of the congregation. This seems to be the predominant guiding model adopted in the interviews in the previous chapter. The second, a form of multiculturalism,[31] suggests that what worshippers need in order to feel part of a church community is some kind of representation of their culture within the worship, that they will connect to this element and as such will feel a valued part of the community.[32]

Historically, much of the contemporary worship movement has sidestepped either of these alternatives by close association with the homogeneous unit principle popularized by Peter Wagner,[33] an idea in which different homogeneous church bodies address themselves to particular sections of culture.[34] The movement initially addressed itself to one particular cultural demographic, seeking to make it easy for them to enter a church environment without encountering any cultural (particularly musical) barriers (Hunt 2000). In such a situation there was no need for either assimilation or multiculturalism as everyone started off with a shared background in a common cultural environment. Despite its avoidance of the tensions that diversity brings, such an approach nevertheless aligns closely with some of the assumptions of the multiculturalist model in emphasizing the importance of cultural connection. The homogeneous unit principle also aligns itself closely to group-based models of identity (see above), and in so doing can tend to underestimate internal diversity within any particular cultural group; by the nature of its logic it defines such diversity out of the range of discourse, viewing those whom it attracts as essentially identical by virtue of their membership within the target demographic (Butler 2000, p34). Even within its own limitations, it is often not quite so successful or as easy as it might seem; Howard and Streck (1999, p60) narrate the way in which contemporary Christian music, despite initial intentions, quickly found itself to be part of an isolated subculture, one which, in its efforts to serve the Christian community, became irrelevant and disconnected from the rest of society. Worship music has thus ended up with a somewhat conflicted relationship with surrounding popular culture – on the one hand wanting to maintain some level of connection, and on the other, being aware of its inability to do so in all respects, thus complicating the dynamic at the heart of this research. In bringing a straightforward connection into question this development requires a greater degree of negotiation surrounding this relationship.

As is becoming increasingly clear with national-scale debates on immigration and multiculturalism in the UK, neither multiculturalism nor assimilation really seems able to do justice to the range of ways in which individuals relate to a community[35] and the complexities of different levels and kinds of identity.[36] We are presented with alternatives in which either people change to become part of the culture, letting go of that which they are attached to, or they hold on to their existing attachments and resist any process of change. These mirror, to a certain extent, the disparity between individual-centred and group-based models of identity, with either the characteristics of the group as a whole or those of the individuals serving as foundational and taking precedence. This polarization, by its provision of stark alternatives, is unable to provide a great deal of space in which dialogue, transformation and learning can occur. Some authors, noticing the problematic nature of the traditional polarisation, have sought to move dialogue into more fruitful areas of discussion and provide us with examples of how it might be possible to resist the problems of both alternatives. Dan Rodríguez-García's description of 'interculturalism' illustrates one such alternative:[37]

> Interculturalism can be understood as the interactive process of living together in diversity, with the full participation and civic engagement of, and social exchange between, all members of society beyond that of mere recognition and coexistence, in turn forming a cohesive and plural civic community. Interculturalism has the merit of focusing on the negotiation and conflict-resolution process, rather than solely on the problem [of how to manage diversity], and of emphasizing the changing nature of cultures and societies.
>
> Rodríguez-García (2010, p260)

Rather than individuals and groups being expected to either assimilate to a culture or maintain their own distinctive world within it, there is a process of engagement and exchange in which they are able to share and debate important issues and thus participate in the negotiation of a shared social existence. Such a model focuses on the process of negotiation rather than on building a community based on assumptions about the inevitable outcomes of such a process. It locates the key to plural communities in processes of exchange rather than individuals, musics or communities as fixed entities. In leaving the questions of the outcome open we are presented with a much messier model, in which the solutions and negotiations of one community will look very different from those of others, and in which, therefore, the varying possibilities suggested by the diversity of identity models within ethnomusicology might find themselves better able to contribute.

The potential of cosmopolitan models

A turn towards intercultural processes is often complemented by a move towards cosmopolitan models of community, and it is these which, I suggest, in seeking to provide frameworks for understanding the interactive negotiation of cultural movement, inter-relation and difference, form a helpful basis for understanding the various negotiations of congregational diversity described in the following chapters. A number of ethnomusicologists have, in recent years, been drawn to cosmopolitan frameworks in order to understand a variety of musical negotiations and practices (Turino 2000; Stokes 2007; Tsiouslakis 2011; Perman 2012; Bosse 2013; Harnish 2013; Webster-Kogan 2014). It is not, however, primarily to these authors which I want to turn in considering worship at St Aldates, but rather to a number of recent thinkers within bodies of social and political theory who have sought to develop cosmopolitan theories not just as a way of understanding global and international relationships and flows, but as tools for understanding social interactions and processes more widely.

While cosmopolitanism often refers primarily to national identities and international flows and exchanges this is not the only level on which it can be a useful concept. Gerard Delanty suggests that:

> It is useful to distinguish three main dimensions of cosmopolitanism: the historical level of modernity, the macro or societal level of the interaction of societies or societal systems, and the micro level of identities, movements and communities within the social world ... cosmopolitanism is not to be equated with transnationalization ... it makes more sense to see it expressed in more reflexive kinds of self-understanding ... it resides in social mechanisms and dynamics that can exist in any society at any time in history where world openness has a resonance.
>
> Delanty (2006, pp41–42)

Vertovec and Cohen make a similar point, suggesting that 'present-day processes ... such as diasporic identification and the rise of identity politics, have multiplied people's interests and affiliations. Now gender, sexuality, age, disability, 'homeland', locality, race, ethnicity, religion - even cultural hybridity itself - are among the key identifications around which the same person might at one time or another politically mobilize' (2002, p12). Beck and Sznaider likewise point out the way in which 'the principle of cosmopolitanism can be found in specific forms at every level and can be practiced in every field of social and political action' (2006, p3). It is not necessary, therefore, to invoke trans-national flows in order to invoke the conceptual frameworks of cosmopolitanism. As a conceptual framework it is capable of application to a range of social scales within which similar sets of issues are present – in the case of this book, the micro-scale of everyday movements within individuals' lives.

Turning, then, to some recent definitions, Onyx et al suggest that 'everyday cosmopolitanism reflects the ordinary interactions that occur between individuals of different cultures routinely negotiating across difference in order to coexist within a shared social space' (Onyx et al 2011, p61) and Anthony Appiah suggests that 'cosmopolitanism imagines a world in which people and novels and music and films and philosophies travel between places where they are understood differently, because people are different and welcome to their difference' (2005, p258). Others make similarly broad and resonant suggestions. Beck suggests that 'The central defining characteristic of a cosmopolitan perspective is the "dialogic imagination" ... The dialogic imagination corresponds to the coexistence of rival ways of life in the individual experience, which makes it a matter of fate to compare, reflect, criticize, understand, combine contradictory certainties' (2002, p18), while Vertovec and Cohen quote Waldron, who suggests that '[cosmopolitanism] means the ability to stand outside of having one's life written and scripted by any one community, whether that is a faith or tradition or religion or culture - whatever it might be - and to draw selectively on a variety of discursive meanings' (Vertovec and Cohen 2002, p4). As we will see over the course of the next three chapters, such descriptions capture important facets of what it means for individuals from a diverse range of musical backgrounds to co-exist for a period of their week in a shared musical environment, drawing attention to the dynamic negotiation of musical community as varied musical spaces and identities are brought into ongoing relationship. This outlook therefore joins the renewed understandings of music, ethics, taste and identity discussed earlier in this chapter in providing new and helpful ground on which to overcome previous obstacles to fruitful discussion of congregational musicking and providing foundational ground for the rest of this book.

To return to the question of this research – how do individuals relate their musical lives outside church to their experiences within – we have seen that, while it is often assumed that experiences of this relationship are relatively insignificant, there are good reasons to bring such an understanding into question and that an alternative strategy might be to approach music from an ethical angle, focusing on the negotiation of meaning and value in community, and in particular the relationship between individual experience and institutional discourse. We have seen that, rather than approaching musical taste as a mere fact of only subjective significance, it may be helpful to approach it with a broader understanding of the nature of attachment in which engagement between subject and object is an important location of significance. Finally, we have seen that the relationship between individual and group identity is likely to provide a multifaceted rather than straightforward location for interaction and negotiation. These understandings will guide much of the rest of this book and, with these established, we now turn to the framework within which I will be discussing the interview data.

The analytical framework

The conceptual categories which guide the following chapters have arisen largely out of my own attempts to do justice to the range of experiences within the interviews and focus on the negotiation of potentially inconsistent identities while allowing sufficient room for discussion of the full range of issues raised thus far under a tripartite umbrella. They are not neat and self-contained and many people's experiences fail to fit completely into any single one of them and instead overlap or cut against any boundaries I try to put in place. This seems to be the price that is paid when creating any analytical framework and my solution is to allow the chapters a certain degree of messiness, to allow the discussion of people's experiences to lead the text astray where appropriate. In this way, I am aware that there are elements in the interviews I overlook; but at least the text hints at its own incompleteness rather than pretending to contain everything within a single frame.

My framework concentrates on three different ways in which people relate their musical lives outside of a church environment to their experience within a church setting and parallels closely one constructed by Rachel Kraus (2010). Kraus, in her study of identity integration among Christian women who belly dance, surveys a range of approaches that have been used in examining the way in which people negotiate potentially inconsistent identities. Kraus's survey of existing approaches, combined with her own focus on an expressive medium, makes her work an ideal starting point for this study.[38] For Kraus, identity is a category which comes into play in any situation where people play a role that is important and meaningful to them. She notes that, while most analysis in this area has focussed on situations where it has been assumed that there will be some kind of initial conflict caused by inconsistent identities,[39] less research has focused on experiences in which such conflict is not assumed. In addition, she believes that little attention has been paid to the process of 'integrating religious identities with identities derived from participation in secular leisure' (Kraus 2010, p458).[40] Kraus examines a range of 'identity integration techniques' that have been proposed in the literature as well as proposing her own set which does justice to her area of study. She identifies the following identity-integration strategies from within prior research: 'maintaining both identities' in which neither of two differing identities is suppressed or emphasized; 'selectively defining religion' in which certain aspects of religious teaching are reinterpreted or highlighted to reconcile identities; 'separating roles' in which there is an occupation of different roles at different times; and 'emphasizing one role' in which one identity is seen as more important that the other. Two of her own proposed categories closely parallel this framework, while the third, 'setting intention', seems to work in a similar manner to 'selectively defining religion' by allowing the secular, rather than the religious activity to be the one which becomes redefined.

While Kraus begins with the assumption that identity integration is key to the way in which people negotiate their experiences within multiple environments, I find the assumption of positive integration to be problematic in the area of congregational music and prefer to begin with an assumption of relatedness, but not necessarily of complete integration. This is reflected in the slightly different form which my categories take.[41] In this book I focus on three broad categories of experience, to each of which I devote a chapter. 'Bridging worlds through common modes of being in music' forms a close parallel to Kraus's categories that are built around the redefinition of religious or secular experience, as I highlight the way in which the malleability of different experiences allows commonalities to be formed between different musical worlds. 'Communal and private, spiritual and secular' focuses on the ways in which separate musical worlds can co-exist, while 'At the edges: value transfer, judgments, discontent' focuses on situations where the transfer of values between different musical worlds can potentially become problematic or in which there is some need to suppress particular aspects of experience in order to positively evaluate an activity.

Each of my categories is intentionally broad in order to encompass a range of different experiences. While there is no particular sense that either musical environment has any priority over the other, it is nevertheless the worship environment in which the musical aspects are pre-defined to a greater extent, meaning that the different experiences do not necessarily start out on an equal footing. In one sense, therefore, the pattern is reversed from that of the belly dance, with the activity of worship within the church being the pole of musical experience that is brought into greater question. Nevertheless, there is a sense in which the church often maintains a greater degree of priority in spiritual formation and it is partly this ebb and flow of 'musical' and 'spiritual' (neither of which should be taken as isolated or self-contained terms) and their intertwining from and between different poles of experience that makes the analytical project an interesting one.

Notes

1 See Chua (1999) for a discussion of the concept of 'absolute music' and its disconnection of music from other kinds of meaning. See Kramer (2003) for a discussion of the ways in which the 'New Musicology' has served in the late 20th century to broaden discussion of musical meaning.

2 As Jones and Webster (2006, p14) highlight, such debates were by no means limited to America; they were also present within British evangelical circles.

3 See Habermas (2006) for a discussion of the ways in which secular and religious viewpoints can interact productively within the framework of a liberal society.

4 Problems which, in my experience, St Aldates preachers can be particularly sensitive to when fearful of the decline of Christian influence in British society.

5 'The performance with its concomitant styles, gestures, and techniques' (2008, p248).

6 Klisala Harrison (2012) is one of many drawing attention to the way in which the applied/non-applied dichotomy that has arisen within ethnomusicology may be an unhelpful one. During my fieldwork a number of interviewees commented that they hadn't thought about a particular question before; some asked for my thoughts and one or two even indicated that maybe there were certain things that they perhaps 'should' do on the basis of our conversations. The asking of ethnomusicological questions has ethical implications of its own, particularly when touching on topics that carry with them deeply felt significance.

7 It is important to note, however, that there is not a complete absence of public discourse; instead the discourse that is present is able to accommodate the schools of belief within the congregation even if they are primarily held in private. The nature of this public discourse is key to the holding together of the congregation, whether or not discussion specifically enters into debates on particular issues.

8 See Baumann (1996, p10) for the distinction between dominant discourse employed by those in positions of status and demotic discourse employed amongst the people. See also Cameron (2010, p53) for the way in which there can be a gap between espoused and operant theological understandings of practice which may be as relevant to the demotic as to the dominant discourse. Positions espoused within demotic discourse may not always reflect operant practice and experience.

9 Rommen notes, for instance, the denunciation of Dancehall music by a number of pastors (2007b, p28).

10 See Leslie Green (2003) for a helpful discussion of these ideas.

11 Rommen cites Simon Frith to demonstrate what this might mean: 'Music constructs our sense of identity through the direct experiences it offers of the body, of time and sociability, experiences which enable us to place ourselves in imaginative cultural narratives. Such a fusion of imaginative fantasy and bodily practice marks also the integration of aesthetics and ethics. John Miller Chernoff has thus eloquently demonstrated how among African musicians an aesthetics judgment (this sounds good) is necessarily also an ethical judgment (this is good). The issue is "balance": "the quality of rhythmic relationship" describes a quality of social life. In this sense, style is another word for the perception of relationships' (Rommen 2007b, pp36–37).

12 Think, for example, of the way in which immediacy of expression in rock music can combine with simple chord structures which can make it easy to form a band and perform this expression.

13 The Anglican Church is particularly familiar with the tension between a variety of viewpoints (most recently over the question of female bishops), and the process of moving towards consensus on particular issues over time. Tension over ethical and theological issues forms a perpetual part of its communal life. The slow process of forming consensus is one which acknowledges the goal of unity and the

importance of discernment and which, although it recognizes the fragmented nature of human communities, nevertheless holds out the possibility of making progress under the hand of divine guidance.

14 Baumeister (2003) is sceptical about this possibility, believing it to neglect the deep level of certain kinds of value conflict. He nevertheless argues for a process of negotiation and compromise which takes into account differing perspectives despite failing to completely reconcile them. Likewise, Schrerer and Patzer (2010) stress the tension between universalist and relativist approaches and, on the basis of this, establish an account of discourse ethics more sensitive to this tension.

15 Habermas's model doesn't immediately account, for example, for a situation in which appointed leaders are expected to carry decision-making authority which is not necessarily directly founded on democratic representation. However, Michele Dillon (1999) examines ways in which Habermas's processes can fruitfully relate to structures of church authority. Within the church, Habermas's processes need to be set alongside ideas such as 'servant leadership' (Matthew 20: 25–27), communal formation of the individual, and preference of the other over the self.

16 Ammerman reinforces the importance of this: 'the ability to use a group's language is basic to what we mean by membership and identity. To participate in the "discourse" of the group is to enter the social world that the group has constructed' (Ammerman 2003, p213).

17 It is important to emphasize that I am referring to worship as distinguished from music – discourse about worship often avoids much discussion of the way in which music contributes to the act.

18 For example, prayers for encounter with God during the worship time and sermons on the need for correct heart-attitudes. See Chapter 1 for an examination of some of this discourse within St Aldates.

19 Frank Burch Brown rhetorically asks 'When it comes to sharing out songs and deciding which songs to sing, are we stuck with power struggles and sheer relativism?' (2009, p60). See the previous chapter for the ways in which questions of music can often be seen as questions of whose tastes to appeal to. See also Rees (1993) for a discussion of clashes of authority between clergy and organists in more traditional settings.

20 See for example Rich's response to a question relating to musical style: 'I think there's something to be said for, for musicians, that it's, that we're not to be selfish, come with selfish ambition when we're leading worship, we're leading people in worship, because that's ... our role is not to bring our own, it's not, I'm going to be careful here. Our role is to serve the congregation' (interview with the author – 10 May 2012).

21 Of course, many conflicts, even musical ones, centre overtly around ethical disputes, as Rommen (2007b) demonstrates. If carried out according to Habermas's proposed framework, however, it is my argument that this level of discourse has greater irenic potential than one that centres simply on direct claims to influence.

22 See, for example, Nekola (2009, p256) and Frith (1996b, p9), a stance echoed by Rich's suggestion that 'I think you have to sort of first of all come to terms with the fact you're never going to please everyone, you're never going to satisfy everyone's personal desires, musical tastes' (interview with the author – 10 May 2012).

23 Although see social-psychological writings such as MacDonald et al (2002) for an approach more in tune with the nuances of ethnomusicological study.

24 Nick Prior positions Hennion as one of a number of post-Bourdieu scholars who are more willing to engage with the specifics of encounters with music rather than considering musical taste simply as a means of large-scale social differentiation; part of 'a new "post-Bourdieusian" analytics where taste and consumption are more than social weapons' (2013, p190). While he suggests that 'Returning to Bourdieu after reading Hennion, one is struck by how flat Bourdieu's analysis of the work of art is, how synoptic, inert and mechanical the cultural encounter can seem' (2011, p133) he also highlights the importance of paying attention to the way in which 'music mediates, intersects with and expresses power relations – power relations and stratified social trajectories that are, moreover, often glossed in accounts considered post-Bourdieusian' (2013, p191). Prior makes it clear that we should not retreat simply into 'another (albeit rather scintillating) form of aesthetic individualism' (2011, p134).

25 Bourdieu's much-used and much-critiqued theory of taste emphasizes the connections between social class, status and their associated dispositions, positing taste largely as a function of an individual's broader social positioning (Bourdieu 1984). Douglas Holt suggests that Bourdieu's theory of tastes can be understood as 'a set of sensitizing propositions concerning the relations between social conditions, taste, fields of consumption and social reproduction that must be specified' (1997, p100); however, such abstraction seems to deliberately side line the question of social status and class which Bourdieu aligns closely with particular cultural forms.

26 Rather than something which is simply about, for example, a recognition of beauty or about music that happens to appeal to the subject's makeup in such a way as to make them feel good.

27 David Looseley helpfully situates Hennion in context and emphasizes the way in which Hennion's framework contributes to public policy debate. He suggests that 'Hennion's pragmatism … implies an ethics of cultural policy … he takes pragmatism to mean that abstract principles – for example, that a particular form of music should be promoted for its intrinsic aesthetic merit – should be replaced by a concern with consequences. I interpret his reasoning here as being that, since music exists not as object but as process or event, what matters is not a declaration of principle regarding the worth of a particular genre … but an on-going evaluation of the effects of a particular policy regarding that genre, which the policy agent must commit him/herself to constantly monitoring' (2006, pp349–350).

28 Rice (2007) contains a longer but less clearly defined list of questions.

29 For example, 'Music may also afford the imaginative projection of bodily movement, as when one "pictures" a type of movement when hearing a type of music. The example of marching music serves to illustrate these points. On hearing march music one may (but not automatically …) be reminded of or begin to imagine – to "picture" – marching. One may, in other words, become motivated or aroused in relation to a type of agency – marching – to a particular movement style, and one associated with a particular set of institutional practices and their particular agent-states, such as bodily regulation, coordination, and entrainment. One may "become" (produce one's self as) a "marcher" – that is, on the occasion of music heard, one may adapt one's self to its perceived properties and so become, via the music, a type of agent, in this case, one imbued with march-like, militaristic agency' (DeNora 2003, p47).

30 'For me, good music-making or dancing is a realization of ideal – possible – human relationships where the identification with others is so direct and so

intense that we feel, for those best moments, as if our selves had merged' (Turino 2008, p19). While Turino is clearly elaborating a personal view here, it nevertheless connects closely to the theoretical frameworks which he chooses to employ.

31 A 'position that rejects assimilation and the "melting pot" image ... and instead prefers such metaphors as the "salad bowl" or the "glorious mosaic," in which each ... element in the population maintains its distinctiveness' (Glazer 1997, p10).

32 On the basis of ethnographic fieldwork in the United States, Gerardo Marti has recently argued against the principle of multiculturalism as the key ingredient which allows people to find a place within a church. He instead favours a much more assimilationist model as having a better basis in reality, finding that worshippers will make themselves at home in a range of environments and that their own habits outside of the church community are largely irrelevant to the social processes which incorporate and welcome them into a particular community (2012, p80).

33 See, for example, Hunt's discussion of the principle's prominence within the charismatic movement (Hunt 2000, p20).

34 According to Kathleen Garces-Foley 'Donald McGavran, the director of the School of World Missions at Fuller Seminary in Los Angeles, developed this principle in 1936. McGavran taught those preparing for foreign missions that forming homogeneous congregations was the most effective method of evangelization, because crossing cultural barriers is too great an obstacle for potential converts. As he explained it simply, "men like to become Christians without crossing racial, linguistic, or class barriers"' (Garces-Foley 2007, p20).

35 See, for example, Joppke (2004) for a description of various twists and turns in national policy-making in response to inadequacies in both alternatives.

36 Negotiating these questions within the musical life of a community of faith might be thought to present a different set of challenges from those that might be faced on a national level. The shared commitment to a common cause and group is one that provides a significant gathering-point which can help to ensure a certain initial level of shared understanding and cooperation within a church community. However, as Penny Edgell Becker suggests, there can still be a significant amount of talking-past one another where different understandings of the nature of this community, its priorities and the operation of authority within it are present (1999, p4). A top-level understanding of commitment to faith, God and church may nevertheless result in very different models of the nature of this relationship. Certain understandings of the church body can tend to minimize space for dialogue and debate, preferring to conceptualize the church body in ways which preclude the importance of individual attachment. These may be successful in minimizing tension for those who adopt them; however when there are those in a congregation who adopt a different model for their thinking about the church they can also lead to conflict.

37 See also Warner (1997) for a similar but less developed or comprehensive attempt to move beyond the assimilationism/multiculturalism binary.

38 Even so, it is worth drawing attention to some key points of difference. In focusing on belly dancing she is choosing an activity which the church is assumed to morally distance itself from. The nature of disparity between the two settings is thus much more explicit than in the area of music in which there is no initial assumption of incompatibility. In addition, belly dancing is not an activity which would often take place within a church setting, while music of some kind is an activity which is clearly present both in and out of the church. In focusing on the

mediating concept of identity, however, Kraus sets such disparities aside and adopts a more egalitarian frame with little implicit weighting.

39 Principally homosexuality and feminism as they relate to the church.

40 A somewhat problematic label, music outside of church may well neither be conceived of either as entirely secular or as leisure, however her description seems, nevertheless, to point in its general direction.

41 The internal conflict that Kraus finds to be minimal within the experience of Christian belly dancers is something that is very present within some aspects of congregational musical experience. The presence of ongoing tensions within the life of congregations, not least surrounding musical choices, is something that anyone who has spent a significant amount of time within a single church body will be well aware of, and these are products of individual experience as much as of the range of relationships formed between congregation members and each other or the church body as a whole. Kraus's distinction between internal conflict (which she finds little of) and external conflict (which is more present) therefore is one that I find hard to maintain in the case of church music, at least within the context of this study – experiences may be framed in discussion as belonging to one particular sphere or the other, but participatory congregational singing is a realm where both spheres inevitably intersect and intertwine as the experience is both personal and collective.

3 Bridging worlds through common modes of being in music

The malleability of music

The first category which I trace through my interview data focuses on the bridges that can be built between different musical environments. The variety of backgrounds which worshippers bring with them through the doors of a church open up a broad range of different experiences. It is sometimes possible for worshippers to form connections between music within the church and musical experiences elsewhere in their lives, enabling them to experience a certain degree of commonality between different musical worlds and thereby experience a level of coherence between different aspects of their musical lives and modes of musical attachment. For some worshippers these bridges enable a positive experience of collective worship with the *goods* (i.e., those things which they value positively) from one area of their life coinciding closely with those of another, thereby allowing multiple forms of music to be experienced and assessed in similarly positive and valuable terms. The ability for this to happen is often rooted in specific ways in which worshippers conceive of and find significance within the different musics that they encounter and the particular characteristics which come to the foreground within each experience. These characteristics are not simply pre-given, and it is partly the malleability of musical experience which can enable strong bridges between diverse musics to be formed. As will be illustrated in this chapter, modes of experience formed in one setting can be brought across to another, or broader ways of being in the world can be brought to the different musical settings which worshippers enter. There can also be a more complex relationship between different settings whereby they (mutually) reinterpret each-other, developing commonalities that might never be found in either in isolation.

The possibility of differing readings of a particular text is one that has been long-recognized within the realms of reception history. The author is no longer usually considered to be the sole arbitrator of meaning, but instead has become one voice among many others who are all empowered to interpret and give meaning to a text. Within the context of sung worship it is not simply the text (musical or otherwise) of an individual author which can be subject to multiple experiences and readings, but socially produced practices within the church body itself. The church congregation is not simply a passive audience which receives and reinterprets a text but instead actively engages in the performance of worship through sung participation. The church body is therefore able to actively engage in the meaning-making activity of performance alongside the receptive aspects of their engagement with the performance of the musicians on the stage; members not only receive performative meaning but play a role in producing it. This active participation implicates members of the congregation strongly in the activity of worship such that their experience of different modes of being in the world is at least as significant as patterns of uttered and received meaning. Differences in understandings of worship will lead to differences on a significant experiential level due to the high level of self-involvement inherent in the activity of sung worship. Such patterns can be inscribed on a deep level within the lives of worshippers due to the way in which musical worship is expected to connect with significant spiritual aspects of a worshipper's life as well as with their deepest feelings.[1]

One process which draws attention to the way in which musical meaning can be flexible and open to re-conception in different contexts and situations is that of musical migration. Laudan Nooshin's work (2011) draws attention to the way in which the meanings associated with different musics can be altered in the movement between un-related contexts in such a way that their significance becomes almost entirely different. She draws particular attention to the way in which mediated technology makes it possible for musical style to migrate without a necessity for it to do so alongside particular peoples or cultures which might serve to maintain its 'original' meanings. While music has relatively little distance to travel within the context of a single church community, as members of the congregation migrate between their everyday musical lives and the experience of a Sunday service they become themselves loci of musical migration as they bring foreign musical worlds with them to the gathered activity of congregational worship. The possibility of flexible relationships between music and people in a society where group allegiances are multiple and fluid means that, in a similar but converse manner to the migration of musical forms, individuals are able, as we shall see in the next section, to bring a variety of meanings with them into this environment without bringing the musics with which they are associated. This migration can lead to a constant interplay of meaning-making between a variety of contexts and has the potential to contribute to a destabilization of any given musical meaning, particularly where a given setting does not form the primary musical home of particular congregation members. The way in which worship music is (re-)conceived by individuals within the congregation therefore has the potential to draw upon meanings which are not pre-given by the church environment within which they find themselves.

A number of authors comment on the way in which musical meaning can be flexible within the ongoing practice of communities. Jonathan Dueck (2003, p63) comments on the possibility of differing understandings of a shared musical practice depending on the generational identity of a group, with different sub-groups conceiving of the music according to different shared frames of reference. Dueck illustrates this using Thomas Turino's example of music in Conima, Peru, which 'for youth ... performs the role of a pro-indigenous folklore, while the older audience of this music, mostly ex-residents of Conima, find it a nostalgic recreation of the activities which informed their own social life in Conima' (2003, p64). In a similar manner Anna Nekola (2009, p30) draws attention to the way in which cultural studies' concern for the political and ideological aspects of meaning-making can help us to come to terms with the multiple ideologies and epistemologies within evangelical discourse about music, highlighting the usefulness of the concepts of 'oppositional' and 'negotiated' readings. This contestation of significance and meaning can – as this chapter will demonstrate with reference to individuals' musical experiences – be significant on a more personal level, as idiosyncratic musical worlds are brought in relation to a shared practice in ways that can be peculiar to the lives of individuals while it can also draw in discourses surrounding music in other contexts which individuals inhabit.

Timothy Rice (2001) draws attention to the multiple levels on which music can be assigned meaning, ranging from the personal individual level all the way through to the level of national governance. For Rice music can exemplify an uncontrollability which allows it to break free of the broader discourses that attempt to define its significance. This becomes especially important when a high level institution[2] seeks to assign a particular meaning to a musical practice but finds itself unable to bring it under control. The ability to assign meaning can, as a result, become a key part of contestations of authority. Within the church such contestations can become important when a shared understanding of music is needed in order for an individual to conform to the expectations of leaders and the wider church. The musical life of the church, due to its prominent role in services, is a key part of its functioning together as a community, and so the way in which church members are able to come together in a common practice is key to the broader functioning of the church body. Rice's category of metaphor can help to understand the way in which competing understandings of music function:

> A given metaphor probably achieves some goals and makes some sense in certain situations but fails to account for the full range of music's possibilities and significance. I further suggest that multiple musical metaphors probably guide action and thought in individual lives, in society and through time. Sometimes, I suppose, they happily commingle; at others they may become alternative, competing strategies.
>
> Rice (2001, p22)

The question of how the guiding metaphors for and understandings of music within the church as used by those in authority interact with those employed by congregation members can illuminate our understanding of how worshippers relate to the musical activity and habits of the congregation. Rice suggests that such metaphors as 'music as object', 'music as art', 'music as emotional expression', 'music as text', 'music as social behaviour', 'music as political symbol' and 'music as sign' serve to make truth claims about the ontological status of music and should be taken seriously as 'fundamental claims to truth, guides to practical action and sources for understanding music's profound importance in human life' (2001, p22).[3] Some metaphors are compatible but others potentially conflict with each other.

Ambivalence towards music's role means that it is hard to pinpoint the guiding musical metaphors of St Aldates precisely. While 'music as worship' might seem the obvious principal metaphor to employ, as we saw in Chapter 1 the musical aspect is often consciously distanced from the activity of worship such that a more appropriate primary (although not exclusive) description might be 'music as a space for worship' or, more strongly, 'music as a neutral canvas for worship'. The implicit disconnect between music and significance which these metaphors introduce both leaves room for worshippers to employ their own metaphors for understanding the meaning of the music and brings the potential for conflict if individual and institutional metaphors are brought into close conversation with each other. While 'music as worship' is a broad metaphor that has the potential to suggest a range of subsidiary understandings, the distancing provided by 'music as a space for worship' offers a metaphor with less content and, as a result, less internal richness for other metaphors to hook onto. As a guide to action and thought (Rice 2001, p22), it stands at a distance from questions of musical and inter-personal engagement, setting such questions aside into a separate realm in which they may or may not be engaged further. Individual musical experience is often, therefore, precisely just that – something which people will keep to themselves or share in the odd moment with close and trusted friends. This aspect is perhaps what led a number of interviewees to comment that they were articulating particular thoughts for the first time in interview – the conversations we were having around music were not a regular or normal part of their life at the church. Such a dynamic is reinforced by the nature of Sunday services – the large and buzzing crowd before or after a service is not an ideal space for deeply meaningful conversation and members of the leadership are often preoccupied with the details of the things they need to get done and the queue of people they need to talk to such that the prospect of a longer engagement there is also restricted. The structures of a large church body run by a professional and busy team tend to militate against anything but the most selective and sporadic individual engagement between leaders and congregation. In addition, the clear dividing line between those employed in positions of authority and those without such status means that the content of congregational gatherings is rarely challenged by unexpected input. Different musical metaphors rarely get the chance to be contested in public space, but instead competing strategies can persist without necessarily coming into situations of conflict.

The flexibility of musical meaning, while it can facilitate individuals' ability to bring different parts of their musical lives together into a coherent whole, allowing different musics to be experienced in similar ways, is not necessarily a requirement for such bridging to occur; some musical environments may contain sufficient commonality in and of themselves that little re-conception is required. Nor does it necessitate that particular musical worlds be bridged in this way (as we shall see in the next chapter). If such slippage in and looseness of musical meaning is common within experiences of music, however, then it should be expected that such connections are likely to be built and, indeed, that there may be a somewhat fluid line between an experience that seems, by exploiting this flexibility, to radically re-conceive a particular music, and one which simply tends to latch on to or foreground certain characteristics within it. If intertextuality refers to the possibility (or inevitability) of the formation of significant or meaningful relationships, through a variety of methods and agencies, between texts, then we might refer to the possible relationship between different musical worlds as a form of inter*con*textuality, highlighting the likelihood that meaning (as we will see later in the chapter) will spill over between multiple contexts. Such a designation would encompass a similarly broad range of possible associations as its textual counterpart, with its terminological scope able to expand as far as the variety of relationships that can be formed. In a similar way to the concept of intertextuality the idea of intercontextuality avoids the necessity of focussing on pre-given meaning, allowing a fluid relationship between constructed, experienced and given meanings. Within the context of worship it does not, therefore, assume that the content of musical worship is entirely given by the church community but allows the church context to be situated in relation to the surrounding (in this case, musical) world. It also allows a similarly fluid sense of the direction of relationship between the church and other contexts, a sense that is perhaps heightened in experiential situations where there is no clear chronological priority of one kind of encounter over another. The analogy between text and context is not a precise one; individuals encounter texts and contexts on different levels, often finding themselves embedded within contexts to a greater degree than they might individual texts. There is often also a lesser degree of authorial agency at work in artfully constructing a particular context, with relationships formed between contexts sometimes being less intentional in nature. The term serves to highlight, however, the way in which a music's context is not merely a passive and semi-neutral background but is capable of becoming meaningful as much as the texts embedded within it. Discussion of the relationship between contexts can often fall to the background as they are often treated as self-contained worlds within which to understand the content they contain, the church service, for example, providing a frame within which songs gain meaning as part of the act of worship. The way in which subjects move between contexts, however, inevitably means that certain relationships come into play in a way that goes beyond simple familiarity or unfamiliarity with particular environments.[4] We now turn to some of the experiences of members of the St Aldates congregation to examine some of the ways in which experiences in diverse musical contexts can be brought into various forms of ongoing, productive relationship.

Building bridges between diverse environments

> I enjoy playing and, I guess, performing as a horn player, and know I can make a fairly reasonable noise. But that's never been the primary purpose for me in terms of worship, or in terms of orchestral playing. You want to play your own stuff well, but you're contributing to part of an overall impact … The same is true orchestrally as was true in a worship context: that you were able to bring different impact through the sound and the quality of what you were able to bring in. And that was then both making for a fuller, richer music, and then hopefully helping people to be able to worship.
>
> Graham – interview with the author, 11 February 2012

Graham[5] regularly plays first horn in the Oxford Symphony Orchestra and, until recently, was the orchestra's chairman. He is also a regular horn player on the St Aldates worship team, improvising horn lines as part of one of the morning worship bands. These two musical worlds occupy separate ends of the traditional art music/popular music divide and, as such, are usually thought to be relatively well distinguished from each other. For Graham they are, however, bridged by their exemplification of a common set of values. Both musical worlds centre on a group of people coming together to create an impact through their shared music-making activity. This value lies at the heart of music for Graham, and is highlighted by his lack of regular engagement either with recordings or as a member of a concert audience – the importance of the communal production of musical affect means that private or passive listening to either classical music or worship music is not something that has a role in his everyday musical life. Evaluations of his experiences within the different musical environments are also carried out in similar terms – Graham highlights the importance of members of an orchestra being both literally and metaphorically in tune with each other when coming together to perform, the coherence of and relationship with the group being the key element in creating good music.[6] In a church setting he finds the quality of being metaphorically in tune with the congregation and with God to be highly important when leading worship, a sensitivity to others serving to open up a meaningful and powerful experience for those present.

The way in which Graham applies the value of 'in-tuneness' to musical worship clearly differs from how he applies it in an orchestral setting; the relationships which it refers to are different in each; nevertheless its presence as an evaluative criterion within both environments demonstrates a significant element of commonality. Graham conceptualizes worship music according to some of the criteria found within an orchestral setting, and he thinks of orchestral music in terms that are not necessarily distinctive purely to itself but can carry across between differing musical worlds. He does not employ the conceptual categories which often serve to distinguish these two musical realms (e.g., art/pop, formal/free, high/low) but instead both musical experiences can be evaluated using this common set of terms. Turino (2008, p95) finds that individuals foreground certain identity-characteristics as they move between a range of situations; however, here it is the music that is drawn on selectively so that the characteristics which are able to connect across a range of experiences are foregrounded. The identity of the music, rather than Graham's identity as an individual, carries with it a level of flexibility that allows it to be incorporated into his musical life. The range of affordances offered by the music gives it a degree of flexibility which Graham can draw on not just in relating to the musics themselves but in relating different musics to each other while maintaining a coherent sense of self.

The connection between the two musical worlds is not simply a uni-directional one for Graham, with his orchestral background affecting his experience of worship; meanings found primarily within the discourse of a worship context can also be present in his orchestral experiences. Later in the interview he described how orchestral playing carries with it the potential for an awareness of the presence of God, and the potential to become a worshipful activity in a way that feels internally similar to his experience on a Sunday. While it is rarer for him to encounter the experience in this setting, the fact that he does so highlights the fact that a certain experience of, and way of making, music carries with it worshipful significance which is not uniquely present within one particular setting. It highlights the potential of spiritual meaning to migrate out of the walls of church into other musics but also suggests that Graham's experience within a church setting may not be experienced in terms which are wholly reliant on characteristics unique to the gathered community, as they are able to be experienced elsewhere. Experiences that might initially seem to indicate a simple one-way transfer of meaning from one context into another may in reality be enabled by a two way dialogical relationship between elements of the different contexts.

Charlotte's experiences of worship seem to function in a similar manner to Graham's. Her main musical interest is in musical theatre, both as an audience member and on the back row of the chorus. For Charlotte both church worship and musical theatre are to be thought of, to a certain extent, as stage-enabled expressions of emotion taking place within an English culture which rarely allows this kind of expression. Both situations are about undergoing a transformative emotional experience and journey which has the power to shift your focus and perspective. The element of having a 'good hearty sing' is also key to Charlotte's experience of Sunday worship:

> Although it's not a style of music that I really listen to in any other bit of my life, I do still enjoy the music at Aldates. And I think one of the things for music that I'm participating in – be that in church, or singing in G&S [Gilbert and Sullivan] or something, it is nice for there to be something that lets you have a good sing. Particularly, I always think it's quite interesting about worship music that on stage you have lots of

people pouring out their emotions and sort of singing love songs or 'O woe is me' type songs [features typical of much musical theatre]. And because that's happening in a stagey context it's inevitably going to be slightly artificial, and it seems to me that worship music is one of the few points I can think of where people in the course of their everyday life will use music as a way of expressing their own emotions and their own feelings.

Charlotte – interview with the author, 25 February 2012

Charlotte's experience of Sunday worship seems partly to be conceived of in terms of musical theatre. Some of the elements which come to the foreground of her experience are already present within the official discourse of the church – emotion, singing and the enabling role of the worship team are all regularly talked about. Their emphasis in Charlotte's experience, however, is very different. The stage element is not generally emphasized in the church for fear that worship might be thought of in terms of a performance; the visibility of musicians on stage will certainly be discussed, but the stage is generally not thought of as a separate kind of space in the way that it seems to be for Charlotte. Visibility of musicians would normally be talked of as something that enables congregational worship as the musicians lead and set an example. In contrast, Charlotte's experience draws attention to the artificial nature of the stage context as she highlights the way in which it enables a different mode of experience from everyday life. This theatrical conception of the stage moves away from the particular ideas of authenticity and natural self-expression inherent within rock and worship music towards one in which artifice and separation become a recognized part of the machinery which allows this to happen. Elizabeth Wollman (2004) highlights the contradictions that can be faced when bringing rock and musical theatre together in a production, contradictions which come precisely as a result of these differing aesthetic bases. For Charlotte, however, both musics can be approached via a common aesthetic stance, without causing significant friction, as elements within discourse are reshaped and reframed according to broader lived musical experience and are appropriated in ways consistent with that experience. In a similar manner, the element of emotional singing is one that is important within the life of the charismatic church, but would generally be considered a secondary-level element – something which has to take place in response to the (primary-level) work of God – rather than something which can itself be a primary transformative element within a service. It receives a greater degree of emphasis within Charlotte's experience. The conceptualizing of worship in terms of a 'good hearty sing' also strikes against the regular patterns of discourse – the importance of singing passionately from the heart is certainly a key element of discourse, but hearty singing would normally be emphasized only in such a way that its secondary role to the activity of worship is made clear. Indeed, as Gordon Adnams (2008, p111) discusses, the idea of 'just singing' is something which can become the very definition of unspiritual engagement within contemporary worship culture – singing is not thought of as the primary transformative spiritual element within worship, but rather the attitudes and experiences which the mind focuses on alongside it. The embodied experience of singing thus becomes significant for Charlotte in a way that may be felt by many others within the congregation but will rarely be expressed in these terms.

Emotions and expression

While the examples of Graham and Charlotte are relatively unique in conceptual clarity they serve to draw attention to a range of similar experiences within St Aldates, occurring at varying levels of experience and with equally varied significance. Amongst those interviewed, the most frequent bridge between different forms of music consists, as it did for Charlotte, of its potential to carry different kinds of emotional or expressive significance. These include a range of experiences such as the conception of singing as an activity which honestly expresses the heart, the potential of music to attach itself to particular emotional life-situations which worshippers find themselves in, its potential for helping to process and reflect on experiences, and its broader power to move and connect with an individual. These patterns of significance, while involving somewhat broad categories, are not, however, simply generic experiences of the emotional power of certain kinds of music but draw upon its emotional and expressive potential in a range of ways so that its significance differs from person to person:

> The same emotional attachment I have to songs; that is carried on to the worship music that I listen to in church I think, I guess because I'm quite an emotional person, my emotions are really – I'm attached to my emotions ... when I got involved with a church and started listening to – it was a thing that mattered ... [to] make new emotional associations with each song and connect, and probably that's why I can get involved with it.
> Nemi – interview with the author, 12 March 2012

For Nemi, one of the key qualities of music is the ability to attach particular emotions and emotional situations to particular songs, and to form ongoing associations of meaning between them. The narrative of music through her life is deeply bound up with the narrative of her personal emotional attachments and struggles as they relate to friendships, family members, relationships and her experiences of migration. The music used in church is different in many ways to the music she would choose to listen to elsewhere, and there are aspects of this which she finds problematic; however, the possibility of carrying this aspect of experience with her enables her to involve herself in the musical life of the church. Indeed, it is largely this element which enables her to involve herself in the church's worship rather than any particular musical characteristics, as she often finds the musical sounds themselves to be somewhat routine. As Nemi became involved with the church the thing that mattered to her was the ability to 'make new emotional associations with each song and connect'. While this process of association is one that most people experience to some degree with different pieces of music, the place it occupies at the root of Nemi's musical life is key to her self-identity and ties into her conception of herself as someone who is highly connected to her emotions.

By contrast, for Hannah, the important emotional element within music is the quality of singing or playing from the heart. She finds this quality to be present in a range of musics in different ways. It can be found listening to a singer like Michael Bublé, listening to worship albums and in her own singing, but she also finds a similar quality within orchestral playing as the musical qualities which singing invokes are expressed through the medium of an orchestra as much as they are through an individual voice. The following illustrates just how freely connections can be made across these different realms:

> People meet God in music, and that's something that I've really enjoyed, is actually being able to sing and for – like help people meet God in music. And I think there is something amazing about how you can play one note, and there's so many notes around it that would just create such a different sound. You've still got – it's almost like you've got the note, the melody note on top, and you've got all these other things underneath it or around it just creating this much richer picture. I think that's the thing about singing from the heart, because, or playing from the heart, is you're playing the notes around it and you're creating this sound that isn't just this one note that is just there which is fine on its own, but it, music was created to be whole, it's why you have symphonies and why you have orchestras all playing all these different, different notes, or even the same note with different instruments you know, that's beautiful.
>
> Hannah – interview with the author, 15 May 2012

For Hannah, the quality of singing from the heart becomes linked in with the ability to meet God in music but also with the potential to create a rich and beautiful sound through the textures that this kind of singing can create. It is hard to tell where one part of her descriptive picture ends and the next begins or whether any of the qualities she describes have any particular priority over any of the others. Instead they are all bound up and woven together in a manner which flows fluidly through the different aspects of experience. These different aspects seem able to evoke each other such that they form a common experiential texture while not necessarily entailing complete similarity throughout a range of different musical environments.

Doing something different in worship

For some singers the activity and mode of singing can be particularly important, and, as a result, they sometimes bring not just a particular internal attitude to the activity of worship but will find themselves singing in ways which don't necessarily conform to the same style or even content as others within the congregation. Rhiana finds particular expressive significance in a very free and personal form of singing, qualities which she finds essential to the life and essence of music and without which music instead becomes mundane and lifeless. During worship in church she will therefore improvise new words and melodies around the music that the congregation and band are engaging in:

> I sing whatever I feel like singing, often I pray over the songs, I pray through them. If there's a particular lyric that's jumped out at me then I, I meditate on that, no matter what everyone else is singing I stay in that place.
>
> Rhiana – interview with the author, 9 May 2012

Rhiana thus brings a different mode of being into the activity of worship, occupying the space of corporate worship in a way which forms connections with her broader musical world and thereby turning church gatherings into locations of significant worshipful experience. Musical connections are made not just on an internal basis but the music is altered on a demonstrable and practical level. Rhiana is not the only member of the congregation to find her own way of participating in worship – in a similar manner Stephen, a rapper in the congregation, finds that contemplating alternative ways of expressing the lyrical content of songs, rephrasing song texts in his head, enables him to find a way of being in the time of worship which helps to turn it into a meaningful experience. Contemplation is also part of the experience of Janet, a member of the congregation who finds herself struggling with her eyesight and her ability to keep up with the repertoire. Rather than joining in with the music and singing, Janet often sits and meditates on the lyrics of the songs, using this as her way of participating in the corporate act of worship. Within a musical environment that, on a stylistic level, is largely homogeneous these individuals find their own ways of producing diversity. Their strategies express a degree of deviance in a setting where there are strong expectations of corporate sung engagement, but they provide ways in which individuals take control of the situation for themselves and find a way of joining in with the communal act in ways in which they feel able to properly engage. They do not completely assimilate to a shared mode of engagement, nor do they hold out for their own musical attachments to be represented; instead, they take commonly held materials and find their own ways of interacting with and moving through them which allow an individual attachment to a nevertheless corporate activity.

The range of experiences surveyed thus far demonstrates some of the ways in which the experience of worship within St Aldates can be very malleable, able to take on a range of significance which is not restricted to a purely abstract spiritual level but finds its place within the context of a broad range of musical lives and activities and connects to them at different points and in varying ways. Value, of varying degrees of 'spiritual' significance, inheres on a range of levels, being found within experiences of the voice, community, and emotion among others.[7] These musical bridges can be productive – they can allow people to move fluidly between musical realms while maintaining consistent ways of being in the world as they move between them, without a need for any fragmentation of musical identity. While the musics may be different, they can be evaluated against a common sense of what is good in equally positive ways. These bridges can also produce a range of meanings which enrich the worshipping experience and experiences within other contexts. Meaning is formed in the multi-voiced dialogue between subject and contexts, reshaping existing meanings and identities as well as creating new ones. Subjects are able to not only interact with differing contexts themselves, but to bring these contexts into mutual dialogue with each other through their inhabitation of and movements between diverse musical worlds. No context stands entirely by itself in such a way as to be able to entirely determine its own meaning in relation to those present within it, but instead all contexts are situated in relation to a range of others which have the potential to redefine and reshape them, meanings spilling over from one to another, just as they have the potential to do the same in reverse.

Fluid relationships: Finding God in everything

Explicitly 'spiritual' framings of music can be equally varied, and cannot always be relied upon to provide a counterbalancing element of consistency and stability to the variety that music brings:[8]

> [Sunday worship] prepares me for being in the presence of God, and it definitely stays with me all week, but then that's what music does for me generally.
>
> Justin – interview with the author, 12 March 2012

> I think, intimacy I think is key, really, as in there's music, I listen to music because it helps bring me back to myself, in a way, and what I know, but also brings me back to God and having a place of intimacy with him. Probably actually all music is, I listen to all music for that purpose of bringing me back to something – ultimately God, because listening to music to bring me back to myself and what I know and what I'm about so it's kind of a bit obvious this, but it's soul stuff, I love listening to music which connects to my soul, but that's what music does isn't it.
>
> Tim – interview with the author, 9 March 2012

The relationship between musical worlds can be particularly fluid when all music is experienced as in some sense sacred. The expected presence of God in

Sunday worship lies on a continuum with the experience of divine presence in other musics within the quotidian events of the week. For some this is the result of a musical life which is strongly centred on the use of worship music to the relative exclusion of other musical genres, but it can also coincide with a strongly theological aesthetic sense which finds an inherent connection between experiences of things such as beauty or emotion and experiences of the divine.

For Justin and Tim, both of whom are visual artists, the experience of God in music is something which is far from unique to their experiences on a Sunday. Instead the power of music to achieve a certain effect is something which is common to both church music and the other musics which they use in daily life. For Tim music opens him up to a way of being in the world which allows him to become sensitive to the things around him, and to God, and to respond to this creatively in his art while painting or drawing or through sung worship within a Sunday service. He finds experiences of extended collective spontaneity during services particularly valuable as they are acts which involve a release of control in favour of submitting to the leading of God's Spirit – an experience which seems to parallel the process of spiritual inspiration that he experiences when creating visual art. While it is not only worship music which opens him up to the experience of being sensitive to God, his own identity and the world, he often finds this form of music particularly suitable for use as a backdrop to the activity of painting. For Justin, music creates a sense of emotional connection which enables him to experience the presence of God, a connection centred around combinations of happiness and sadness that bring aspects of joy and melancholy together in the same music:

> I feel worship in a way is melancholic – it's our depravity and our sense of, you know, every world religion says God is holy, every world religion [including] Christianity says man is depraved. Every world religion apart from Christianity says how is man gonna get to God. And it's the only religion which says God will reach you ... I do feel quite strongly that, in sets, I am taking the week, my pain, my joy, my gratefulness to God, thankfulness, which I think is the key to everything, I give all that to God, I think that comes across in worship.
>
> Justin – interview with the author, 12 March 2012

While this particular form of emotional connection is as much to do with his particular personality as it is to do with spirituality it nevertheless seems to be something which Justin connects to the way in which Christians are called to experience the world, combining the troublesome experiences of everyday life with the hope that is to be found in the gospel.

The spirituality of worship music for both Tim and Justin is not a unique defining characteristic over and above other forms of music, but becomes, instead, part of a continuum of experience. They do expect to find particular spiritual experiences within the gathered Christian community; however, these are expectations that are not completely unique to that setting or its associated music. Worship music is not, for either of them, the sole determiner of spiritual meaning in music but has, instead, to share this role with the other musics and art forms of daily life. The spirituality of worship music becomes defined, to a certain extent, by broader expectations of what music is able to achieve spiritually. As visual artists there is the potential for Justin and Tim to find the meaning present in a range of art-forms particularly strong.

While this kind of continuity can be a productive one, uniting different musical realms together through a common depth of purpose, both Tim and Justin are also aware that it can produce dissonance. For Justin, the presence of God in music connects to a broader picture of a God-infused world in which the church can often define the sacred too narrowly. The role of music has a very direct spiritual and theological significance for him, not simply on a personal level but also in broader terms of soteriology and ecclesiology. He draws attention to the presence of Christ in those outside of, and often put off by, the church, an emphasis that he also tries to convey in his photographic work. For Tim, the artistic sensitivity, creativity and spontaneity which music can unlock can often be constrained within a church setting, with the church not always succeeding in exploiting fully the potential spiritual power which he has learnt to find in music. Continuity between musical environments, in both cases, leads to a sense of limitation and a desire to break down boundaries and expand horizons.

Anna Nekola has discussed the way in which evangelical definitions of worship as lifestyle combine with worship music's increasing role as a consumer product such that individuals gain 'individual authority [not only] to define worship as a musical genre but also as a spiritual practice' (Nekola 2009, p365), deciding whether or not to accept readings (in the sense of understandings) of the music preferred by leaders and producers. While this process of free definition seems to resonate closely with Tim and Justin's ability to imagine the spirituality of worship in the light of broader (extra-ecclesiastical) expectations, their experiences don't necessarily implicate current worship culture as their primary catalyst.[9] Instead, it seems that a broader range of perspectives and practices can enable a similar fluidity – the connection between art and spirituality invoked by Tim's experience is common, in differing ways, to a number of historical periods. Any process by which spiritual meaning can migrate (or be produced) beyond the confines of the church walls seems capable of serving this function, and such processes are found in a range of spiritualities and aesthetics. This ability of the individual to define spiritual meaning in the light of extra-ecclesiastical realities can be present while maintaining a distance from consumer culture. Tim specifically affirms that he puts aside attitudes of consumerism and self-satisfaction when approaching church worship, instead seeking to be a part of the practice of worship in a way that is set apart from any particular engagement with his individual musical desires.

Soul, worship and (divine) presence

Ben experiences spiritual continuity between musical worlds in another way; for him the experience of playing music is one that has to flow from the soul, it enables him to enter into a state of flow in which he is connected with others. It allows him to be truly present in the moment and for the constant work of his brain to be set aside in favour of an abandonment to the experience of the music. This state of being is one in which God can in some sense be present, the experiential qualities of the moment being a potential location for divine encounter. As similar experiences of musicking are possible both within a worship band context and when gigging elsewhere, the church service is not the sole location for this kind of experience:

> When I play music properly in any setting, it's about the connection between your soul and the other band and whoever's there, and just expressing yourself truly honestly ... I totally let go when I'm playing, and that could be in a church setting or a contemporary music pub scene. The difference is that I actually felt for a long time that the church was a better connection, [that it] was a more true and honest connection to worship, whereas now I'm finding at the moment it isn't necessarily.
>
> Ben – interview with the author, 6 March 2012

This manner of conceiving of an encounter with the divine is something which carries a different theological emphasis from that usually found at St Aldates, centring as it does on the musical experiences of playing and interpersonal connection as the keys to the encounter. The spirituality of the worship service is therefore shifted to focus around a broader framework defined, in part, by experiences of music in other settings but which is also shaped by a Christian spirituality found within the experience of a church community. This serves to open up potential comparison between the spiritual power of music within church and the power found in it elsewhere, with the church music sometimes coming out positively, but sometimes coming out as less powerful than non-ecclesiastical musical settings as, for Ben, they embody to a greater degree the experiential qualities associated with divine encounter. The relationship can operate equally powerfully in the opposite direction – for Alex it is much more clearly weighted towards the church's music:

ALEX: I don't think I knew anything about rock music until I started listening to Christian rock music, and I've tried listening to secular rock music and I don't like it nearly as much, but there's something about Christian rock music that I just find absolutely fascinating.

MARK: Do you know what that is?

ALEX: Some combination of the fact that there's great rhythm, great music, great lyrics, everything working together like you can get some interesting music elsewhere, but rock music just has the steady beat which I find, like I say, helpful and useful for me in terms of concentrating and just reflecting on things.

Interview with the author, 14 June 2012

Alex's musical life is predominantly centred on worship music, but he also engages in other musical activity, often instrumental. For him the offering up of music as worship is the defining spiritual feature of music in general, whether or not it contains worshipful lyrics. Having prayed over his guitar as an act of dedication, all music making takes place in a posture of worship. He thus carries the attitudes inculcated within a worship service over to other musics, and these shape the meanings and define the roles of other musics within Alex's life. As a result music which is unable to maintain the same kind of spiritual focus of worship fails to provide Alex with any significant meaning or purpose. On the occasions where Alex plays or learns secular songs these are closely connected with the purposes of worship – either in developing skills to offer up to God in worship or in finding reason to thank God for the experience of a particular moment. Music as a whole becomes a tool for personal devotion and the aesthetic of Contemporary Worship Music also becomes, to some extent, the standard to which some other musics can be compared. Alex finds secular rock music, for example, to be too loud and 'thrashy' in comparison to the musical qualities exemplified in Christian rock. The spiritual priority given to Contemporary Worship Music seems to connect to its acquiring a corresponding aesthetic and musical priority, partly due to the way in which these qualities are informed and shaped by spirituality, but perhaps partly also due simply to worship music's place of significance within Alex's musical life as a whole.

Relatively direct connections between spirituality and music such as this are not the only kind that it is possible to make, and the existence of more complex and less direct relationships is equally important to acknowledge. For Luke aesthetic enjoyment of music when listening can often be defined by the 'presence of another' – of God alongside the music:

> It sort of creates emotions that are enjoyable and there's a ... I don't know ... what to call it, an aesthetic pleasure and perception in that, in the reception of beautiful things like appreciating the lyrical content and the melody and the intricacy of how it's put together, but also just the sort of visceral ... impact that the sounds have ... I think there's a qualitative difference in worshipful experience while listening to music ... it's not just enjoyment on its own or enjoyment for enjoyment's sake, it's enjoyment that's defined by the presence of another ... the sense of the presence of God, the presence of this being, this person who I'm communing with and asking to be near to me and in a sort of love relationship ... and so they kind of intersect, because that is an enjoyable, pleasurable experience, but it's also something more. There's this dimension of otherness to it,

and also, I think there's an effect much more profoundly of stillness and calming and it's like medicinal in a sort of spiritual and emotional sense.

Luke – interview with the author, 14 May 2012

In many situations there is a close connection for Luke between enjoyment of the aesthetic aspects of music and divine presence, in a manner that seems to draw in both contemplative aspects and a specific framing of music as art. The experience of God in worship music, by contrast, is not strongly connected to its aesthetic qualities and yet worship is a situation which can offer him an even more powerful experience:

> I think worship music is odd, because some of the most powerful experiences of God I've had have been in a context of worship music and where worship music is being played, and there's nothing like worship music, it seems to me, for mediating that encounter with, with the presence of God which I was talking about, but at the same time often it's a very, I find, if I'm not so much in that frame of, worshipful frame of mind worship music isn't as aesthetically pleasing and interesting and maybe even well-crafted a lot of the time and beautiful, as some of this other music that I listen to, which is sort of secular, bordering on the Christian, or just completely secular.
>
> Luke – interview with the author, 14 May 2012

While the quality of divine presence may be the defining feature in both situations Luke's experience of worship music and his aesthetic enjoyment of other musics have a sense of qualitative difference and thus neither takes priority over the other in its ability to define spiritual meaning. There is a sense of spiritual commonality between experiences in different musical settings and therefore some sense of mutual interrelation between the different experiences; however, they also maintain a degree of independence in which a direct connection and commonality isn't expected. Any connection between settings is instead mediated so that each can maintain this independence while nevertheless sharing certain experiential qualities with the others. While for many worshippers a connection between different musical worlds also entails a certain degree of value-transfer, Luke's experience demonstrates a way that this connection and commonality can happen without necessarily entailing a wholesale transfer of expectations. Luke also finds that there are musics which are able to share both the aesthetic quality found in non-church musics and the worshipful quality found within a church setting. In particular he finds this within Russian Orthodox music and in the music of the worship leader and recording artist Misty Edwards. The possibility of this combination can open up questions about the relationship between the two worlds and the potential value of a greater degree of connection between the two. It can also bring into question what it means for worship music to lack aesthetic qualities which this music demonstrates that it could potentially adopt without losing its integrity as a worshipful medium. The raising of such questions, however, is a matter of enriching already-valuable experience and builds on an already productive understanding of these different musical experiences which already have some experiential elements in common.

Selective resonance: Moments of connection

For many within the church, deep connections between their musical lives in and out of the church are not a regular part of experience but instead they are found in particular moments, artists or songs on a much more selective basis either within the music of the church or within the musics which they encounter and use in a range of other settings. This occasional coming-together of values and experiences can be a significant encounter at the specific times and points when it occurs.

Kathryn regularly participates in a number of different musical settings, each of them providing different qualities for her, and each also having its points of weakness, the things that it does less well, as well as strength. These settings are, to a large extent, independent, with the significant qualities within each one generally being unique to that location and not something found within any of the others. In her hierarchy of value, however, things are taken to a new level when aspects from the different settings come together to combine the positive aspects of each:

> It's so cool, when the Schola [the chamber choir she sings in] matches with the Aldates, that is the best thing ever, because like with the Rach[maninoff] Vespers and with this piece we're doing now because it's like what I love about Schola is that it sounds amazing and it's difficult, and it's like interesting and the lyrics are actually like something, and then that combines with the spiritualness of Aldates ... some of the stuff we're doing in Schola at the moment is really spiritual but no-one there is Christian, very few are, but I think it gives you, so when you're sort of just singing calmly and when you like know the notes so you're not worried about the notes, and you get to actually think about what you're saying, I think that's a more powerful way of worshipping.
>
> Kathryn – interview with the author, 5 June 2012

When two modes of being[10] which are usually distinct and separate are combined in this setting the experience is made particularly enjoyable in a way that surpasses the abilities of either experience on its own. A bridge is formed which allows music to exhibit a greater power. The experience of worship itself is made more powerful through the ability to inhabit it in a different way, the spiritual content being able to take on a greater degree of significance through resonance with modes of being which Kathryn is at home with elsewhere. While this is something that, for Kathryn, happens primarily outside of

St Aldates, it also has the potential to occur in the church setting if the music there were to adopt reflective or celebratory emotional qualities with which she is at home.

Nick talks about similar moments in his worshipping experience at St Aldates. He highlights the particular power of the song 'Stand in Awe' which was written and introduced by previous worship pastor Martyn Layzell. Upon its introduction this song consistently over a period of months moved Nick into a state of tears. Nick finds specific pieces of music elsewhere in his life can have a similar effect – a JC Bach setting of a text from Isaiah, his first hearing of Beethoven's 9th Symphony:

> There's something there that is not just about the music, but something about, I would express it in terms of how I think about who I am, my spirituality and it connecting with that, and being very important.
>
> Nick – interview with the author, 18 May 2012

For Nick these different musics all connect to a similar sense of who he is and what he is about in the world which he says is to do with a sense of loss, and of smallness before something much bigger than himself. In this moment the music, for Nick, becomes in some sense a place where he is at home, a potential which is shared by a range of musics by virtue of the ways in which he explores, experiences and selects them as part of his personal musical life. Nick's sense of self exhibits a degree of complexity, connecting to a way of being in the music, to a position before the divine, and to a musical life which finds its home in exploration and eclecticism as much as in particular emotional and spiritual musical qualities. His sense of self and his sense of the divine are closely connected, each being informed and shaped by the other. Specific moments are able to evoke some aspect of this connection and thus become particularly powerful to him.

Liz builds connections between her experience of going to gigs and her experience of worship that exhibit a degree of asymmetry. For her the connections are formed in two different directions but with differing levels of effect:

> I remember updating my Facebook status after a gig saying 'I love it when gigs feel like church' like, I get the same feeling in my chest as actually when I'm really worshipping and I feel God.
>
> Liz – interview with the author, 3 February 2012

The two settings can result in similar qualitative experiences for Liz, relating primarily to joy, thankfulness and a sense of being created in God's image. The experiences arise, however, out of different qualities – Liz's descriptions during interview highlighted how at a gig they arise largely out of the experience of particular musical qualities which excite and inspire, whereas at church it is much rarer for these experiences to arise through the foregrounding of particular musical events. While specific musical qualities can resonate with Liz's own musical attachments and world within a church setting, these have potential to distract from worship as well as to inspire and create a feeling of home. The commonalities between settings can relate to the music but they are more about the resultant feeling than any characteristics of a specifically musical nature. Moments of resonance occur when non-church music is able to achieve the same level of emotional power 'just because of the music' as church music is able to through its more direct focus on God – both of these are then turned into a response towards God and achieve a similar spiritual purpose as aspects of experience become focussed around Him.

Selective moments of resonance between different musical worlds such as these could potentially be used to reinforce particular notions common within churches adopting a more 'multicultural' approach (Marti 2012, p82) which highlight the importance of worship music being the same as an individual's music elsewhere to truly express their heart and create valuable musical experience. The examples discussed highlight the way in which the coming together of elements from different parts of someone's life can result in particularly powerful and noteworthy experiences and could thus reinforce the importance of combining Christian spirituality with individuals' 'own' music as the way to go about creating these. The nature of the experiences, however, problematises any straightforward definition of what this might mean. In the experiences outlined in this section the sense of what is valuable can arise from qualities and values formed in a range of settings and on a number of levels. While particular combinations of these can produce especially powerful experiences, some of which connect closely to an 'authentic' sense of self, in many cases the relationship is less straightforward and the experience of worship music is as much able to form a sense of what is authentic and good in other settings as experiences in those other settings are of forming a sense of what is authentic and good in worship music. Values from different settings are sometimes able to mutually reinforce each other; however, it is often the case that it is not the wholesale equivalence of the music or experience of different settings that becomes important but of particular individual qualities within the different contexts. It is not simply the use of a particular kind of music combined with a spiritual attitude of worship that will result in an effectively powerful combination, but a much more nuanced relationship between the different qualities that become significant to the worshipper and the effects which these can produce in certain combinations.

Musical malleability, community involvement and authority

This chapter has highlighted the way that, for some individuals within the church, the terms on which worship music is experienced are not entirely defined by the manner or form of its presentation. As Nancy Ammerman summarizes in relation to religious identities and institutions:

Because no situation is rigidly bounded, multiple public narratives are always present, and no institutional field is defined utterly in its own terms. All situations are characterized by a fluidity of boundaries and the presence of story lines gleaned from the multiple contexts in which modern and postmodern persons live ... While religious organizations generate and sustain powerful narratives, the intersectionality of identities and the permeability of modern institutional boundaries guarantee that these narratives will not remain singular or untouched ... While powerful authorities keep existing stories in place, new narratives are constantly emerging. Ongoing stories are disrupted by unexpected events and deliberate innovation. Accounts from one arena are imported into another, as new participants carry plots from place to place.

Ammerman (2003, pp216–223)

While much flexibility is achieved by worshipers being able to selectively foreground certain characteristics afforded by the worshipping environment within their experience, the emphasis can also shift to incorporate values from other settings which may differ more radically from expected emphases. This can often occur in a relatively unproblematic fashion as worship music is more often engaged in than authoritatively defined. According to Rice, official discourses are powerless to completely control the meaning of such a multiplicitous form as music which brings with it an inevitable plurality of meanings (2001, p35). Unless a worshipper specifically comes into direct relationship with the structures of church authority, then, the experience often remains open for them to reframe and reshape as they wish. They shouldn't, however, necessarily expect their experience to be acknowledged or taken into account by the leadership of the church and made part of public discourse. As Matthew Guest has suggested: 'while the congregation is united by a common set of symbolic boundaries, members relate differentially to the symbolic resources available to them' (Guest 2004, p76). It may be, then, that the relative lack of music-talk within the church environment is part of what allows it to hold together in its current form, enabling a multiplicity of connections, such as those seen in this chapter, to be formed in relation to a set of common practices. Members of the congregation are thus able to unite around the gathered practice of musical worship while interpreting it in ways appropriate to their broader ways of being in the world.

Such a model does not, however, neatly account for all experiences and members of the community and it is, perhaps here that questions of discourse ethics assert themselves. The degree to which the worship experience is open to differing conceptions by congregation members varies depending on the particular involvement of worshippers within the life of the church. The boundaries alter at progressive levels of involvement – a greater level of conformity is required as greater responsibility is acquired. While it is expected that there will be a certain level of diversity within the congregation, it is also acknowledged that certain qualities are required for someone to become involved in the worship team and to publicly lead worship. The introduction within the last few years of a worship team contract which musicians are expected to sign highlights the importance placed on an acceptance of a centrally produced set of values and principles in order to participate actively within the musical life of the church (see Appendix B). While it is possible to experience the music in different ways within the congregation as a largely private matter, within the context of leading and making music differences in experience are likely to give rise to differences in practice and emphasis which will then be open to critique by leadership and team members. This can then lead to encounters with the discourses of worship which may bring into question individual experiences and emphases which would otherwise be able to exist unquestioned. Musicians within the church can be aware of this tension, knowing that there are limits to the level of involvement they can expect to be offered given the particular foci and ways of doing things which they would bring to different roles.

Alongside the theoretical perspectives discussed in the previous chapter, the range of positive experiences possible within the congregation very quickly begins to challenge the assumption that the way in which people form evaluations of the music is simply a matter of personal preference or that the music in some sense floats above a common shared attitude of worship which can be adopted regardless of musical content. Rather, the musical experience itself can be a key element in formations of what it means to be meaningfully worshipping in ways which transcend a simple 'take it or leave it' state of affairs. Few of the experiences described in this chapter are to do with a like or dislike for various kinds of music; musical taste instead becomes about broader ways of being and values, thereby bringing us back to questions of ethics.[11] Very few of the experiences discussed thus far have focused on 'the music itself', but centre instead on these ways of being in the world which it enables, and the values embedded within them. While it is possible for the musical activity of the church to express certain values of the community, it will not necessarily be the same values which are picked up and foregrounded in the same way for all worshippers; and even here it is possible for elements of these values to be embedded in broader contexts which reshape the way in which they are thought of and conceived.

Notes

1 See, for example, Ingalls's discussion of expectations of sincerity in singing and their connection with God-centred feelings (2008, pp297–298).
2 In Rice's case the 1944 communist government in Bulgaria. See also Nooshin's discussion of Iran (2011).
3 Rice gives a number of examples: 'among the Navajo of the southwestern United States music is medicine, a form of therapy; it is performed to heal the sick. It doesn't represent something; it does something ... Among some strict Muslims, music is the work of the devil; its performance and appreciation signify apostasy

and contribute behaviourally to it. For some African-American jazz musicians, a musical performance is a story and, if you are not telling a story, no matter how technically accomplished you may appear to be, your playing is not part of the tradition' (2001, p23).

4 While Bourdieu's habitus (an interesting discussion of which can be found in Lizardo 2004) may be the natural conceptual tool to turn to for this kind of work, and can be useful in talking about movement into novel contexts or ongoing involvement in one particular environment, it seems to me that the implied unification of dispositions within the self leaves less room for foregrounding the diverse range of ways in which relationships between experiences of varied contexts can be formed (see Bennett et al 2008 for a discussion of similar critiques), particularly when there is potential for some kind of ongoing tension or dialogical relationship between multiple, potentially diverse, settings.

5 Some, but not all, names have been changed in order to achieve some degree of anonymity. Complete anonymity is hard to achieve in a community of this size in which individuals are likely to be recognizable to their friends and acquaintances simply from the transcriptions of their interviews.

6 See Turino (2008, p28) for a discussion of modes of evaluation in participatory performance. While it is hard to express Graham's experiences completely in a singular metaphor, the ideas of 'music as community' or 'music as alignment with another' seem to be lenses that shed at least some light on his experience.

7 Such an understanding, in which things in the world are endowed with spiritual significance, is not a novel one within Christianity with its incarnational tradition. However, such traditions have yet to make their presence felt within the world of Contemporary Worship Music other than in a somewhat fixed and narrow form in its denunciation by opponents.

8 See the interviews with worship leaders in Chapter 1 where this seems to be the suggestion.

9 Indeed, consumption of worship music recordings and of Christian music more generally seems to be something only selectively engaged in by members of the congregation, perhaps indicating a selective engagement with aspects of evangelical culture.

10 My use of this phrase is loosely inspired by similar usages by Gordon Adnams (2008), whose own work draws on the traditions of phenomenology. I intend with it to draw attention both to the texture of experience and to the adoption of varying intentional (in the philosophical sense of 'aboutness') stances that worshippers adopt in themselves and in relation to the surrounding world.

11 Jeffrey Summit offers a similar perspective from his research within Jewish congregations: 'I found again and again, when these non-specialists spoke about music in Jewish worship they were in fact talking about the deepest spiritual questions in their lives. What tunes and chant represented the essence of who they were and what they believed as Jews? What music constituted authentic practice? What was their relationship to their ethnic and religious history? Where and when did they feel truly comfortable and fully at home? In my many conversations and interviews, we spoke about music, but the real conversation was about the locus of core meaning in their lives' (2000, p18).

4 Boundaries

Communal and private, spiritual and secular

Worship and ritual separation

While many worshippers form a close connection between musical experiences in and outside of the church environment, for many the establishment of significant boundaries is an important key to their experience of worship music, their ability to maintain attachments to multiple disparate musical environments and their ability to evaluate and experience multiple musics in a positive manner. The distinction between communally-expressed religion or spirituality and everyday (secular) life or individuality is a familiar, if sometimes problematic, one, there being a much greater potential for inter-relation and overlap than it, strictly, suggests. In churches which employ an elevated sacred style of music this is a dynamic that can often be deliberately cultivated, with the sacred space of the service intentionally set apart symbolically and aesthetically from the world of everyday life.[1]

Catherine Bell, drawing attention to the close similarities between ritual and other performances, comments on the dynamics which often underlie this kind of ritual separation:

> Another feature of performance lies in the dynamics of framing. As noted with regard to sacral symbols, distinctions between sacred and profane, the special and the routine, transcendent ideals and concrete realities can all be evoked by how some activities, places, or people are set off from others. Intrinsic to performance is the communication of a type of frame that says, 'This is different, deliberate, and significant – pay attention!' By virtue of this framing, performance is understood to be something other than routine reality.
>
> Bell (2009, p160)

The rationales of Contemporary Worship Music work, to some extent, against this separation; the use of Contemporary Worship Music is not justified by an appeal to ideals of the sublime or beautiful or of standards of musical-writing appropriate to the divine, but instead has the ideal of a close relationship with the worshipper and the experience, routine or culture of their daily lives at its heart (Nekola 2009, pp306–307; Ingalls 2012a, p147). The use of popular music in church is intended to establish a closer connection between the sacred worship of the service and the activities of daily life. Anna Nekola describes, for example how worship albums are often marketed in a manner that emphasises the continuity of experience between worship in the church and the kind of experience that can be had at home or while driving a car, a trend that fits into a broader rhetoric of 'worship as lifestyle' (2009, p370). While the use of contemporary popular styles might indeed facilitate the building of such a connection for those who have a close allegiance to certain forms of soft rock, the diversity of musics enjoyed and employed by congregation members means that for many this music is very different from the music of their daily experience. This musical world can thus often become a distinct realm within their musical lives – it becomes a specifically sacred music precisely because of its genre, even whist maintaining a popular aesthetic.[2] As the stylistic distinction of worship music from the music of daily life works against much of the grain of Contemporary Worship Music's rationale for existence, the ways in which such a distinction functions have the potential to vary greatly between different congregation members. In the gap between ideal and experience a potent site for individual meaning-making is opened up in which worshippers form their own understandings of the kinds of distinctions to be made between congregational musicking and their broader musical lives. Boundaries are often put in place that express individuals' understanding of what the church community is about in distinction to other areas of their (musical) lives.

Gerardo Marti, in his study of multi-racial congregations, finds this separation to be an almost pervasive experience:

> Church worship music does not at all correlate with the music most people listen to outside of church or to what they grew up hearing.
>
> In talking about music, members consistently separated the music of worship from music in other arenas of their lives. Many, like Judy, an Asian member of her church, distinguished between music that is for worship and music that is for entertainment. Judy told me she mostly listens to jazz music, and when I asked if she heard anything similar in church, she said 'Rarely.' Yet, it did not bother her that the music she listened to outside of church was not found in church.
>
> The importance of the setting, in contrast with the 'music', is evident in that even people who are the most moved by the worship in their church do not listen to such music outside of the congregation. In talking about Christian music on the radio, Kristina said, 'I'm not really that into it.' Sue, who attends a church with mostly contemporary Christian music, said, 'No. I don't really enjoy Christian music all that much'
>
> Members simply accept the music of their church as it is. Hearing worshipers talk about how they learned to worship in their church moved

me to pay less attention to the dynamics of race as accounting for inherent differences to the response to worship music and more the dynamics of anticipation and socialization among members of particular churches.

Marti (2012, p80)

Marti highlights the way in which the social setting of the congregation can be formative as worshippers learn to appreciate, adapt to and inhabit the music in appropriate ways. The communal dynamic enables a shared social experience as individuals learn to assimilate to the culture of the church despite their differing backgrounds. Musical boundaries are negotiated by a common process of socialisation and Marti finds these boundaries to be relatively insignificant in comparison to processes of social inclusion. Marti's findings are important, and serve to counter simplistic views which assume a direct and immediate correlation between the musics people experience and employ outside of church and those that they are able to relate to within it. However, I want to go beyond Marti's analysis and the mere fact of individuals' acclimatisation to the music of the church in order to examine the nature of such movement and how the separation between different musical worlds can take on a range of significances in the musical lives of congregation members. This separation can be significant, productive or problematic because it is often musically, spiritually, personally and socially meaningful and not simply natural, universal and obvious. Its significance, moreover, depends on how the music of the church is conceived and with which other musics it is brought into relation. Since separation is often viewed as simply a lack or absence of connection, it is very easy to think of boundaries as neutral and without quality; this is, however, far from reality. When asked whether the difference between music in church and music outside of church bothers them, many congregation members agree with Marti's suggestion that it doesn't; however, there are wider realms of meaning and significance that can make such disavowals seem superficial in comparison to the broader tapestry of experience.

The (continuing) significance of boundaries

Janet, an older (retired) member of the congregation, is one person whose experience does, in many ways, echo Marti's writing:

MARK: How do you find the musical setup with, so with the bands, with the electric guitars, with this kind of slightly rocky style that we do. What do you make of that?

JANET: well I suppose it's not everybody's cup of tea, is it. But again, no it just doesn't worry me now, I think it's part of me now, it's St Aldates and it's part of me, and it's my home and it's the music that I've become accustomed to and quite, and I do like. We [older members of the congregation] might complain a little bit about, as I said, and what I said about. But other than that it's what I … occasionally I must admit occasionally I think it would be quite nice to have a nice quiet service and not have it quite so loud and quite so noisy, and people have adjusted the noise levels I think, from time to time, and it's been fantastic, but no, I've just got used to it.

Interview with the author, 7 March 2012

Outside of a church context Janet more often listens to classical music, with her listening habits slowly evolving to include more recent composers. St Aldates music is very different from what Janet would enjoy elsewhere, but it has become part of her life in the church community over time, and she has begun to enjoy it. Her qualifications, however, indicate that there is still some element of distance between her and the music; her appreciation is largely mediated by the community life, rather than one that necessarily appreciates any qualities of the music more directly. The musical boundary between different areas of Janet's life, while negotiated via processes of social inclusion nevertheless maintains some degree of significance, with her relationship to the musical activity appearing, sometimes, to be of a tentative rather than completely certain variety. Despite this there are also specifically musical characteristics which she finds compelling within the communal environment:

MARK: And so what do you most value about the musical life here, if you say you love it, what qualities of it?

JANET: Well I think it, I think if they ever change, I don't know, I just like the fact that it's alive and vibrating and it's, you know, it gives you a buzz. I like it.

MARK: It gives you a buzz, you haven't mentioned that before. What kind of a buzz?

JANET: Just a buzz, you know you sort of, and if you hear something that really, you know sort of grabs … takes your attention then … hmm, there is something after all.

Interview with the author, 7 March 2012

This element of musical appreciation is one that Janet held back from expressing until an off-hand remark towards the end of the interview, suggesting that it is a characteristic which is far from the centre of her own understanding of what is important about St Aldates worship. The realisation comes as something of a surprise to her, perhaps because these aren't the terms in which she is used to thinking about the music. Interestingly, the quality of 'buzz', when associated with qualities of aliveness, is one that would often be conceived of as pre-eminently social in nature and, while this isn't something that she articulates, hints that it might be the combination of a certain kind of social and musical experience which serves to make musical worship compelling for her. It might therefore serve to reinforce the way in which worship music is defined by the church environment, and made compelling, for Janet, largely by the context within which it is engaged.

Tom, an English graduate and former intern at the church, finds the musical boundary between church and daily life to be loaded with other kinds of significance. Tom tends to listen to music that he describes as 'indie', 'literate', 'witty', 'alternative', 'melancholy' and fairly introspective. He specifically contrasts this kind of music-making, which often takes place in a small, cramped room, with the atmosphere at a stadium gig. Giant musical collectives in which the intimate relationship between music and self is de-centred in favour of a large-scale group atmosphere are something he would generally avoid. However, expressive charismatic worship in a Sunday service seems to be unproblematic for him. When I commented on the similarities between music-making in a Sunday setting and some of the qualities he avoids in the larger stadium context, Tom responded:

> I'm quite an introvert, and I tend to process things quite inwardly. [But] I love the joy of being able to come together in a stadium setting [correcting himself] well, I say in a stadium, in a church setting – and declare [shared purposes] with others, knowing that this is something I've thought through deeply in my own time ... I think the music I listen to personally helps me process and helps me work out what I'm actually thinking, or shapes my thoughts. And then the music I respond to in church, I appreciate that, because it's got a congregational dynamic. It is a response; it is designed to be with a range of different people all coming together to affirm one common faith.
>
> Tom – interview with the author, 15 February 2012

For Tom, there are two counterbalancing poles to this musical life. At one pole is the introspective way in which he processes things and deals with life, not just musically but intellectually and emotionally. At the other is the confident expression of faith within community. For Tom, neither the reflective music he listens to in private nor the expressive worship music in church is completely adequate on its own; instead, he finds that they each fulfil a role in relation to the other, together completing the pattern which helps him to navigate life as a believer. Both contribute to his faith, but in different ways that are appropriate to their setting. The musical expression of the church can function for him because of its corporate and sacred setting, and is not a music that he would engage with either privately or in a group setting outside of the church boundaries.

Combining analytical categories – both bridged and bounded

Nemi outlines a similar divergence between the public and private aspects of her musical life. We saw in Chapter 3 how for Nemi, music is something that takes on a large degree of emotional significance as it becomes attached and associated with different people, events and situations. Her own tastes in music take her a little away from the church style to music that is often more 'messy' and 'unpredictable' but the church music is still able to become important to her due to its potential emotional significance and attachments. There is thus some level of commonality between the way she experiences music within and outside of church. For Nemi, however, the music of St Aldates doesn't migrate out of a worship setting, either in terms of listening or of significance; in fact, she even goes so far as to say that listening to some of this music elsewhere would be weird:

> Maybe it's not my style of music, and other than the church and what God is doing in Aldates it doesn't have any other significance to me personally. With [traditional] hymns on the other hand, I've been singing hymns with my family since I was younger, so it, I can travel, I can remember things but with the church and Aldates it's just Aldates.
>
> Nemi – interview with the author, 12 March 2012

St Aldates music, while meaningful within the context of the church is unable to take on any significance outside of that context, and Nemi doesn't listen to it outside of that setting; it is not part of her broader network of significant personal associations. During the course of the interview I discovered that this musical boundary has parallels in the personal realm: Nemi forms and enjoys significant friendships, even with members of the congregation, outside of the services rather than finding a place for them in the church. Emotional, relational and musical boundaries are bound up together. For Nemi, as for Tom, the divergence in musical style between church and other parts of her life is laden with deeper significance for the way in which she negotiates the world and conceives of the church community. The corporate spiritual life of the church is something distinct from the experiences of daily life in specific and meaningful ways. While both Nemi and Tom's experiences within the church services may conform quite closely to church expectations, musical features and style carry with them additional significance in relationship to other parts of their lives. This relationship is of particular ethical and spiritual significance in a context where the living out of faith is a primary concern – there is a deep connection between questions of musical style and significance and personal, social and theological relationships and attitudes. The music that Nemi and Tom employ and encounter outside of church is important to the way in which these relationships become significant.

In the previous chapter we saw how Liz builds connections between different musical worlds, and in the next we will see how these can be problematic for her. She is, however, simultaneously aware of the boundaries around and distinctive characteristics of her experience at Aldates. Her experience demonstrates how the categories I am employing in these different chapters are by no means mutually exclusive and can be subject to a great deal of interplay:

LIZ: Going to Aldates is very different to going to a gig, because during a gig I am watching what the people on stage are doing, particularly because, the sorts of music I really like, there's generally at least one guy with a series of boxes and loads of pedals and you're trying to work out exactly which bits do what and he's pressing things and there's synth music coming out everywhere. And at Aldates, partly because your eyes are on the screen so you can know the words, partly because [at a gig] you're more likely to have your eyes closed, I close my eyes at quite a lot of gigs. Like, it's less about the band [in church] and more about kind of the songs whereas it's very much about the band and the music rather than the songs they're playing at the gigs.

MARK: We talked quite a bit about things that these two musical realms have in common and the things that they don't. How would you characterise that relationship, so that relationship between sacred and secular music for you. Would you say that these are two things that really do have quite a lot of overlap for you, or are they things that are quite distinct realms, or how do they inter-relate?

LIZ: They're quite distinct realms for me at the moment. When you started that question I was sort of – what went through my head was 'you couldn't do worship if it was like a gig' and that's sort of true, like if my focus is on the band it wouldn't really be worship, it would be worshipping them, but then I thought about actually 'you definitely could do worship with like, with dance music, or with industrial music, or just with more' because I can envision it, and it is beautiful.

Interview with the author, 3 February 2012

Liz inhabits these different musical worlds in different ways, her visual and mental focus differs, her physical attitude is altered and she is aware that each world defines what it is and what it does in its own distinct manner. This separation echoes common worship discourses which encourage individuals to focus themselves and their attention on God in worship rather than on musical characteristics but Liz articulates the differences in terms of genre, instrumentation and physical attitude in a way that makes it clear that this distinction touches on a large number of realms. Liz is both aware of how this differentiation works productively and serves the particular aims of each occasion and unsure whether it is entirely inherent and necessary. The fact of some kind of boundedness and its current utility does not mean that it is an essential boundedness; it is instead one that is shaped by the current dynamic of the different occasions and environments. This is, perhaps, a result of the mixed nature of Liz's experience, the connections between different musical realms that we saw in Chapter 3 preventing any kind of essentialising tendency within her own thought processes.

A desire to separate

Some individuals within the church find that they have an active interest in maintaining boundaries between church music and the other areas of their musical lives. Jules, who has been employed for a number of years as the church chef, has a strong sense that the music of worship should embody different values from the music of other areas of life:

JULES: We're so chronologically territorial about the music we play in church ... we'll quite happily play something that's 300 years old, but 3 or 30 years old, things start becoming problematic ... it makes you wonder about the longevity or the built in obsolescence of worship songs, I mean when you write an album how many years will it be before no-one's going to play your music in church. So you could argue it hasn't lost any of its validity, it's just out of vogue.

MARK: In a way doesn't that happen with any mainstream though? If we think about mainstream popular music it follows similar kind of fads but ...

JULES: It does, but should we be having, shouldn't there, should those rules apply to the house of God?

Interview with the author, 8 February 2012

In later email correspondence Jules further emphasised the discomfort he feels when worship music is evaluated according to criteria drawn from popular music; patterns and standards which might be acceptable within secular musics are not, for him, things which should always be carried over to the music of the church as they violate values important to the space of worship. Jules has little desire for the music he values elsewhere to make its way into church services, and expresses a sense of uncertainty and slight discomfort at the prospect:

MARK: If someone said 'we are going to have a late service, and it is going to be [your] style of music' ... How would that make you feel?

JULES: Intrigued. I think I'd probably go along to check it out, maybe, I'd like to think that I would. I don't know, maybe I'm a bit of a musical snob, maybe if everyone started liking it I'd chop my own arm off to, you know, to not like it. Who knows ... as soon as something becomes massively popular, it sort of loses a little bits of its mystique or curiosity value doesn't it.

Interview with the author, 8 February 2012

While Jules does have desires for the music of the church to evolve in certain ways and according to certain musical values that he holds, the idea that a public such as the church might adopt something which he values partly for its niche nature is something he is unsure about. The music he enjoys on an individual basis is specific to that realm and bringing this music into the church would not enhance and affirm its value or foster a sense of personal connection with the church's worship but instead has the potential to violate the kind of values applicable to the different musical spheres.

Drew's sense of musical boundaries is based much more upon the ideals of the elevated, liturgical environments in which he grew up and now finds himself more at home. For Drew, the sacred and the profane exist as distinct musical realms, embodying aesthetic values appropriate to their own particular functions and context. The implications of this for him, however, are very different from those which Jules experiences as the music that he might enjoy outside of the church environment matches up much more closely to that used within it. Drew's tastes are rooted in the Radio 2 culture of his parents[3] and popular music is something which he connects quite strongly with a sense of the profane rather than the sacred. The experience of this music within the worship of the church is thus something that he often finds disconcerting or jarring. The church context is one in which reverence and distance is appropriate and where words should be eloquent in order to fit this dynamic:

> I mean I don't have anything against the simple band setup of guitar, bass, you know, someone singing. Someone could be singing secular themes very similar, you know, about love and forgiveness, but because of my background, or because I can't incorporate, I can't integrate this with my background, I seem to think that God would be better off with, I don't know, something holier, as if the way I, as if the organ is inherently holier, when you know, I don't know.
>
> Drew – interview with the author, 2 June 2012

This experience is part of a broader struggle with a charismatic spirituality, an environment in which Drew doesn't, despite his best efforts, feel particularly at home. He thus draws quite a strong separation between musical worlds, and struggles with the fact that the church doesn't seem to do so in quite the same way. Drew has a sense that, within a charismatic frame of reference, the worship is supposed to convey an emotional experience to him, something *more*, but finds himself unable to grasp hold of this element of experience. The music thus becomes an avenue for disappointment as it fails to be able to fulfil the expectations with which it has been endowed by the church. It is, perhaps, unsurprising that it is unable to live up to these when set against a background expectation of transcendence – for Drew, the church's attempt to bridge musical worlds is unfruitful precisely because it is trying to reach out to a musical world that is built upon values irrelevant to what he expects of worship. Timothy Rommen explores the separation between musical worlds that can be an important part of negotiations of style on Trinidad. He proposes the idea of 'negotiation of proximity' in which churches on the Island deliberately employ North American Gospel music rather than local styles of music in order to avoid styles which are complicated by being loaded with local meaning and utilise, instead, those which are able to embody a spirituality untainted by the realities of island living (Rommen 2007b, p66). This seems to form a close parallel to Drew's experience with his seeming need to avoid music closely associated with everyday life in divine worship.

Drew's sense of sacred and profane separation, while it causes problems for his experience of worship music, seems to operate only in one direction. He is happy to find a sense of the spiritual in popular music:

DREW: I don't mind the spirituality being in the pop sphere, it's like I don't, I don't like the pop being in the spiritual sphere.

MARK: Yup. Because pop embodies another set of values?

DREW: Possibly, and that doesn't quite make sense, because pop can incorporate spirituality, it doesn't need to be set apart from it. I suppose I see the spirituality as enriching the pop and pop is debasing the spirituality.

Interview with the author, 2 June 2012

An expectation of transcendence and separation within the liturgy of the church does not lead to the cutting off of other aspects of his musical life from that same sense of spirituality. The spiritual is allowed to flow out from gathered worship and infuse other aspects of life, but popular musics are not able to be brought back into the realm of worship because they are felt to be in some way unworthy of it. They are not, then, under judgment as bad or evil, but are instead appropriate to a realm in which the mundane, rather than the divine, is often the more immediate reality.

For both Drew and Jules there is a sense that, in bringing certain kinds of music into particular settings, musical and/or sacred values are brought into question. Value is closely connected with context and not something which is able to be maintained independent of setting; value becomes a relational quality. Musical boundaries are thus the result of broader contextual boundaries that exist between the communal and the personal or sacred and profane. To re-work musical boundaries would also necessarily involve a re-working of these broader categories of existence. Music may also serve to construct or reinforce these boundaries in the first place, with the values and meanings embodied in particular musics serving to characterise different realms of existence and the forms of relationality appropriate within and in relationship to them.

Claire also finds the ability to draw distinctions between differing musical realms to be important, if not always something that she is entirely capable of achieving:

Because I do the kind of degree where I spend half my time doing really mindless things and I've done a lot of exercise where music is used to motivate, and I've done a lot of like processing as an adolescent where music is used to process, and then a lot of worshipping where music is used for something else and I guess what I would've been trying to do for since I became a Christian is figure out how to approach those things differently, so like the stopping listening to worship music over Lent was to try and teach myself how to detach myself to listen for arrangements, or to engage with it to do something else, how it's ok to do that.

Claire – interview with the author, 24 May 2012

Claire finds a tendency to engage with different musics in the same way to be unsatisfactory and self-consciously seeks to modify her approach to different musical settings so that her mode of engagement with music in each can be appropriate to its context. This has required her to undertake intentional work, denying herself a particular music for a period of time specifically in order to separate it out from other patterns of engagement. For Claire it is the common stance of listening to different musics in the same way that causes potential conflation between them. The interplay in her life between such activities as listening to live music on the radio, using recorded music, often Christian, as physical motivation in the gym, and watching live-streams of Christian worship online means that there is no single straightforward participatory/passive or corporate/private division within her musical life and it is partly this multiplicity which leads her to seek out a clearer sense of distinction. In order for worship music to become something which she can use to engage in the activity of worship this is a necessary task, otherwise modes of engagement from elsewhere get carried across and prevent her full involvement.

Alternative outlets, scales of community

For some individuals the music-making of the church is balanced and complemented by other communal musical outlets. For Dom, a musician and student of fine art, the music of the church is something that seems to follow very different rules from the music he enjoys creating and making elsewhere. For him, the ideal music-making setting would be thought of in terms of a big family singing together on stage, an ideal which draws on elements of folk traditions. This combines with a vision of creativity within that setting which seems to connect to his broader life as an artist, something which, in turn, often touches on areas of significance within his faith and spiritual life.

The fact that Dom has a range of musical outlets,[4] however, means that he doesn't feel the need for St Aldates to embody all the qualities which he might look for elsewhere. When I suggested that he might find St Aldates services more problematic if they were his sole musical outlet he quickly agreed. Alongside this Dom seems to have a strong sense of the strengths and weaknesses of different settings and how these fit together. He is conscious that these are determined by the different natures of the communities that he is involved in:

It's like different scales of community, so the church is like, I'm never gonna like say that I get more out of something which isn't church because it's kind of all church ... The Sunday services are so important in my eyes for being together as a whole body, and there like I really enjoy that and I sometimes think that God does an overall bigger work in those services ... Sunday services can be so good, and worship can be so good, and can be intimate, but I definitely love the Bezalel meetings and the prayer room meetings because you can fully receive, and you cannot stop, you cannot stop until you've received kind of thing.

Dom – interview with the author, 18 May 2012

Bezalel is Dom's pastorate group within the church,[5] consisting of a small number of like-minded individuals who come together in student rooms and other smaller venues to express their spirituality creatively and freely in ways that include a number of art forms. The prayer room (to be discussed in Chapter 6) allows a similar freedom of creativity, and these settings are important to Dom such that he finds the need to repeatedly affirm the importance of Sunday services in the interview as a counterweight to the depth and significance he attributes to these smaller scale meetings. An awareness of the nature of the church community and the significance of its corporate gathering keeps this central to his spiritual life, while key musical and creative elements of his spirituality tend to be located elsewhere.

This musical separation seems to be something which carries with it significance for Dom's understanding of church and the church community. The church body is thought of as something which is big, and perhaps slightly impersonal, and which needs to be supplemented by other, slightly separate and unrelated, kinds of Christian meeting in order to do justice to what is required of it. Sunday gatherings are thus, to a certain extent, de-centred, and become one of a range of settings of different scales and purposes rather than being the location which ties them all together. Dom's understanding disperses the notion of church such that it is found within different contexts, each of which expresses different elements of what Christian meeting-together should embody. This understanding is one that is, in many ways, encouraged by St Aldates – the relative scarcity of widespread input to Sunday gatherings in the form of spiritual gifts (such as prophecy), for example, being balanced by an understanding that this is a function, instead, of the smaller pastorate groups which meet fortnightly in people's homes.

Hannah's pastorate is an environment where there is the potential to stray from the patterns and repertoire of Sunday gatherings and where she finds the potential to contribute in a way that isn't always possible in church. She acknowledges that these different kinds of gatherings have different roles and therefore different kinds of associated worship and creativity. This is carried alongside a dispersed notion of church life which seems to resonate fairly strongly with Dom's:

See, I'm a youth worker, so I come, like the whole concept of church, when you say church, I think you mean church on Sunday as a service.

When I say church I mean the body of Christ, and that this is church, this is a looser form of church. Evangeline [her daughter] and I got on the bus at quarter to, it might have been 11 yesterday so we got into church at quarter past 11 and we were there until 3 o'clock and we had lunch with the vergers and stuff like that. My concept of church has expanded, so, so from that my concept of worship and worshipful music, and if I'm listening to Linkin Park and it's stirring my soul towards God, and I can feel myself becoming more alive then that's worship.

Hannah – interview with the author, 13 August 2012

While there is some kind of separation between these different settings and the ways in which they are expected to function, they are also held together and bridged on a much larger scale through the ultimate purpose which they are expected to serve. The differing levels of community are all expressions in different ways of what it means to be the body of Christ. This notion is able to hold the different settings together while simultaneously allowing each to have its own particular priorities. Because they function on different scales and levels it is possible for them to retain these priorities without any implied contradiction or conflict: the priorities of one would simply be inapplicable to another due to the way in which the scale of each dictates its nature. The core functions of the church are thus dispersed and distributed between a range of locations. There is not an expectation that a Sunday gathering will fulfil, or necessarily be the climactic point of, all the core functions of church; instead, the latter are separated off and fulfilled within other gatherings and relationships.

For Hannah, part of the key to engaging with the different forms of worship that individuals within her pastorate group bring (some musical, some not, some participatory, some receptive) is centred closely around relationships with members of the group:

I've had times where I've gone 'I don't know what the heck you're doing there, but I love you as a person so I'm gonna roll with whatever you suggest, because I want to support you. You've supported me in the past and I want you to be supported in this.' So I think that [unintelligible] a lot to it, so, it's not the church, this nebulous body, it's my friends who're playing me something that's intimate to him, and loving someone means that you'll try and engage with the way that ... I guess.

Hannah – interview with the author, 13 August 2012

This stands in contrast to whole-church gatherings which, for Hannah, can become powerful because of 'the anonymity of standing in a sea of noise' in which 'there's something really beautiful in being swept away with everyone else'. In a similar manner as for Dom, a distinction is made between different scales of community such that features and dynamics from smaller groups are not simply scaled up and projected on to larger ones. Each has a dynamic unique and appropriate to its size, and the capacity for certain kinds of interpersonal relationships in each setting seems to be reflected by the way in which musical relationships, and therefore also style, are able to function. Notions of church become dispersed through these different settings as each is able to contribute some, but not all, of the ingredients necessary for Christian community.

Questioning models of musical eclecticism

The question of how to conceive of boundaries between different parts of individuals' musical lives can serve to problematize and complicate common understandings of individuals' increasingly eclectic or omnivorous musical tastes. The editors of the volume *Culture, Class, Distinction* (Bennett et al 2008), in their follow up study to the work of Bourdieu, examine patterns of musical allegiance in contemporary Britain. As part of their work they examine the rise of the idea of cultural omnivorousness and the possibility that it might now stand as a symbol of class in a similar manner to earlier allegiances to art music, a position that has become known more-generally as the 'omnivore thesis'. The book is part of a growing body of research on the idea of cultural omnivorousness and the editors display mixed feelings towards the idea, suggesting, for example, both that 'insofar as there is a dominant expression of cultural capital in Britain, it is perhaps the adoption of an omnivorous orientation' and that 'the prevalence of cultural omnivorousness as a form of distinction cannot be accepted in any simple form' (Bennett et al 2008, p254). They both utilise aspects of the idea and highlight the ways in which musical and cultural allegiances are often more complex than the idea by itself allows for.

For the purposes of my own research, the idea of cultural omnivorousness helpfully highlights the often diverse nature of individuals' musical lives; however, by applying the idea of eclecticism or omnivorousness the fact of boundary traversal rather than the significance of particular traversals can often be foregrounded. While the notion of omnivorousness is helpful in highlighting this traversal, taken by itself it goes relatively little distance towards providing a framework to understand exactly how these different musical realms fit together. In contrast to the more nuanced understandings of musical taste presented in Chapter 2, it often presents a perspective within which all musics are, at least in some sense, the same kind of thing. Musics are thought of as a selection or range which can be consumed, expanded or restricted according to desire, and 'liked' or 'disliked' in similar ways, rather than music carrying with it a diverse range of environments that someone might move between, adapt themselves to and juxtapose in different ways according to the specific nature of musicking involved. In his study on musical boundaries, John Sonnett examines the nature of such omnivorousness and the varying degrees to which it can operate (2004). He goes some way towards looking at the kinds of values that can form particular kinds of boundaries around people's musical tastes and, as such, makes an important contribution to discussion. Sonnett seems to assume, however, that the main significant boundary markers are to be found around someone's musical life as a whole, rather than boundaries existing within that life that are to some degree external to the self and which individuals might need in some sense to traverse. Bernard Lahire suggests that:

> [The] idea of the 'omnivorous' consumer falls into the trap of essentialism. Cultural practices and preferences are produced when incorporated inherited dispositions, partialities, and competences, meet with fixed institutional or relational contexts; they are not intrinsic characteristics of the individual. The zoological metaphor [of omnivorousness] leads [us] to see only a variety of tastes, while variation in cultural practices and preferences is as much explained by the diversity of contexts and reasons in/for which consumers are led to act than by personal eclecticism or by a multiplicity of interiorised cultural propensities ... This serves to create a two-dimensional social reality and to equate practices or tastes that are in no way equivalent. The intellectually tempting zoological metaphor, is therefore potentially dangerous in the extent to which it suggests – as the findings of surveys have widely demonstrated – that consumers practice everything that they claim to practice or like everything that they claim to like to the same degree, in the same conditions and for the same 'reasons'.
>
> Lahire (2008, p182)

Concepts of fluidity and omnivorousness therefore, although increasingly popular, by themselves often fail to establish a comprehensive framework within which to understand the diversity of individuals' musical lives and, in particular, the internal boundaries, distinctions and separations that may exist within them. As such they, as yet, provide little advance over older frameworks based around fixed ideas of identity and allegiance.[6] Collective practices such as worship music bring this problem into sharper relief – worshippers cannot simply include a Sunday service as part of a diverse selection of music which they listen to through a pair of headphones in a relatively uniform manner. The inhabitation of the collective act of worship on a Sunday sets it apart in a way that cannot be entirely privatised or contained within the self. As we have seen in Chapter 3, there are indeed ways to unify diverse experiences; however, this is not a simple given but the result of particular ways of inhabiting and conceiving of musical activity. Rather than moving towards pictures of people's musical lives as simply eclectic or omnivorous, we need to look at the diverse ways in which individuals either unify an eclectic musical life or the ways in which boundaries which they habitually and frequently traverse between different parts of their musical lives themselves become meaningful.

I want to suggest that ideas of musical eclecticism manifest themselves in two main ways within the lives of worshippers and examine how these function for a selection of individuals. In the first, the music of the church (or parts of it) can be thought of as one of many different musical elements which go to make up the whole of the worshipper's musical life. In the second, the music of the church is thought of as a realm of musicking which should itself embody an eclectic ideal. These two models demonstrate very different conceptualisations of the church and of the music that takes place within it. To the extent to which they address the life and role of the church, they place it in very different relationships to the rest of life and society – either constructing the church as one musical location among many or, instead, as a paradigmatic community which should embody within itself the ideals and concepts expected to be found elsewhere.

Nathan's understanding of church music is much closer to the second and, while he seems to place most musics on a unified and level plane, he seems aware that there are differentiations to be made between what different musics do and embody:

NATHAN: Well, I listen to a range of stuff, I think it's important not to be defined by one style, I think the more styles you have an interest in, I think the more creative a musician it makes you ... I think that it would be wrong, I think, or it would be at least detrimental to creativity to say that you should really listen to one style, you should only listen to indie music, you should only listen to emo music, I think that's just an impoverishment creatively if that's the line you go down, and I think it can only make you a more interesting musician, or a more interesting person generally if you have, you know, a range of styles under your belt.

MARK: So what about eclecticism, I mean you, very much something you're into in your own life, is it something you'd miss within the church?

NATHAN: Yeah, very much. I think growing up in an environment where people had very different music tastes and very different music styles that kind of came together on a Sunday to create something very collaborative, but also very individual. And I think we run the risk, I think nowadays, of stamping out eclecticism, and stamping out individuality in order to fit a model and I think we need to ask ourselves 'is this model a good model? Is this a creative one, is it allowing room for individuality? Are we just trying to become somebody else, are we trying to become another model? Are we trying to become like HTB [Holy Trinity Brompton]? Are we trying to become like Hillsong? Or are we actually allowing our musicians to express themselves individuality, so that the church, or St Aldates looks like St Aldates rather than HTB or something else'. And that would be true across the board I think.

Interview with the author, 25 February 2012

Eclecticism here is tied to ideas of being an interesting musician and person, of creativity, individuality and authenticity to the self as well as to allowing a community to express the full capacities of its members and allowing them to flourish. A range of music is able to bring out a range of capacities in people both collectively and individually, thereby allowing them to become their full selves, and it is only natural to connect this ideal to the enrichment of the communal life of the church. Here there is indeed no significant boundary to be erected between the musical life of the church and other musics: both church and non-church environments are called on to embody ideals of creativity linked to individual and collective human flourishing. However, it is notable that in Nathan's private musical life he expects to encounter diverse musics as a single individual whereas within the church life it is individuals themselves who have the capability of bringing their own (presumably distinctive and not completely omnivorous) individuality to the activity of sung worship.

Tim's understanding follows the same general outline as that of Nathan, but he begins to distinguish between the functions of different kinds of music such that they are clearly distinct:

TIM: So I think, so for me what is, what I like to see in church is just a rich diversity of different types of music, and I like to see that feeding in with creativity generally ... not just different types of music, but different ways in which it's conveyed, so spontaneity in music ...

MARK: Is there a rationale for you behind valuing diversity? I mean, is there something you think 'this is the reason why I want it to be diverse'?

TIM: Yeah, I think partly because that then appeals to all people involved in church but I think also different, the different types of music, as an individual it's good to just, it's good and healthy to have like the sort of, you know, liking for different types of music. 'Cause I think they feed different aspects of your character and they release different things. So an example would be: so I would often go to evensong, which I love and in some ways I look at it as like this counterbalance to all the loud drums in St Aldates but it's not really, it's just I go to evensong and what do I love about the music? I love that it puts me in a place of reverence really, and humility and puts me in a reflective mode ...

MARK: ... what about this kind of soft rock style that we fall into?

TIM: I think it's quite interesting how we, how that has become just the flavour of the month, like for worship leaders and people who are composing the modern songs. It's kind of interesting that there is such a strong similarity in it all, I find that all quite bizarre really if I think, thinking about it. And I don't really know why that happens, obviously there's a reason, because it's popular I guess, as in I think young – I say young people, as in younger than me, it's their [unintelligible] full of popular music, and it's those young people who are generally also involved with often composing these songs.

Interview with the author, 9 March 2012

Tim's eclecticism is closely connected with his spirituality and his sense of what a community should look like, but within this it is noticeable that he finds different musical worlds do different things to him; he values the balance that can be provided by one music alongside another as they appeal to different significant qualities of human existence. Different musics are inhabited in distinct and different ways and achieve a variety of different formative outcomes – the music of evensong at an Oxford chapel does something very different from the music of St Aldates – however they form part of an eclectic whole that is needed in order to feed and nourish the full range of healthy human characteristics and attitudes. Eclecticism doesn't, then, here collapse boundaries but, instead, becomes a higher level form of organisation and unification.

For Simon, the specific functions of church music and his own self-consciousness about the goals behind his own exploration of a range of musics mean that his normal sense of exploratory eclecticism is specifically set aside from the music of the church. This music becomes, instead, something different which does not form part of the same eclectic whole:

MARK: A lot of your interests revolve around discovering music and things. How does something like St Aldates, which seems to have a very standardized sound, how does that ... how is that for you?

SIMON: That's fine for me. What I need to be cautious here is to not tread too much into my own kind of ideas about worship theory. I don't see the primary role of the church service to artistically challenge my preconceptions about what a church service should be. It's not to say it should never do that, but on the whole what I would look for from a church is a variety of theological teaching, a sense of fellowship, a chance to worship, to approach the throne, to meet with God, to meet with the Spirit, and not necessarily to, yeah, do a whole host of other things, so specifically with music not necessarily to be introduced to new sounds and new things. And I think part of the reason that I make that distinction is that it took, it could certainly be very tricky to regularly introduce those aspects without detracting seriously from some other requirement of a church service.

Interview with the author, 28 May 2012

Simon is very aware that his own eclectic priorities are based around desires and priorities that are different from those appropriate to church experience. His exploration of diverse musics is based upon a desire for novelty of experience which seems to be framed primarily in terms of personal enjoyment whereas he believes the function of music within the church to be largely to make the congregation feel at home with what they are doing and comfortable within the worshipping environment. He separates church, too, from other corporate musical experiences, suggesting that:

A lot of modern event organizers, so primarily this will occur in a large evangelical event, aren't conscious, aren't as conscious as they should be that they are almost artificially generating in a secular way a feeling of inclusion for the people who are going to their Christian service and that that could be damaging for the congregation.

Interview with the author, 28 May 2012

The wrong kind of connection with broader culture then, is not only undesirable, but potentially harmful. For Simon, worship music exists as not only one of a range of musics, but as one of a range of ways of engaging music, a sort of meta-eclecticism. This is significant, because the music of the church is not one that is supposed to fit into a single existing musical life and world, but instead is expected to exist as its own realm and system of engagement. It has to sit as a defined musical world rather than simply as one music amongst others.

A clear sense of differentiation is also evident within Kathryn's musical life. Despite the moments of connection examined in Chapter 3, her musical life is, on the whole, clearly stratified into very different areas with their own purposes and roles. Kathryn describes a much more specifically defined eclecticism. She sings with Schola Cantorum, a high-profile chamber choir within the University of Oxford. When singing with Schola the sense of creating very high quality music with others is, for her, at the centre. She has also, in the past, sung with Univ choir, a chapel choir within her college, however she subsequently left this group due to the problematic nature of spiritual singing in a group of non-believers. Kathryn enjoys listening to 1990s pop; however, she describes this music as a 'guilty pleasure' which she uses for mood control accompanied by a knowledge that it is 'rubbish' music. Alongside choirs and private listening, Aldates music finds its place as a music of spirituality, closely associated with the goals of her church membership. Kathryn doesn't evaluate this music in entirely positive terms; there are times when it can become problematic for her because of its emotional character and she finds parallels between the way the music of the church manipulates emotions and the typical effects of music at clubs and gigs. This leads her to be suspicious of the way in which the music works on the mind rather than always reflecting true spirituality. She articulates a need for the music of worship to accomplish a different task from the state-inducing music of secular pleasure.

Such evaluations play an important role in guiding Kathryn's eclecticism. In describing the range of her musical activities, Kathryn is quick to evaluate both the strengths and weaknesses of each – with the possible exception of Schola which is perhaps unique in receiving little negative evaluation and so, perhaps, being the setting with which she would most closely identify. The ability to weigh up both the strengths and weaknesses of the different musical settings which she finds herself in, combined with a sense of each having a particular role, means that they are able to sit together in a manner which is often complementary, and in which there isn't always a strong expectation that the values of one would carry over to the realm of another. Each music is, to a certain extent, allowed to define itself, rather than being defined by the others with which it comes into relation. There is a sense that the holding together of different musics in this way is partly a pragmatic response to the state of the world – holding out for particular ideals of music making would do little good as, by themselves, such hopes have little power to shape institutions or situations. As seen in Chapter 3, Kathryn searches out moments and places which embody a more ideal convergence of different values in a single place but nevertheless, as a participant in musics over which she has little control, she pieces together different elements into a whole which is able to fulfil different needs, desires and values in different places and situations.

Eclecticism, then, has the potential to operate in diverse ways in relation to the worship music of the church. While the concept helpfully problematises the notion that standard generic boundaries are inviolable and provides a conceptualisation of the fact that a range of musics can in some sense co-exist, it fails to do away with boundaries completely. Important distinctions often can and still need to be made in order to do justice to the ways that eclecticism functions in the musical lives of individuals and as they operate in different contexts. Indeed, it might be wiser at this stage to talk of eclecticisms in the plural, highlighting the diverse manners in which they can function. For some individuals the single coherent musical whole that it seems to suggest is indeed quite close to the truth, but for many it is a complicated notion such that there are important boundaries to describe and traverse within or even in addition to eclectic elements.

The interplay of similarity and differentiation

This chapter has illustrated some of the ways in which musical boundaries between different areas of worshippers' musical lives can carry with them a range of different kinds of significance. These significant boundaries can be key to the ways that worshippers negotiate multiple musical worlds – meaningful conceptual distinctions associated with varying forms of attachment and engagement can allow different musics to be evaluated according to different criteria and thereby allow a variety of different musics to be evaluated positively rather than coming into tension. They allow different parts of worshippers' musical lives to have their own significance in relation to others without any necessary direct spill-over of meaning from one area to another. The church often becomes a location that is set apart, but one that is defined in a variety of different terms, carrying a variety of schemes of value sometimes related to, but not necessarily continuous with the surrounding world.

While this process seems to operate counter to worship music's ongoing attempts to relate in some way to music in the surrounding culture, social anthropologist Anthony Cohen, writing about the nature of community, suggests that it is precisely within situations in which a high degree of surface similarity is present that we should expect to see processes of differentiation at work:

> Within any country, the language, family structures, political and educational institutions, economic processes, and religious and recreational

practices of communities come to have a certain apparent resemblance to each other. ... Such apparent similarity may well lead people to suppose that the old community boundaries have become somehow redundant and anachronistic ... But this homogeneity may be merely superficial ... a veneer which masks real and significant differences at a deeper level. Indeed, the greater the pressure on communities to modify their structural forms to comply more with those elsewhere, the more are they inclined to reassert their boundaries symbolically by imbuing these modified forms with meaning and significance which belies their appearance. In other words, as the structural bases of boundary become blurred, so the symbolic bases are strengthened.

Cohen (1985, p44)

In losing some of the distinctions that might traditionally set musicking in worship apart from activity within other spheres of life, boundaries are instead reasserted in other ways. The kinds of boundaries and distinctions that worshippers describe occupy a similar status to that of the musical meanings discussed in Chapter 3 in their significant variation between different individuals. While I have suggested in the chapter title that sacred/secular and communal/private distinctions may be at the root of much of this, it is clear that these categories are themselves open to varying interpretations and out-workings. Cohen suggests that:

The community boundary is not drawn at the point where differentiation occurs. Rather, it incorporates and encloses difference ... The boundary represents the mask presented by the community to the outside world ... But the conceptualization and symbolization of the boundary from within is much more complex. To put this another way, the boundary as the community's public face is symbolically simple; but, as the object of internal discourse it is symbolically complex ... In the public face, internal variety disappears or coalesces into a simple statement. In its private mode, differentiation, variety and complexity proliferate.

Cohen (1985, p74)

The boundaries around corporate worship, then, provide a location where different symbols can be employed in order to attribute them particular significance. Cohen suggests that such difference is inherent to the nature of boundaries, which are defined oppositionally, in relation to other communities rather than themselves possessing any absolute status (1985, p58). Clearly, the diversity of individuals' musical lives contributes to the varying ways in which these boundaries are constructed. The distinction between worship music and the music of a rock concert can't help but be different from the distinction with music-making in a semi-professional choir. Once the assumption behind much Contemporary Worship Music that the music of church either does or should ideally form a close direct parallel to the music of everyday life is brought into question by reality,[7] the possibility of productively understanding the kinds of distinctions that are put in place between these musical environments can usefully be opened up.[8] The boundaries drawn between worship music within the church and the other musics of a worshipper's life can have social, emotional, relational and spiritual significances which suggests, in contrast to Marti, that while worshippers may often happily separate out different spheres within their musical lives unproblematically, these differences in style are indeed significant. These significant characteristics are not to be construed as completely separate from the music but are carried along closely with questions of style and stylistic difference. They may not arise directly from the musical 'sounds themselves', implicating a variety of social processes along the way; however, music is very much caught up in the social processes that Marti identifies as important, and becomes meaningful precisely because it is caught up with a range of other mechanisms and processes. It does, indeed, often matter if musical style within church departs from the musical styles of everyday life, but this chapter has, hopefully, shown that this departure need not always be interpreted in a negative manner and that the ethics of such boundary-making are therefore more complex than the question of whether or not church music connects closely to individuals' other musical attachments. The virtue that worship leaders found in being able to set aside one's own musical attachments in order to better serve others seems, here, to involve little sense of setting aside an ever-present musical affinity but, instead, to centre around the ability to find significance in the music of the church specific to that setting. Rich's suggestion in Chapter 1 that individuals can potentially find specific values embodied in the music of the church is one that is much closer to the reality of these experiences. However, such boundary making happens in diverse ways, with different aspects of experience coming to the foreground for different individuals. These are placed in relation to, and not simply separate from, the other musical environments that they inhabit. The process of identification often requires an understanding of worship music's nature as related yet separate from other musical settings in order for it to find a place in broader structures of evaluation and experience.

Notes

1 Again, this is not to imply that there is no relation between the two, but simply that within the service these distinctives are maintained in order to distinguish it.

2 Accessibility, relatability and everydayness remain key elements of worship music's aesthetic just as the music also maintains an element of ritualization even where it integrates more closely with the musical lives of worshippers.

3 Radio 2 is a BBC station that has a reputation for playing popular music that might appeal to a middle-aged audience.

4 These include his band The Wooden Chairs, the prayer room (see Chapter 6), and a smaller church group called Bezalel.

5 St Aldates has around 28 pastorate groups of 15 or so members each. Pastorates are described as follows on the church website: 'In a world where people yearn to belong, we believe in building a "community of communities" – large numbers of small groups which act like extended families. These authentic, accountable families of faith, meeting regularly across the city, are called Pastorates. Please consider joining one. What do all Pastorates have in common? A desire to make friends and enjoy fellowship with other members of St Aldates; A hunger to get to know the Lord better through reading the Bible together, worship and prayer; A willingness for every member to play their part and use their gifts within the group; An openness to allow the Holy Spirit to work i[n] us and through us; A heart for reaching out to others in our locality and/or through our friendship networks' (St Aldates Church n.d.). It is probably worth noting that while pastorates are a musically significant space for some such as Dom, my enquiries suggested that many pastorates avoid music-making either through lack of leaders with the appropriate skills or through a general sense of embarrassment and awkwardness when singing in such a small and intimate setting.

6 See also critiques of the omnivore thesis in Rimmer (2012) and Atkinson (2011). Rimmer, in particular, highlights the limitations of purely quantitative approaches to analysis of musical taste 'typical of much omnivore research' (2012, p301).

7 Something that is acknowledged by some of the worship leaders in interview but which, nevertheless, has yet to be fully explored.

8 This is not to say that Contemporary Worship Music doesn't bear some ongoing relationship with widespread cultural forms, but simply that this is not a straight-forward relationship in which most people will immediately recognise the music as their own.

5 At the edges

Value transfer, judgements, discontent

Meta-evaluation of musical value judgements

The third category that I trace through my fieldwork interviews encompasses a broad range of experiences in which musical value judgements formed largely outside of the church either become problematic for worshippers or need to be consciously suppressed in order to maintain a positive experience of Sunday worship. This is, perhaps, the most pastorally sensitive of the three categories of experience as it can sometimes lead to frustration and alienation on the part of musicians and congregation members. The question of what to do with value judgements in a context in which they are not a regular part of public discourse is something that can create tension for those who find them to be part of their experience and it is the area in which ethical dilemmas are most readily present both for worshippers and for the leaders shaping the church's musical life and values. It is here that the musical practices of the church or the individual's relationship to the church community are most readily brought into question. We saw in Chapter 1 how worship team leaders described the way that they would encourage worshippers (and, indeed, themselves) to set aside problems encountered in relation to musical style in favour of a direct engagement with God that can happen regardless of musical context. Beliefs about the nature of music shift discourse away from musical evaluations and instead frame music simply as a tool for worship. If worshippers regularly experience tension between the music they value and the music sung in church, they may learn to regularly suppress key aspects of their experience (or may eventually move to a different church as a way of escaping these tensions). This habituation is likely to have consequences for the way in which these worshippers learn to relate church and world, spiritual and material. Some of these consequences may be positive, fostering self-discipline, selflessness in community and the development of attitudes that allow them to relate to the divine in a broad range of situations. Other consequences are likely to be negative, where congregation members are forced to hold back key elements of their experience and activity from dialogue with the church community, refraining from valuing important aspects of experience and preventing Sunday worship from being a place of fully open and honest coming before God as community.

The title of the volume *Bad Music: The Music We Love to Hate* points to the ambiguity that often surrounds negative evaluations of music (Washburne and Derno 2004a). In ascribing positive value to the practice of making negative value judgements the editors suggest that such judgements can help to solidify identity and position individuals within a broader discursive field (Washburne and Derno 2004b). They also draw attention to the way in which it is often possible to indulge in music that on one level we are willing to judge as 'bad' but, on another, intentionally immerse ourselves in.[1] Negative evaluations of music, and the musics which engender them are not, then, necessarily always an unwelcome part of musical life. The first chapter in the book is an essay by Simon Frith, who argues, first, that 'there is no such thing as bad music. Music only becomes bad music in an evaluative context, as part of an argument', and, second, that '"bad music" is a necessary concept for musical pleasure, for musical aesthetics' and is part of what it means to be a musical fan and of the process of establishing oneself in a musical world (Frith 2004a, p19). Frith's first point is on the one hand intuitively obvious and, on the other, slightly incomplete. While an evaluative context is key to the evaluation of music such contexts are so closely allied with music that they can rarely be detached and float free in the manner which Frith seems to suggest.[2] Music is itself closely associated with, and is embedded within arguments such that it is unable to be completely distanced from these and reattached elsewhere in a completely free manner, but relates to its context in specific ways, inviting specific kinds of arguments and judgements to be made around it. Moreover, evaluative contexts are themselves subject to negotiation and valuation such that it is rarely the case that all have an equal seat at the table of musical evaluation. Contexts are inherently bound up with the process of forming appropriate kinds of relationships and engagement with a range of different settings, people, materials, communities and subjectivities. All of these are themselves subject to forms of ethical and political critique which by their very nature assume that, while different things are often valuable in different ways, it is still possible to say something meaningful and more than subjective about such value.

Frith suggests that we listen 'on the basis of who we are and what we musically know and expect, and we respond according to how and where and why we're listening ... musical judgements are also ethical judgements, concern the perceived purposes as well as sounds of music ... judgement is, by its nature, an attempt to persuade other listeners of the rightness of one's own responses' (Frith 2004a, p33). Such a picture, which ascribes ethical significance to musical argument, hangs in tension with Frith's description elsewhere of popular music fandom in which such persuasion is less important and in which the trading of value judgements is part, instead, of the life, energy and fun of musical appreciation (Frith 1996b, p6). Frith both contends for the significance of musical evaluations and describes situations in which the contents of the evaluations themselves bear relatively little significance. This ambiguity is partly due to Frith's focus on consumer-centred situations in which individuals are largely free to establish and contest their own identities from a solo standpoint. Frith can see that for some people (particularly musicians), there is a greater level of self-investment, but also that for many people the situations they are part of don't require a similar kind of commitment. If evaluations are assumed to be rooted largely in the specific subjectivities of individuals then judgements can be traded relatively consequence-free, their individual basis meaning that they have relatively little claim to compel others or devalue their enjoyment of the music.

Within a context of communally significant music-making such as St Aldates, this ambiguity begins to fade and the balance is more clearly weighted towards significant self-investment. Here there is much less room for the play of irony such that the self can find pleasure in pushing the music away as bad while also engaging with it as good or in seriously contesting the value of music while enjoying the contestation for its own sake. Tastes and positions can no longer remain a matter of play as they do for Frith's fans, because individual identities must find themselves a place within a process of communal rather than largely individual musicking. The ethical is no longer simply a matter of contending for one's own value judgements regardless of the ability to persuade the other, but a realisation that one's value judgements encounter and participate in a communal practice of musical activity. Within this process the question of whether to ascribe different elements simply to subjectivity or to elevate them to a more objective level (despite the somewhat false nature of the dichotomy) is frequently encountered. The ambiguity which the editors of *Bad Music* draw attention to is a very present one, with judgements relating to music occupying a whole range of statuses and meta-evaluations which can involve self-critique as well as critique of the music and associated processes of engagement with it. Individuals at St Aldates often face a decision as to what status to attribute to their own judgements and not simply to the judgements of others.

Within the situation of a church community individuals are not free to retreat into their own musical world which accords with their own sense of the good as they are instead caught up in engagement with a common music, which either offers significant potential for participation or a level of alienation from the process of musical engagement. While it may therefore be problematic to single out a musical object and say simply that it is 'bad music' in and of itself, it is quite a different thing to look at an interconnected web of people, music and processes of engagement, which the music is already embedded within, and ask similar questions. Music contributes to the ways in which people are able to negotiate these situations, and judgements surrounding it often focus on these engagements while also drawing in musical sounds, processes and subjectivities. Judgements about music are fundamentally relational in nature, but these relationships include and incorporate the parties, both human and musical, which are implicated within them and the relational should not become an excuse for considering just one of these elements. By taking the relational as primary, we can reach beyond the subjective/objective divide which leaves negative value judgements problematic and find a meaningful place for the ambiguity which is often felt by different individuals.

Ambivalence and ambiguity

Kathryn's assessment of music at St Aldates displays some degree of ambivalence:

KATHRYN: So I think the music in Aldates is even more lame [than 1990s pop], but I don't think it's important that it's lame in the same way, as in, the tune isn't interesting, the …

MARK: harmonies.

KATHRYN: the harmonies are awful, you know, the, there's no like, there's a verse, a chorus and a bridge and that's it, and there's no attempt to do anything different, but I don't think that's a bad thing, I think it's good because it means that people can just learn four chords and can play like most worship songs, which I think is great, and I don't think it's the function of worship music, it doesn't need to be harmonically interesting. I think it should be about the lyrics.

Interview with the author, 5 June 2012

Kathryn's application of value judgements relating to quality is more significant when applied to how others might perceive the music. She finds the music to be 'lame', but this is unimportant, because its simplicity facilitates other purposes – she makes judgements but fails to find them particularly significant. However she would avoid talking about St Aldates music within the context of the choir she sings in (Schola Cantorum) because she knows that according to the criteria of that environment St Aldates music is bad music. Kathryn does find other kinds of judgement relating to the music to be much more significant, however – the overly-emotional nature of it can be something that she finds problematic, preferring the less emotional mode of being that singing in Schola Cantorum represents. A distinction between abstract notions of quality on the one hand and analysis of the modes of being that music offers on the other, mirrors a public-private boundary in Kathryn's analysis of the music. One kind of judgement is significant personally, while the other only becomes properly significant when it combines with self-presentation in other settings.

A different kind of ambiguity is demonstrated by Liz, who we have encountered in previous chapters. As a dancer and clubber with particular interests in heavier rock, Liz has a broadly positive experience of the worship music of the church but, nevertheless, in certain situations is able to express negative value judgements towards the music:

[My] first year at university I gave up non-Christian music for Lent … it nearly killed me … because I love music and I had almost no music. And actually I don't like worship CDs … it's often a bit … wet round the edges. There's not much punch or bite to it … To me it feels quite generic and quite samey and often quite predictable, and it's not the sort of … There are bands who are like that in the secular world, and I don't listen to them … because I don't like that, because it just feels boring.

Liz – interview with the author, 3 February 2012

Liz is, on the whole, able to express incredibly negative judgements about the music while also expressing a very positive evaluation of the activity of worship on a Sunday. She employs value judgements formed in her broader musical life in specific and selective discursive situations relating to the music of worship, but has little need to employ them in the context of corporate engagement with it as its role within that setting shifts the focus away from such evaluations. This differentiation is partly illustrated by the relationship between Sunday worship music and Liz's consumption of worship music CDs. She seems to find the latter much easier to form judgements about due to the way that the mediation of recordings disconnects worship music from the activity of communal worship, placing the same sounds within a different context (see Feld 1995). At the same time, her perspective and subjectivity alter between different contexts as different internal and external priorities are foregrounded and employed in relation to aspects of life and experience. In interview Liz highlighted how even positive value judgements of elements of worship music can be problematic, since they can lead to distraction from what she sees as the principal purpose of worship. She needs the music not to be too 'good', otherwise it potentially fails to fulfil its purpose in relation to the setting.[3] This need, however, seems to be specific to the setting of Sunday worship. In other contexts she finds that similar kinds of positive musical features can lead her to spiritual experiences:

I think sometimes it can distract me, but sometimes it can be a benefit, I think it can definitely do both. Like, I'd say I've had spiritual experiences at live music events just because of the music, because of actually how it makes me feel and how much joy it brings me and just that kind of … I remember updating my Facebook status after a gig saying 'I love it when gigs feel like church' like, I get the same feeling in my chest as actually when I'm really worshipping and I feel God … but that music isn't anything like the music in church.

Liz – interview with the author, 3 February 2012

As I discussed in Chapter 3, there seems to be a one-way passage of experience in which it can be a wonderful thing for a gig to become like church, but for church to become like a gig doesn't function in the same way. The framing of a gig allows Liz a different ordering of experience, with the relationship between music and spirituality being altered such that musical features can become positive spiritual inspiration in a much less problematic way than they might in a church setting. A different arrangement of priorities within the church setting means that features that would be inspiring in a gig context become out of place and distracting, even though they are clearly not inherently unspiritual. In either setting particular musical sounds[4] seem to be what it takes for something to be evaluated as 'good music', however the category of musical judgement seems to be set to one side within the church setting. A dichotomy between music which is merely acting in a utilitarian function and that which serves no such purpose seems to be employed such that the intentionally functional music of the church seems to barely qualify as music at all unless taken out of that setting and consumed in an alternative manner. Liz's ability to frame value judgements about congregational music seems to be partly conditioned by this dichotomy, with 'musical' evaluations largely focusing on specific sonic features, while other evaluations are held together in a separate categorical space.

The fear of distraction

The fear of distraction by musical features is a common theme across a great many of my fieldwork interviews and often serves to restrain worshippers' desire for worship music to exhibit particular features which they clearly value in other contexts. Any musical feature which stands out as in some way different from the St Aldates norm – either positively or negatively, stylistically, as a demonstration of creativity or simply as a matter of skill or competence – carries with it the potential to distract worshippers from their key task. This awareness is often held in tension with the desire to do something which serves a musical, expressive or spiritual purpose, but nevertheless seems to always gain the upper hand:

> [As a bass player] I'm inevitably interested in the bass lines so I'm trying to lose myself in holy worship, but actually I'm thinking 'well that was quite cool' or 'ooh, I'm not sure he got that quite right', so that can be a distraction, actually, sadly, but I think that's probably almost inevitable.
>
> John – interview with the author, 25 April 2012

> The worship band ... itself [can be] doing such a performance that it potentially distracts the congregation, or the congregation are then aware that they're doing a drum solo, they're doing a guitar solo, they're doing something else.
>
> Simon – interview with the author, 28 May 2012

> Obviously people who aren't accustomed to [the prayer room] style of worship [which forms the heart of Joseph's musical life] may find it a distraction, or they wouldn't necessarily know how to engage with it so it wouldn't necessarily be the most helpful thing to bring that into a Sunday.
>
> Joseph – interview with the author, 2 May 2012

I think being a worship leader is so different to being an artist. I would say that I would probably ... don't do anything spectacularly ... anything that stands out, because when you do that you're taking the attention off God and onto me ... I try to sing well and lead well, but not do anything that's going to distract people.

Dave – interview with the author, 29 February 2012

Any feature which has the potential to inspire a reflective or critical distance between worshipping participants and the activity of worship has the potential to distract and take worshippers out of the state of spiritual flow that musical worship helps to initiate. This stems largely from the charismatic evangelical ontology of music which conceives it largely as an accidental feature which occurs alongside an internal act of spiritual and emotional devotion rather than something which fundamentally participates in that process. Anything which might engender a specific evaluation or value judgement is potentially problematic and therefore the musical processes of the church must be designed in such a way as to avoid such moments. Paul, a drummer on the worship team who thrives on playing in a range of different musical environments, questions this ontology:

At church I feel like I'm being creative in a box ... it feels like I'm massively boxed in in my creativity, it's almost like I know in my head 'oh it would be awesome if I could do this groove here', but like you know, whoever will definitely say no and it definitely won't be deemed to work in a worship context. And I kind of get what they mean when people say that, I guess it's just overly flamboyant, or distracting, but I don't know, I feel like yeah, my creativity is limited.

Paul – interview with the author, 23 May 2012

Paul understands something of the rationale for these musical and spiritual priorities but clearly finds that they fail to do complete justice to the potential that music has within the context of worship. Indeed, the very ideology of distraction seems, itself, to distract from the worshipful musicking which he often feels the potential to engage in.

The value of negative evaluations

The experience of Stephen, a rapper and medic, illustrates the kind of inner struggle that can occur when the balance shifts so that the negative experience of the music is foregrounded to a much greater degree while the worshipper is still seeking to engage with the other purposes that the music is aiming to facilitate:

I don't enjoy it [worship music] at all; I find it very cheesy. The jazz part of me finds the chords incredibly boring and the melodies incredibly boring. The hip hop part of me finds the lyrics dreadful and generally empty ... I feel that God has helped me to get past a lot of my own silly judgements in these ways and actually to say, 'well, these [worship songs] are still truth, and this is still' ... and you know, singing truth is a wonderful thing. I love the church and I love joining in with my brothers and sisters to praise God, and so I've kind of found joy in that, but in the music itself, it's a battle.

Stephen – interview with the author, 10 April 2012

Stephen has a desire to engage well with the music of Sunday services but feels that he lacks the tools to be able to properly understand or get into it. He has a strong sense of what jazz and hip hop are able to achieve and the qualities that are important within them, but when asked the same question about soft rock he answers that:

If we're talking about the sort of, if we're talking about Contemporary Christian Music in the sort of Matt Redman, Tim Hughes side of things, I don't really know, I don't really know, I've never been stirred as such by that music, other than this sense of we're all worshipping together. And maybe that's, and maybe just not knowing what it's meant to do for me or how it's meant to stir is a flaw in myself that I need to sort of just somebody to show me how to enjoy this music, but I don't really know is my answer.

Stephen – interview with the author, 10 April 2012

While judgements surrounding worship music are sometimes framed as purely musical in nature they often connect to broader modes of being in the world. For Stephen, his judgements concerning lyrics – judgements that come from his hip hop background – connect very closely with the importance of expressing good theology in songs, while his hip hop background also carries with it a desire for music that does justice to the darker sides of human existence. While he is quick to label his judgements as 'silly', in reality they seem to be meaningful in a way that is far from insignificant but which instead touches on fundamental elements of Christianity. Stephen adopts an attitude of humility and lays the blame for this situation at his own feet, but in doing so he highlights quite strongly the absence of music from the discourse of the church, and the lack of provision of any reflective tools with which to begin to grapple with the musical element of corporate worship despite a desire to fully engage with musical worship and relativise or even set aside his judgements. He has navigated similar hurdles elsewhere, learning to appreciate hymns which he initially thought of as elements of dead tradition. Positive experiences of worship at St Aldates for him, seem to centre on not noticing the music and instead becoming absorbed in other aspects of what he and the congregation are doing. While on the one hand this resonates well with the suggestion of worship leaders that individuals should be able to do precisely this (see

Chapter 1), it nevertheless seems to sit uncomfortably with a church environment in which music is prominently deployed as a key part of worship and is clearly intended to in some way facilitate and contribute to worshippers' engagement.

In Chapter 3 I introduced some of the experiences of Ben, and the close connection he finds between music making and spirituality. Such connections can serve as the basis for negative as well as positive experiences. Ben's musical home is in such genres as funk, soul, reggae and disco, and in playing at gigs. He feels stylistically constrained by the imposition of a uniform pop-rock style within the church and his experiences serve to highlight the close connection that can be felt between musical value judgements and deeper questions of spirituality. We can re-read the material I quoted earlier in order to focus on the more negative aspects of Ben's experience:

> When I play music properly in any setting, it's about the connection between your soul and the other band and whoever's there, and just expressing yourself truly honestly ... I totally let go when I'm playing, and that could be in a church setting or a contemporary music pub scene. The difference is that I actually felt for a long time that the church was a better connection, [that it] was a more true and honest connection to worship, whereas now I'm finding at the moment it isn't necessarily, but that's more of the style and the system.
>
> I think church music is quite [like] a lot of folk music in some respects, in the contemporary kind of if we're talking Aldates, but it does it in a slightly different way, of the elements of that community kind of behind it. But the problem is when you stamp out the fun, that community fun, and instead you've got a regimented 'this is how we'll do it' there's, most of St Aldates songs are now, they're robotically, logically put together, you know what I mean, the soul can be taken out of them ... but I think that's that control, these worship, coming from the soul but at the moment it's all coming from the finger tips.
>
> Ben – interview with the author, 6 March 2012

The close relationship which Ben feels between musical experience and the soul leads him to feel the imposition of stylistic constraint that emerges from a system of authority within the church as a constraint of the soul, with music-making in a pub setting becoming a more authentic location of worship than the church itself. This deep connection between music, spirituality and patterns of authority and community leads to a strong sense of right and wrong in church music practice, with music becoming, by its very nature, a matter of ethics:

> I was incredibly upset [over aspects of the running of the worship music and team] two years ago, I mean I've never in my life as an adult, in not a relationship with another human being kind of setting, been so upset as I was with it. And the answer was – I had to disconnect myself from it,

because I cared so passionately about being part of it, speaking on behalf of the team ... my problem is I've got an incredible, a very acute sense of right and wrong even though sometimes I might not appear to – like for me racism, sexism, homophobia, all those things to me are just – they repulse me and I think for me I think there's that sense of wrongness that gets me, not always, often it's actually because I feel other people shouldn't have to go through this. But the irony is now I feel there's so few people that have to go through it because so many people have just left. Like in one month four [players of a particular instrument] left – a year ago – and instead of them sitting down and thinking 'what on earth are we doing here that has made all these people leave?' they're like 'oh isn't that sad, four [instrumentalists] have left in one month' and I want to go 'look at what is happening, figure out ... ' and but that's not the case. They would literally, they will literally be amazed to think that it's anything in their choices.

Ben – interview with the author, 6 March 2012

The control imposed within the worshipping structures of the church is connected very closely to a lack of appreciation for difference not just of musical style but of and between people themselves. A lack of proper listening and responding to other musicians within the period of a musical rehearsal therefore exhibits the same qualities as other forms of social discrimination and thereby takes on some of the ethical weight with which such discrimination is often loaded. While Ben succeeds in disconnecting himself to a certain extent from applying this judgement, doing so comes at a price, not only disconnecting him from standing up for the justice he believes that others deserve, but also from soulful immersion in the process of music making. Musical, spiritual and communal structures are closely intertwined such that patterns relating to one often map onto patterns in the others. Ben is torn between different courses of action whether or not to stay and whether or not to voice his opinions knowing that his choices have consequences for his own community attachment and involvement as well as for others involved in that community. Just as some worshippers are aware of suppressing musical value judgements during times of worship, Ben seems to be aware of the need to suppress ethical judgements, even framing his own sense of right and wrong as something potentially problematic.

Responsiveness and freedom in worship

The experiences of Claire, who we met in Chapter 4, also connect musical choices closely, but in a different manner, with matters of spirituality:

I think it might just be an Aldates thing that they just take on arrangements from CDs ... Like all the introductions we do, ever, are ones from, unless [a particular instrumentalist] has come up with something, they're pretty much just all from other things ... I just think that you don't do a song the same way whatever emotional state you're in, and whatever the band has been praying about before a service, they should be able to bring some of that to the arrangement and the worship.

Claire – interview with the author, 24 May 2012

Claire follows certain elements of popular music very closely; in particular she finds the way that pop artists perform covers of songs and re-work them to make them suitable for specific events and performances an important and meaningful practice as artists respond to the needs of particular situations. Claire contrasts this with St Aldates' way of doing worship music which more often centres around imitating other people's arrangements or using a standardized form of a song. This means that the music of the church, for her, no longer feels like it is responding to the situation in which the worship is happening and makes her wonder whether the rationales behind musical decisions and arrangements are often relatively trivial or meaningless. The failure of the church to build meaningful connections between musical characteristics and spirituality means that musical decisions are made on a relatively arbitrary basis rather than flowing from an appreciation of God and of the spiritual situation of the worshippers. Claire feels the music in some ways, therefore, to be somewhat superficial in comparison to that of other environments such as Radio 1's Live Lounge[5] in which the musicians demonstrate a strong awareness of the particular setting in which they find themselves and adapt the music in ways appropriate to that situation.

This feeling that the music at St Aldates lacks spiritual depth is shared by Rhiana, although for different reasons. Rhiana's desire for free and spontaneous individual expression is connected closely to her ideal of spirituality but, in addition to this, it also connects to her own practice of music-making as a singer and song-writer away from the Sunday environment of services. She finds that the Spirit is most able to move and work in this freedom, and that without this the Sunday worship becomes dry and dead. This finding of spirit and soul within music seems to carry with it an implicit critique of certain kinds of authority – when dragged to piano lessons as a child, and placed within the constraints of classical style, she 'rebelled against any kind of form of classical and ... was like "I wanna do my own thing."' Similarly, Rhiana finds it problematic when having to perform in a public setting in pubs or clubs where her singing will be in some way defined by the expectations of those in authority above her. The spirituality of music-making is such that for it to take place in a setting where there is little room for individuality or spontaneous expression is almost to destroy the very essence of what music is about. For Rhiana, music is defined, almost by its nature as a somewhat private activity. This doesn't seem to preclude the possibility of music-making in a group situation – there are settings, people and spaces where Rhiana finds the necessary individual space or mutual understanding for music to fulfil its core purpose of free expression. However, the Sunday service setting seems to be somewhat marginal to her musical engagement with the church due to its highly structured format that involves constantly moving from one item to the next. The kind of music produced in church is closely related to the way in which its life and community is structured and is thus reflective of broader patterns of authority and group dynamics.

Reducing music to the lowest common denominator

One commonly voiced judgement about worship music serves both to express ideas surrounding the perceived poor quality of the music and, at the same time, to acknowledge some of the rationale behind current practices. This is the idea that the music used in church is 'lowest common denominator' music: that is to say that musical choices are based around finding a style which is both playable and singable by and inoffensive to a broad audience who come from a wide range of musical backgrounds. Worship music, according to this idea, finds the common ground between different people's musical abilities and tastes however, in doing so, it fails to be in any way musically substantial or unique. The music is reduced to the abilities of the least able participants:

> I always struggle to quite locate it, so I listen to worship albums quite a bit and to contemporary worship albums, and I just think where does this really fit, and part of me thinks, you know it's the, it's almost a bit sort of Snowpatrollish, there's a lot of U2 in it that's, I think, thanks to Delirious it's quite a lot of U2 sort of influence. But yeah, stuff like, yeah, that sort of pop rock, and some of it ... definitely is more sort of on the easy listening thing. I think that is the closest we can get to being where music is in a popular scene, but it's still being acceptable to people that don't listen to that. So there's a sort of lowest common denominator thing where we want to be contemporary and have a band which is drums, bass, guitar led but with the kind of musicians we have available. The kind of cross-section of people in the congregation there's sort of a certain level you can get to in terms of how far you kind of go into the rock.
>
> Dan – interview with the author, 4 May 2012

> Everything is always about the lowest common denominator, because everyone needs to sing it, which I think is wrong sometimes, I think we should have complicated lines and then the problem is with soft rock is it's easy, it sounds good if you keep it clean and easy, everyone can sing it easily, so they get stuck in it.
>
> Ben – interview with the author, 6 March 2012

> I don't feel like Brenton Brown puts enough changes in his songs. No, that's slightly facetious, yes there are. I feel like they often lack depth,

they lack creativity, they have to be almost lowest common denominator because they need to be played by worship musicians across the world with varying skills, and also because you don't have that much time to practice.

Tom – interview with the author, 15 February 2012

This is a situation in which the simplicity and accessibility of the music and, as a result, the potentially poor quality is considered to be mandated by the situation in which the music is made. There is a feeling that music is constrained by the abilities of the musicians and the congregation. This introduces a pressure which those in control of organizing the worship can feel they have little control over and, instead, are themselves constrained by. Ben, nevertheless, expresses a desire to escape this set of priorities, even questioning whether it is always ethically acceptable. The frustration is one that Thomas Turino discusses, suggesting that 'if there were only simple roles, people who are deeply engaged with music and dance would likely become bored and not want to participate. If everyone is to be attracted, a participatory tradition will have a variety of roles that differ in difficulty and degrees of specialisation required' (2008, p30). Turino suggests that this is the norm among participatory musical cultures and that it is only within cultures where participatory music-making is no longer so common that an ideology of uniform simplicity in order to enable participation is assumed. The failure to offer an appropriate variety of roles, for Turino, leads to some participants being unable to enter into a state of flow with the music – an immersive state which is enabled by an appropriate balance of an activity which is neither too challenging nor too simple.

If St Aldates' chosen route of simplicity is not the only route to harmonising diverse musical abilities, it is nevertheless one of the most readily available solutions within the toolbox of a broader musical culture that is often more consumption-driven than it is participatory and a church that has adopted models from that environment. Musicians within the St Aldates team are, as we have seen, encouraged that their task is not to be a self-serving one in which they can indulge their own abilities and tastes but is, instead, one in which they are called into a role of service for (what is assumed to be) a congregation that has little musical ability and lacks the same musical drives and desires. The priorities of the musical life of the church, not just in terms of simplicity but of style, are thus, slightly paradoxically, determined by what is assumed to be an unmusical body. The dichotomy that seems sometimes to be drawn between musicians on the stage who might be tempted to indulge their musicianship and non-musicians in the congregation fails to conceive of the church body as a fully participatory musicking community in which all are engaging in the activity of music alongside one-another. Rather, the musicians are encouraged to be as non-musical as possible, resisting the majority of musically-motivated impulses, while those in the congregation are encouraged to engage in a primarily spiritual (non-musical) act of musical worship.

The effect of demographics

A similar demographic dichotomy is often employed to account for the usage, in church, of popular styles which will appeal to younger people.[6] A duty to focus the musical life of the church on young people who are assumed to be at a vulnerable stage where they might easily turn away from the church results in a writing-out of other musical priorities as relevant to the church's core mission:[7]

> As a church leader I'm aware that I'm getting older but we want to draw in the young people, so when I was growing up and going to church the old people liked singing the old hymns, but I, the young people didn't, that's why there were only about four of us and they were all in my family. But, maybe the older you get, the more staid in your ways – you've got to be careful and fight against 'well, I liked the other better' because you want to have in church young people, and therefore even if I don't like the noise, the volume, the edgy thrashy kind of driving music that we would have say at the late service, there are 300 18- to 25-years-old who do like it, and that's a great thing, and therefore, not that we're simply there to feed consumerism, but we're there to somehow help reflect and articulate and enable the people of that age-group to express their worship in a way that they find most fitting.
>
> Simon – interview with the author, 8 February 2012

Simon sets aside his own musical priorities because of a desire for the younger demographic not to be turned away from the church for life. Catering to any musical priorities which he might be drawn to is unimportant and almost irrelevant to the task of evangelism and outreach. Simon finds himself led into different modes of being in the worship, alternative forms of involvement which reflect the way in which he experiences the music:

> When I say 'this isn't really my cup of tea' I try not to just opt out, so it's not as if I'm doing my own thing while this is going on as the main congregational thing, so the main congregational thing is celebration, and I'm being more meditative so I'm choosing not to celebrate. I guess I am, I would be choosing to celebrate, but I might only have one foot in, so to speak. You know, so whatever is, whatever we're doing in church I'm trying to, I'm not sitting down and sitting out and taking a back seat until a song or a style comes along that I like, I just am aware that, you know, it's a bit like meals, you know, every now and again, you know, once a week I might eat one of my favourite meals, well the rest of the time I'm eating because I need to eat. The worship styles in church or the songs chosen may not be my preferred choice but I participate because that's what we're doing collectively, and because ultimately true worship is to God, and therefore God may like it a lot more than I do.
>
> Simon – interview with the author, 8 February 2012

There is both involvement in and a distancing from the times of musical worship. With one foot in, Simon isn't carried along fully by the music, but instead participates in it as a deliberate act. His experience thus echoes, to a certain extent, those described in Chapter 3 in which individuals find alternative ways of occupying the space of musical worship, in this case transforming a lack of musical compulsion into a deliberate act of the will.

Marco Antonio's alienation from the music seems rooted in a sense of cultural rather than generational identity; in a theological sense of what worship should be expected to do and in his aesthetic sensibility. Listening to Middle Eastern music is able to give him 'the sense of being in the presence of one's father, of being at home',[8] and this is contrasted with not just the music but the environment of the church:

> Often when I used to go to church in the early 1990s at the same place that I go to now [St Aldates] I would almost have to shut my eyes and blank out everyone else and imagine that the architecture was very different from what it was. When I came back, that was from sort of 1990–1994, but because it was such a challenge actually I became rather disillusioned with the existence and identity of God in a cultural sense because I felt I do not identify with the person that I am apparently meeting here.
>
> Marco Antonio – interview with the author, 1 February 2012

Marco Antonio doesn't listen exclusively to Middle Eastern music; however, his aesthetic sense seems to be shaped, to a certain extent, by particular musics from that region so that he relates well to forms of dance music that draw on similar aesthetic priorities, particularly that of being 'evocative', a word he connects to beauty, landscapes and emotion and which seems also to carry with it a sense of gentleness. He contrasts the invitation held out by the musics he engages with and listens to with the intrusive aesthetic of rock music:

> I mean, yes, you go to nightclubs and the music is too loud. But for me one is invitation to enjoy life and one is an intrusion, even though ironically worship is meant to be an invitation to God of life, Lord of life when actually the main reason why I would go to church is to listen to the sermon.
>
> Marco Antonio – interview with the author, 1 February 2012

As a result of this Marco Antonio often deliberately avoids the extended worship time at the beginning of a St Aldates service. The ways in which he evaluates St Aldates' music are rooted in values that affect him deeply and connect to strongly-held beliefs, relating in different ways to a crisis of faith, cultural and ancestral identity, patterns of church attendance, his sense of God, his sense of personal boundaries and his theological self-understanding. They are thus deeply rooted in very personal qualities while also being bound up with elements which have the potential to claim much wider validity. This combination makes his evaluations particularly potent as felt significance combines with an authoritative sense of conviction. It would likely be a highly problematic process for Marco Antonio to suppress such evaluations as so many elements would be at stake in doing so. This isn't to say that his musical attachments are un-open to negotiation. Marco Antonio demonstrates a degree of openness to the invitation of a range of musics, but these are largely those which he finds to offer an appropriate invitation to enter into patterns of engagement which he feels at home with. The nature of the church community means that there is little room for him to have any kind of ongoing dialogue with those who establish the musical patterns of the church in order to create a sense of mutual understanding and awareness. This comes partly as a result of the size of the church body,[9] but also as a result of the kind of community which it has chosen to be.

David Hesmondhalgh observes that 'Modernity weakens the doxa of tradition, but also entrenches class division and widens the gap between cultural producers and consumers. This combination of factors creates a crisis of value' (Hesmondhalgh 2007, p513). These features of modernity can, arguably, be seen in the patterns of Contemporary Worship Music with its rejection of many traditional features of church music and implication within broader patterns of consumption. The crisis of value which Hesmondhalgh suggests this can lead to seems to be exemplified by the way in which the principal option open to Marco Antonio is one of absence and non-engagement. There is some degree of space for dialogue between church members and those in authority but members remain, for the large part, consumers within a culture that is not geared towards practical response.[10]

As well as issues of cultural and generational identity, issues of gender can also be present within musical experience. Becs, who is on the worship team as well as the church staff, is into pop and finds the dominance of rock within the church's music-making can be problematic:

> I think worship music's got stuck in a rut of this kind of epic soft rock stuff. And I think that's partly to do with the fact that the people who are writing our worship music, that is what they listen to and that's what they're influenced by. So I always joke about how for example at Worship Central[11] people are like 'oh I went to a Coldplay gig last night, it was amazing' ... and I'm like, 'of course you thought it was amazing because you try and write worship music to sound the same as it.'
>
> Becs – interview with the author, 13 February 2012

Becs tends to prefer singing along to female singers, who are generally not heavily involved in epic rock styles, and relates the kind of music made in church quite closely to the kind of gigs that those making and writing the music (generally men), will be attending. A rock-focused musical culture, then, carries with it a certain kind of gender bias which has the potential to engender alienation. It is symbolic of a certain kind of male subjectivity embodied, for Becs, particularly through the male voice, which she finds hard to participate alongside. By contrast, Becs highly values pop music not just for the novel sounds produced as it evolves, but for the way in which it connects to trends in society and things that are happening at particular moments, allowing a relationship with culture on a wider scale. This principle of cultural connection is important to her:

> I can't remember what it was, but a church in America, in a state in America and said that all of their worship music was very much in the minor key. And when he first went he said 'this is really weird, I don't get it' but it's because it's, that's like the culture of that place where they live is blues music, and so their, the music that they were singing was reflecting like the kind of cultural identity of the place where they were living, and he said after a while I just saw that people were really connecting with it because that was the type of music that they listened to day in, day out.
>
> Becs – interview with the author, 13 February 2012

The question of how closely the musical style of the church should attempt to adhere to current trends in popular music is one that is frequently raised in my interviews. In particular, the connection between the rise of Mumford and Sons[12] and the new folk/pop style and St Aldates' recent reintroduction of a brass section (a feature used by the band) on a Sunday morning as well as a folk arrangement of 'O Little Town of Bethlehem' at the church's 2011 Christmas carol services came up in a number of conversations. While these seem to have been broadly welcomed by members of the church, there is often a level of scepticism at the idea that the church's music should be bound up too closely with broader musical trends because of a feeling that simply following fashion in this manner fails to carries any real depth. Those musicians who feel that a trend towards folk offers something in terms of musical or spiritual importance which would usually be lacking in the church's worship are often the ones that appreciate the welcoming of the style into the church. For Becs the style's benefits centre around cultural connection, however other interviewees focussed on different aspects such as melody and cheerfulness, acoustic honesty, poetry and rawness. For Becs, a desire for cultural engagement between the music of the church and wider society alongside a desire for creativity seem to have theological roots in her understanding that the church should be pursuing these kinds of relationships as well as roots in her love of popular music:

> I think my biggest problem with it is that we are perhaps two years behind current trends of music, trying to be popular and accessible for people outside of church coming in, but just somehow being a little bit dated, and I think, like if you look at the early church, it was always the

early, so like at Notre Dame, it was the church influencing the secular, and also loads of crossover, like in madrigals and stuff of different like secular and sacred mixing. And I just, I don't see that now, I see that we listen to stuff and then we're like 'Ok, we need to try and recreate that' rather than harnessing some of our own creativity.

Becs – interview with the author, 13 February 2012

Stasis in the evolution of worship music has, at points, led to boredom for her, with a process of creative engagement 'being part of the worship team and trying to mix it up a little' helping to revive her interest. Similarly the music in the church can make her cringe at the thought of what others might think of it as it tries, but fails to connect with the evolution of popular culture. It doesn't necessarily make her cringe for the sake of her own feelings, but on behalf of the feelings she believes it might engender in others. Within Becs's reflection on St Aldates' music her thoughts surrounding theological ideals, musical habits and subjectivity intertwine with questions of ecclesiology, patterns in the life of the worship team and broader cultural relationships. Becs engages with these issues in a manner that is self-aware such that she can self-critique and reflect on her own priorities and that of the worship team. She is aware that others on the team struggle with the music of the church and that, as a result, they can struggle with questions of musical integrity. As a result she has a desire to initiate a deeper process of engagement within the team as a whole in which there might be space for greater creativity and freedom alongside the moments of creativity she begins to see emerging. The ability to channel frustration into both dreams and actions means that Becs's value judgements can operate in a productive rather than pernicious manner, with reflection becoming an opportunity to find vision for the future.

Juggling perspectives and priorities

With such a range of reactions to and assessments of the church's music, founded on wide-ranging criteria which draw in many dimensions of life, community and spirituality the formulation, by those in leadership, of a musical rationale which sets most of this to one side and asks the music, instead, to be engaged on the church's terms is a very understandable response. The task of juggling such a vast array of perspectives is one that could easily become completely unmanageable and overwhelming for those in leadership. As Rich highlights, it is impossible to please everyone and, indeed, pleasing the congregation is far from the central mission of the church. It is precisely the range of judgements that has been discussed here, however, that serves to undermine such a response and create a significant gap between experience which, as we have seen, finds significant value in musical encounter and discourse, which leaves such value largely unacknowledged. In terms of the discourse ethics introduced in Chapter 2, this creates a problematic situation. While some of those interviewed did seem to experience the music on a level such that negative value judgements could be set aside with relative ease; for the vast majority to set aside their value judgements around music would also be to set aside meaningful priorities which the church would often want to embrace in other aspects of its work and ministry. Evaluations of worship music are tied to the range of issues I listed in Chapter 2 – spirituality, justice, authority, cultural and contextual engagement, theology and gender amongst others – and often represent struggles with these issues through the music of the church.

As Nancy Ammerman suggests in her work on religious identities and institutions: 'Where significant collective identities stand in opposition to one another, individuals who find themselves in both warring camps at the same time must engage in active identity work' (2003, p208). The occupation of multiple disjunct musical identities entails the need for active work if they are to be brought into more harmonious relationship. A process of deeper engagement by the church with questions of musical experience might, therefore, provide a way to do justice not only to individuals but to the broader priorities of the church. The earlier chapters of this book demonstrate how some individuals manage to utilise the flexible nature of musical meaning to move between musical worlds or form boundaries in their musical lives in ways that can sometimes be productive. These accounts have the potential to serve as a model for possible ways of helping worshippers to grapple with their musical experiences. They point towards the possibility for worshippers to engage with musical meaning rather than stepping away from it. It may be, however, that the reason that some worshippers' interviews end up in this particular chapter is precisely because such strategies fail to be workable given their backgrounds, values and situations. Some concerns may simply not be amenable to this kind of re-working, although they may nevertheless be open to contestation in relation to other priorities. If so, then rather than dismissing these valuations as simply the result of personal preference it may be more truthful to affirm the importance and meaningfulness of these different perspectives while also conceding that it is not possible to properly engage with everyone and everything and that there are at least some meaningful reasons behind current practices.

At the same time it is important to take these worshippers' experiences seriously as critiques of church practices and not simply private struggles. These experiences demonstrate ways in which it is possible to gain critical purchase on worship music and musical style in a way that is valuable and can serve to open up some of its weaknesses in constructive ways. As such, they are valuable for the church to hear. In Chapter 2 I drew attention to the work of David Hesmondhalgh who suggests that some negative evaluations of musical qualities which initially look as though they have the potential to lead to social closure and the cementation of division have the potential to be redeemed through attention to deeper meanings and social critiques which may embody positive social potential and a search for solidarity which surface-level articulations can often conceal (see page 34). In other words, the kind of investigation undertaken in this chapter may bring to light ways past a state of unresolved tension as individuals' concerns are shown not to be simply about judgements of others and their musics in the light of their own tastes but, instead, to be concerns that might be shared and which there might be some level of desire to share.[13] Such a perspective carries with it the potential for an associated renewal of social space. As Hesmondhalgh suggests:

> The great advantage of [Habermas's notion of] the public sphere, when used appropriately and with attention to other Habermasian concepts such as discourse ethics, is that it can encourage us to think properly about the institutional conditions that make it possible for people to question simplifications and projections ... The idea of an aesthetic public sphere relates ... to the degree to which a social space provides those participating in ... debates with the resources to undertake discussion in a thoughtful and informed way.
>
> Hesmondhalgh (2007, p524)

Thomas McCarthy describes the public sphere as 'a sphere between civil society and the state, in which critical public discussion of matters of general interest was institutionally guaranteed' (McCarthy 1989, pxi). While this definition is specific to particular kinds of national governance, it can be understood more generally to function as a place of encounter between the discourses of those in authority and the viewpoints and concerns of those within a particular community. Hesmondhalgh finds the development of a public sphere to be important due to its ability to link up ideal discourses with the actuality of how people talk about their experiences. This kind of space needs to be resourced by appropriate institutional conditions in order to function, it does not simply exist automatically, and it is within this kind of space that processes of discourse ethics such as those described in Chapter 2 are able to happen. If we follow Hesmondhalgh's suggestions, then the simplifications surrounding the significance of individuals' relationships with musical style that persist in St Aldates' discourse may serve to indicate the currently underdeveloped nature of the church's musical public sphere and possibly therefore also the virtue that might be found in its further development.

The perspectives outlined in this chapter illustrate quite strongly the way in which such dialogue can potentially uncover perspectives which are more capable and deserving of engagement than seems to be implied by their absence from church discourse. These perspectives have the potential to open up important areas of significance within the church's worshipping practice rather than simply demand attention to the self. However, such dialogue carries greater consequences than the interactions of largely independent peers that Hesmondhalgh's work seems to centre around. As a function of a participatory communal musical body it instead, necessarily, carries with it a high level of self-involvement in an institutional environment that carries with it the risk of destabilising existing patterns alongside its redemptive possibilities. Such conversation is unlikely to bring about a musical community that realises the ambitions and desires of all its members in one harmonious whole. It is, rather, a process where such frustrations are acknowledged and engaged, placing them on a level with the concerns that members of the church might have in areas of theology, community or spirituality. Musical ontology is at the root of the possibility to have fruitful conversation: if music is to occupy a role within discourse, it needs to be conceived of as the kind of thing about which it is possible to meaningfully converse. Hesmondhalgh makes the comparison between his proposal of an aesthetic public sphere and ongoing conversations around issues such as climate change and HIV. The idea is therefore one which brings the musical onto the level of other everyday conversations and resists assigning it purely to the aesthetic realm. Music may sometimes matter in different ways from other areas of debate; but, as I have shown, the degree of overlap with other common areas of concern suggests that such conversation is well within reach. Individuals already have an abundance of important and engaging perspectives to voice, and are more than happy to express them in sensitive ways if offered an opportunity.

Notes

1 As exemplified nicely by Kathryn's use of and judgement of 1990s pop in the previous chapter.
2 While part of my argument in this book is that musical contexts have some degree of flexibility, this should not be taken to imply complete indeterminacy. The nature of the church context plays a key role in the way that worshippers' experiences play out and, while it comes into dialogue with other musical contexts, it is an important player in this dialogue.
3 See also Rich's comments in Chapter 1.
4 Liz gives the example of 'warbly guitar kind of distorty sounds' which demonstrate some kind of experimentation on the part of the guitarist.
5 Live Lounge is a space and regular Radio 1 feature in which famous artists perform covers of their own and others' songs in a relatively intimate environment.
6 See the interviews with worship leaders in Chapter 1.
7 While a number of those interviewed articulated a similar understanding, one interviewee remained less convinced by this rationale, suggesting that older members of the clergy want the church's music to appeal to young people without really understanding how to go about doing so in a way that doesn't simply reflect themselves. For this interviewee a potentially worthy goal is implemented in such a way that rather than reinforcing genuine engagement, it does the very opposite as it is imposed by an older generation on a younger group rather than opened up as an opportunity for younger people to offer genuine kinds of expression.
8 Marco Antonio's ancestry includes English, Norwegian, Portuguese and Middle Eastern elements.
9 Around 1000 people.
10 This is not to say that there was a lesser gap prior to the advent of modernity, but that modernity structures this gap in a particular manner which leaves open particular avenues for response.

11 Worship Central is a ministry attached to Holy Trinity, Brompton, that involves a number of prominent worship leaders. As well as producing music and touring major cities, they also provide a range of resources and workshops for churches across the UK and internationally.

12 A chart-topping British band with family connections to the charismatic church scene. Their early releases feature what can be described as a folk-pop style, although they have subsequently branched out in other directions.

13 It is important here to include Hesmondhalgh's qualification that 'this is not to claim that any kind of negative comment can be redeemed in this way as a sign of a search for potential solidarity ... it has to be remembered that aesthetic experience and discourse may also reinforce social divisions' (Hesmondhalgh 2007, pp522–523). If the experiences described in this chapter are ones that resonate with some of the theoretical priorities of the church, then hopefully there is the possibility that at least some could lead in a positive rather than divisive direction.

6 Alternative musical spaces

The experiences of worshippers within Sunday services are complemented by other musical spaces within the church. While the St Aldates leadership aim to keep the style of the church's music largely consistent and predictable there are a number of alternative spaces in which different kinds of musicking can find expression. More-marginal locations within the life of the church are able to provide different varieties of musical environment from those found in more visible or more closely supervised outlets and provide the opportunity for different negotiations of musical style than those of the main services. As such they provide an important complement to the experiences discussed in the previous three chapters, both as musical outlets for individuals and as contrasting structures against which to examine the practices of the main church services. Within this chapter I briefly examine two such spaces – Sing O Barren Woman, a week-long musical prayer event which took place within the church's prayer room; and Word on the Street.[1] Each of these embodies a musical dynamic distinct in some way from the mainstream life of the congregation and, therefore, a different way in which individuals can relate to the communal musical life of the church. These spaces both complement and challenge the patterns of Sunday services, not only allowing a greater range of musical styles but offering differently-nuanced musical ontologies within which such diversity can take place (Born 2005; Ingalls 2008, p425). Within each setting, music is understood to be, and to be capable of, different things as the veil of neutrality is lifted and music is allowed to take on, more openly, forms of significance that this discourse serves to mask.

Marginal/third spaces

The two venues which form the focus of this chapter represent in-between realms, standing at the intersection of the music of the church and individuals' broader musical lives. As such, I want to suggest that they can helpfully be understood through the idea of 'third space', as locations in which discourses and knowledges from two usually-distinct spaces encounter one-another and interact. Moje et al (2004) outline three principal ways in which such third spaces can be understood. First, they suggest that third spaces are sometimes understood as a means of building bridges between conventional institutional discourses and discourses marginalised in such settings. Second, they put forward the understanding of third space 'as a navigational space, a way of crossing and succeeding in different discourse communities'. And, third, they suggest that 'third space can be viewed as a space of cultural, social, and epistemological change in which the competing knowledges and discourses of different spaces are brought into "conversation"' (Moje et al 2004, p44). According to these understandings third spaces are largely productive in nature, a means of reconciling disparate identities and belongings.

While Moje et al's understandings position third space as a relatively stable structural phenomenon, other authors highlight its potential to destablise. Routledge, following the lead of Homi Bhabha (Bhabha 1994), suggests that it is 'a place of invention and transformational encounters, a dynamic in-between space that is imbued with the traces, relays, ambivalences, ambiguities and contradictions, with the feelings and practices of both sites, to fashion something different, unexpected'. Hoover and Echchaibi likewise highlight Bhabha's understanding that 'third space displaces the histories that constitute it, and sets up new structures of authority, new political initiatives, which are inadequately understood through received wisdom. [it] gives rise to something different, something new and unrecognizable, a new area of negotiation of meaning and representation' (2012, p.13), suggesting that playful and negotiative practices in which signs and symbols are subverted and re-read stand at the centre of such spaces (2012, pp12, 20). This chapter will, therefore, consider the relationship of these two marginal spaces to the mainstream musical life of the congregation, and, following the divergent understandings in the literature, assess their potential to operate both productively and disruptively.

Sing O Barren Woman

The Oxford prayer room is a basement room located within the St Aldates owned Catacombs building. The Catacombs is a site that has long been owned by the church but which for a long time was left derelict and has only recently been redeveloped to provide a regular site for prayer and youth work. It is set a short walk away from the main church building and as such has been able to develop an identity which is both connected to and slightly independent from the main church.

The naming of the Catacombs' basement as the 'Oxford prayer room' demonstrates a vision for the site to be a place which is not exclusively designed for St Aldates' use but is open to churches across the city to use for prayer. According to the website: 'Hosted by one city-centre church, but freely open to all churches across the city, we have a deep love for Oxford and are here to serve the city through prayer.' The room, then, has an explicit geographical, ecumenical and missional identity, intentionally situating itself in relation to the secular world around it and deflecting attention from its relationship with St Aldates, referred to here euphemistically rather than by name.[2] The prayer room website suggests that 'there is something about the room's location ... right in the city centre of this historic city, yet in a basement, hidden from the city – that lends itself to praying for Oxford'. The room is both a space that relates to the city and the world around it and does so in a hidden and private way. Its connections with the wider world are not visible or mediated ones, but exist through the intangible medium of prayer and the spiritual.

The room is also situated within the context of broader international networks. The establishment of the room is closely connected to the vision and goals of the 24–7 prayer movement which centres on establishing cycles of non-stop prayer and intercession, primarily amongst young people. Within the UK, 24–7[3] has acted as an important driving force to encourage the setting aside of particular rooms for such purposes and the movement serves to connect individual projects with an international network of rooms designed to establish a continuous praying presence around the globe. Much of the ethos and dynamic of the room also connects closely with the International House of Prayer (IHOP) in Kansas City which has championed the adoption of free-flowing models of prayer and worship, combining extended periods of improvised musical worship with scriptural readings and prayers. Events within the building therefore connect with broader currents and identities than simply that of St Aldates.

The Catacombs is set apart from the main life of the church in a number of other ways. It has its own website, created using tools provided by Google rather than relying on the expensive custom-designed content management system of the main church website. The website thus has a much more grass-roots feel, hosting a blog, open calendar and a selection of media produced in relation to different prayer room events. The room also possesses its own logo and branding, giving it a visually-distinct identity both in publicity and on the building itself. A series of concentric, boldly-coloured 'C's create a strong visual impression that contrasts with the church's own more-reserved typographic rendering of its own name that it uses as a logo. This represents a deliberate attempt to give the building its own, separate identity, not simply as a part of the church but as something with a life of its own. Inside the room, the scheme of decoration hints in a similar direction – the building has been decorated in a minimalist, Scandinavian style which, again, contrasts with the pink and green shades used to decorate the church itself and the parish centre – another visual cue that this building has different priorities from other spaces within the church.

The Catacombs building is occupied and managed by a number of church staff, but the ordained clergy rarely take a direct supervisory role and, while the worship department does play a role in some of the musical life within the building, there is also much music that is organized independently of them. For the particular 24–7 prayer week that I will be discussing (Sing O Barren Woman), while the space was opened up for musicians to play music every alternate hour, this invitation was opened up not by worship team leaders to those within the worship team but by prayer room leaders to anyone who might want to become involved. During a 24–7 prayer week,[4] members of the church are invited to sign up for an hour-long period of time in which they will come to the room and pray. The aim is to form a continuous chain of prayer that continues day and night throughout the week. During this period the room will be decorated with art, scripture and other items designed to inspire prayer and strewn with materials encouraging individuals to creatively express their prayers or in some way make a record of their particular prayers or answers to prayer that they have received during the week. Often there will be just one person in the room at a time or sometimes a few individuals scattered around the room contemplatively engaging in prayer and intercession. On occasion those within the room will join together for a shared act of prayer or devotion, but such acts tend to be much rarer.

A blog post on the prayer room website describes the chain of circumstances that led to the instigation of this particular music-heavy prayer week:

> We were in the middle of our 24–7 Prayer week for the term, and I was sitting in the corner, wrapped in swathes of bright and loud cushions. I was doorman for the day, and I was noticing something strange: people kept on coming to the prayer room with an instrument in hand, spontaneously wanting to lead worship. 'Sure' I said, 'come on in'. It was peculiar – just like someone had got organized and invited them to come or something.
>
> So there I was thinking to myself ... 'what's up with the musical theme God? Why so many people turning up at the door with guitars?' And then came an unexpected reply ... 'Sing O Barren Woman'. It's an odd verse at first sight. But I knew roughly where it was ...
>
> 'Sing O Barren Woman, you who never bore a child; burst into song, shout for joy, you who were never in labour; because more are the children of the desolate woman than of her who has a husband', says the Lord (Is 54:1)
>
> ... I suppose I got the singing reference straight away. The guy who had just brought his guitar down was now going full pelt, worshipping God with all his might. That kinda linked quite well with 'Sing'. But what about all the stuff about the woman, children and giving birth? Was this relevant?
>
> Looking further on in the passage, the identity of the barren woman became clearer: verse 5 and 6 says 'for your Maker is your husband ... the Lord will call you back as if you were a wife deserted'. This is not just one lady then. Rather, it is the nation of Israel, the people of God. Throughout their history they had constantly been straying from God. And here, in Isaiah 54, he is declaring that he will call them back again. In effect, he's saying, 'even though you as a nation are not fruitful (are bearing no children), shout for joy, sing aloud, because I will be making you fruitful – much more than you could imagine'.

And this, I thought, was a pretty wonderful inspiration for our worship. God says: 'sing, even though you are barren, because I am going to make your lives fruitful again', and so we do.

Within the week one of my close friends, a pillar of our church community here, had been killed in a bike accident in the centre of town. We were devastated. As we travelled through the months of grief the other side of that tragic day, we wondered how to respond as a community. And this verse hit home to me again: sing o barren woman. Was God speaking ... ?

Coming into the New Year, we looked forward to another 24–7 Prayer week ... And a mad plan began to hatch. We felt like God was calling us to sing out of our loss and grief, to 'shout for joy, and burst into song', even though we weren't necessarily feeling like it ... so how about we try singing throughout the week of prayer?

The idea hatched into a plan: find around 70 worship leaders to lead an hour of prayer every other hour for the whole week, day and night. Our prayer rota was coloured in to reflect the fact that every even hour (2 am, 4 am, 6 am ...) would be devoted to worship, and every odd hour (1 am, 3 am, 5 am ...) would be devoted to prayer. And the response was overwhelming! Musicians came from everywhere to help lead the worship slots; bands camped out to cover the night slots; those who had never publically led worship before plucked up the courage to lead God's people in worship. And over the week, an amazing rhythm of prayer and worship began to be built.

Key (2012)

The musical focus of the week, then, was motivated both by very particular things happening within the communal life of the church and by a strong sense of divine leading. The event is significant for the community as a whole but becomes so in the form of a temporal rhythmic succession of many individuals. This is all unified by the understanding that God is at work amongst it all, in a range of different individuals coming at different times, all co-ordinated by the work of His Spirit. Indeed, it is the fact that many disconnected individuals are somehow all doing the same thing that provides the initial clue that this is indeed something that is being done by God.[5]

Somewhat fortuitously for me, the church decided to document, for curiosity purposes, the music of this particular prayer week by keeping an MP3 recorder in the room and asking musicians to record their sessions. As one of the musicians who had been part of the week I was both appreciative of the space and intrigued by some of the music I heard in the overlap between sessions. In the moments of administrative confusion when others were playing music in the slot that I was sure I had been signed up for I was intrigued to hear styles and see individuals that I hadn't encountered before at the church. This led to exploration of the prayer room during interviews. During my interview with her, Nemi, who helps to coordinate the prayer room, highlighted very clearly what an exciting musical space she had found this 24–7 week to be and was able to grant me access to the recordings. On the basis of this I contacted specific individuals who had been involved in some way with the room and asked them about their experiences of the space.

Listening to the recordings of the prayer room,[6] I found the range of musical styles exciting and intriguing. During my time in the room the most striking example had been one particular individual who seemed, to my ears, to be modelling his worship on the style of the then-newly-emerging Mumford and Sons, a style very different to what I had grown used to expecting at St Aldates. This contrasted with my own flute improvisations over the jazz/gospel harmonisations of a close Polish friend and, through further listening, I discovered music that reminded me of musical theatre, a vocal style that reminded me of particular jazz singers, someone displaying their interest in hymnody and a range of others who seemed to be giving voice to personal styles of musical worship that exhibited aspects of their individuality in relation to the worship of the church. Some prayer room music was improvised or drew on repertoire unfamiliar within the church, but much of it also involved a reworking of familiar songs in ways peculiar to individuals. The music of the prayer room seemed to mediate the relationships between worshippers' everyday musical lives and the musical life of the church in a different way from regular services and I was interested to find out in what ways this was significant for those participating in the prayer room space.

Experiences of the space

In interviews a number of those creating music within the room expressed the kinds of significance that they found there. In particular there seemed to be a small subgroup of musicians who identified particularly strongly with the prayer room space both in the prayer week itself and in the broader ongoing life of the room in a way which differed from their identification with the main church body. It provided an environment in which they felt particularly spiritually enlivened or in which they found freedom from some of the frustrations or limitations that they experienced within the environment of Sunday services. Dom, who we met in Chapter 4, expresses his relationship with the prayer room like this:

> I love, I love the prayer room, I think that particular 24–7 was an amazing 24–7 because I felt like the church just like stepped up and just equipped all its worship leaders to be able to do, have freedom, it just gave them complete space to do, have freedom in whatever they do and I was like really honoured by the church for letting, for being allowed to like step in and worship the way I want to worship, and, and that kind of really says something about the church, and it actually says something about the way they worship on a Sunday and on a Thursday that their heart is

actually that in the 24/7 prayer week everyone was allowed to do it whatever way they wanted, if that makes sense.

Dan – interview with the author, 18 May 2012

Dom's musical expression during the prayer week reflected some of the passion for folk styles and folk models which he employs in other contexts. For Dom the prayer room space seems to provide an affirmation of his own musical expression on behalf of the church, demonstrating that the 'heart' even behind larger corporate forms of worship is one that affirms the importance of these expressions. There is a clear corporate element in the church's provision of a frame for individual expressions of worship, the church giving these expressions status and validation through that provision. For Rhiana, such affirmations are nuanced differently – rather than the authorisation of the church it is the freedom from evaluation that is important in setting the prayer room space apart:

> The prayer room is an absolute gem. I love it, I think it's exactly what I need, and I've finally found a setting where I can do whatever I like, and I can be free with God, and no one's going to really judge me about it, and so Lauren said it would be, it would be great for me to go there, and so I went there, and from the moment I started playing I just knew that it was a really safe environment to experiment, to be creative, which is amazing for me.
>
> Rhiana – interview with the author, 9 May 2012

There is less sense here of the need for any kind of community involvement, but it is, nevertheless, the church that is able to provide a space specifically set apart for her to be with God. The church is thus a provider of sacred space, a place set apart from anyone else's opinions or evaluation in which God can be approached as an individual without having to worry about the insecurities that come with negotiating these expressions in the presence of others.

A hybrid musical environment

The prayer room, while providing a degree of freedom for individual musical expression, achieves this precisely by setting itself aside as a place of individual rather than communal engagement. Individuals' sessions in the room are not expected to be shared by the church body as a whole, and are clearly the responsibility of the individual leading them. Indeed, while each session is open to whoever wishes to attend, the expectation of individualised prayer and reflection in the room can mean that those within the room often do their best to avoid any kind of contact with the others who might be there for fear of disturbing their personal reflections and engagement. This can make the prayer room a somewhat awkward social space, particularly when attempting to enter, leave, or move around within it. There is an awareness that any physical activity will be noticed by others, and that such activity should, on the whole, be avoided. In providing a space for alternative musical expressions, then, the prayer room does so in a way that provides little overt contact between these and the church community. Nevertheless, as suggested by the earlier blog post, overt contact does not preclude other methods of conceptual and spiritual bonding between these disparate expressions and the broader life of the church. Nemi, who in her role overseeing aspects of the prayer room took time to review many of the recordings herself, suggests that:

> I think it's almost like people have three, three facets to their musical lives, so they have a personal one, they have the church music, and they also have their own, which sometimes is a combination of both, which is not too personal, like what people do in the prayer room, it's almost personal meets church, and they have, there's this new style or new relationship with music that they have, and I think after the prayer room, after the stuff we saw or we heard, we were so impressed that we wanted, we want more people to do that, because something was, something amazing happened when people mixed their personal style, personal taste to like what we're doing in church.
>
> Nemi – interview with the author, 12 March 2012

While individual expressions have little opportunity here to make a direct impact on the broader musical life of the church community, the prayer room can nevertheless be a place in which individuals find personal ways of negotiating or articulating the individual/communal relationship. The combination of aspects of personal and church musics suggests that at least some worshippers may, within the prayer room, be drawing on aspects from each of these settings that are important or accessible to them in order to bring them together. The exact significance of this combination, however, is one that is hard to gauge from the fact of combination alone. Nemi suggests that the combination has to do with individuals' 'relationship with music', hinting with this phrase that it potentially draws in a range of dimensions. As such it fits well with my argument that style is never simply a matter of 'personal preference' but embodies a range of other significances. The encounter between personal and church style is one that demonstrates the possibility of encounter and negotiation between these different musical worlds, an encounter that, for Nemi, clearly seems to unlock something with a great deal of potential. She describes more fully what exactly this looks like:

> I've been going through the last 24–7 and editing the audio, and I found really exciting things from everyone that has done a set, cause you find that they always start with a worship, worship like we do in church, but always end up somewhere like, even with you and Patricia, you started

with a worship song, but you guys went on this journey that was so beautiful, and you stopped singing, and it was almost an instrumental and you played, and it just almost showed what was inside, and I found that with everyone, with Rich White as well – could start with a worship song but you could actually know what he's into from how what came out of him.

Nemi – interview with the author, 12 March 2012

The prayer room in providing a space for stylistic expression also, for Nemi, provides a space in which musicians' true selves are expressed and revealed – stylistic authenticity, in the use of styles individuals are attached to, and personal authenticity, in the possibility of genuine expression, come together. This pattern is somewhat different from that typically expected of Contemporary Worship Music. Nemi's suggestion that stylistic expression might be connected to expression of other aspects of a person's makeup differs markedly from the idea that stylistic connection can be important but that style mainly provides a neutral vehicle for whatever textual meaning is set alongside it. The transformation of the music of the church through the journeying process that Nemi describes could, perhaps, be seen as an outworking and expression of some of the different significances attached to this music by worshippers in earlier chapters, a concrete realisation of the varying significances of the music of the church and its varying relationships and potential relationships with the other musics of worshippers' lives. Nemi's understanding seems to resonate with that of Moje et al; the prayer room operates as a productive rather than disruptive third space; it is a place where it is possible to build bridges between elements of the church institution and musical realms and understandings often marginalised within the congregational setting, and it provides a realm in which individuals can negotiate the relationship between these different realms. On this level it can sometimes be seen as an almost unequivocal good, strengthening individuals' ability to identify with the church body as it enables creative hybrid forms to emerge.

Matthew Guest suggests that the alternative worship scene in the UK 'is concerned with reclaiming sources of significance [such as images and the material] eclipsed by the overly rhetorical theology of Protestant evangelicalism' (2002, p48) and it may be that it is appropriate to conceptualize the prayer room space within this broader trend in alternative worship.[7] Sebastian Schüler agrees that there are important differences between the kind of authenticity[8] present and hoped for in prayer rooms and the kind expected within more traditional forms of charismatic expression, suggesting that prayer room authenticity embodies a much more holistic conception of authenticity that takes into account emotional, spiritual, social and missionary experience and action (2013, p261). There is, in other words, a desire to express and find a place for each of these aspects within prayer rooms in order for them to be places of genuine expression and action. Some of these aspects seem to be at work in the St Aldates prayer room, establishing a differently-nuanced ontology of music from that found in the main church body. Musical expression, within the prayer room, is allowed space to take on kinds of significance it is elsewhere denied. Interestingly, Schüler also connects this altered authenticity to a more general aesthetisization of life that is present within the creativity of prayer room culture, such that it is in spaces such as this that creative processes are bound most strongly with broader holistic concerns. Prayer room cultures vary, and the missionary aspect is sometimes less strong within the Catacombs than in the prayer rooms that gave birth to the movement, however this general description seems nevertheless to hold.

Such holistic potential should not, however, be too quickly idealised or universalised. For Nemi, the potential for full expression of self in the prayer room is closely connected to her own ways of engaging with prayer room music:

> I think with the church, because I've been singing in Aldates for quite a while, it's almost become routine, and I'm just an anti-routine person, I just don't respond, so yes, maybe I'm drawn to the IHOP [International House of Prayer] sort of free, not chaotic, but unpredictable worship ... I think another exciting thing about the worship and intercession style, or the IHOP harp and bowl,[9] it just gives a lot of room for creativity, because everything is so spontaneous, and I think it brings out what's inside of you.
>
> Nemi – interview with the author, 12 March 2012

There is a close connection between her own desire for the spontaneous and the anti-routine as a means of expression and her ability to see this as bringing out what is truly inside other people. The expressions of others while varied, and clearly significant for many of those engaged in them, are here evaluated through criteria which Nemi herself finds significant.

Joseph, while having a strong involvement in and attachment to the prayer room acknowledges that this is a space that tends to draw in particular kinds of people:

> I think the prayer room draws a certain kind of spirit, I don't know if it's a certain kind of person, but I think it's definitely a place where, yeah where a lot of people who have perhaps struggled to engage with church in the past can suddenly find 'oh, right I get this', or 'this is where I feel comfortable'.
>
> Joseph – interview with the author, 2 May 2012

It provides a valuable outlet for those experiencing particular kinds of frustrations within the main church body to engage and feel at home, but this is clearly something for particular kinds of individual and not for the church body as a whole. Some of the limitations of the prayer room environment are highlighted by Dan. During the prayer week Dan used the space as a location in which he could engage his love of hymnody within the life of the church. While doing so, he was also clearly aware of the limitations and boundaries he faced:

DAN: Another thing that has been quite a big thing for me in my musical and worship life ... is this sort of the whole movement of hymn reconstruction, they call it, sort of half tongue in cheek, but taking hymns which are some of them very old and basically unused, so discovering words in old hymnals that haven't really been used and putting new music to it, and so, so did some of that in the prayer room.

MARK: Did it feel quite a personal thing to be doing in the prayer room?

DAN: Yeah, it did, yeah, I was aware of that, and I did think it's possible no-one will show and I'll just be indulging my interest but as it happened I felt it was quite personal but was it, quite, I felt quite able to share that with people and they entered into it so it was a sort of sense of vulnerability about it for me, something that I haven't ever really unleashed at Aldates before, although I think that people know that I like hymns so yeah there's a sense of it being quite personal, yeah that's right ... I think, I think with the prayer room there are certain expectations and parameters, even though it's, think of it as being very spontaneous, there are still certain parameters and a kind of tone, almost that's expected. And that sort of, that's partly dictated by the sort of, the harp and bowl IHOP stuff that we've got into and I, yeah, so I was aware I was breaking with that to some extent. But hymns, like I say hymns are still quite comfortable for people.

Interview with the author, 4 May 2012

The spontaneous style of typical prayer room worship, then, is one that doesn't necessarily easily welcome hymnody into it. Hymnody brings with it particular pre-existing structures and expectations of involvement that strike against the kinds of individual spontaneity that seem to be prayer room norms. The eclecticism of the prayer room, while providing a welcome to some otherwise marginal individuals and styles does not manage to provide a completely universal invitation. Dan nevertheless finds the prayer room space one in which he is able to try out new things and push boundaries in ways that he would not be able to do so freely within the environment of a Sunday service or other group-centred worship events. There are boundaries, but they are flexible and not rigidly enforced – they are driven by sensitivity rather than authority. Dan feels able to bring something of his more personal music life into the prayer room and to share it while also making sure that he does so in a way that is sensitive to the expectations of those around him and the norms present in the dynamic of the room. While I have highlighted the individual-centred nature of the prayer room, it is significant that Dan doesn't feel his session to have been as much of a private space as some of my other interviewees, and he feels instead that this was indeed a moment of community engagement. That he highlights this is, perhaps, in part a result of the particular kind of music he was engaging in. By using a musical genre that is traditionally designed for communal participation rather than as simple self-expression his focus is drawn to the communal dynamic that is possible in the space in a way that those more intent on free and spontaneous harp and bowl singing might not be.

Community and the potential for disruption

For Claire there is also an element of awareness of community in the prayer room. The room provides a space in which she can engage in the kind of devotional music that she believes the church as a whole should be practising and the lack of which she has found problematic in other worship settings. Indeed, she finds that she can tend to visit the room the most when she has been aware of some kind of lack in the worship leading at a particular event. She finds that the room provides a place where she can respond in musically appropriate ways and with musically appropriate arrangements to the dynamics of what God is doing in the life of the church around her:

> So sometimes you can sing about love in a really like exciting way and just praise God for his love, and sometimes you can sing about it in a really desperate way and be like 'no I really need this and I really need to believe it'. I think that's the difference. So when I led the devotion the day that Jo died, and loads of people were in the prayer room, and all the songs I'd arranged I was going to change them because I was arranging songs about faithfulness and love, and they were kind of not, but they were kind of celebration songs, but you can sing the same songs and just turn them around like instead of singing come, like 'you've opened my eyes to your wonders anew' like singing like 'come and do this for me now', and just like in the way you play it you can make, you can adapt the, especially the scriptural, scriptural songs, you can change them ... I think you can hear a song in the prayer room that you've heard a thousand times before and just the way they arrange it which is like, that's just revealed something completely different to me.
>
> Claire – interview with the author, 24 May 2012

The mention of Jo's death references an important recent event in the life of the church community and highlights that for Claire this is not simply a space where she finds individual expression, but one that has an important role within the shared life of the church and carries the potential to perform an important function within that. The flexibility and freedom that the room offers means not just that personal and individual ideas and desires and tastes can be indulged but that the musical characteristics of the room can be reshaped to reflect spiritual qualities that Claire believes the church as a whole is in need of. The prayer room, here, provides both a cathartic function and carries the seeds of more disruptive potential, providing the ability to embody, within shouting distance of the church, practices which stand as challenges to regular patterns. Alongside this Claire is keenly aware of a sense of connection with those who have already been in the room before her and the ability of their preparation to make her task and involvement easier. The sense of joining in and taking over from those before her affects the way in which she is able to go about worship, offering an existing dynamic which she can dive straight into.

The dichotomy that seems to exist between the top-down and relatively fixed musical style of the Sunday services and the grassroots-focussed fluidity of musicking within the prayer room led me to ask the church's musical leadership about how they thought of the space and whether they might see it as having some effect on the corporate practices of the church as a whole. Lauren described some of the reasons why she finds the prayer room to perform a valuable function within the life of the church, beginning by describing her love for the work of IHOP and the model that they provide:

> I think a lot of people haven't really heard of the kind of IHOP music scene, especially over here in the UK, and I think, maybe I'm wrong, but I get a sense that they don't. I think the diversity that the music has there just shows how much they're actually in touch with the Lord and what the Lord is doing creatively and musically in the church where we allow him, and I think that shows how, you know, a vibrant picture of, you know, joy and despair, and intercession and response and whatever. And I like that – I think their language is slightly different to what we're used to in their songs, and so that's kind of a divide that can't just be jumped over, we have to like build a bridge to move that, and I think, I think I really love the diversity of people that come in to the prayer room, because there's so many different backgrounds, and it seems to me that the IHOP stuff is something that a lot of people can engage in in different ways, and that's kind of ok, and in the prayer room there's space for that to happen because it's not so rigid, it's not so structured, and that's why I am really passionate about doing that stuff, it's because I want, I want a response to be natural, and not felt like it has to be reflective of the person five seats down from you, and my hope would be is that that's a place where people can go and find a bit of refuge in worship.
>
> Lauren – interview with the author, 6 June 2012

A couple of different strands come together here. First, that diversity and creativity, qualities which are closely connected, demonstrate the work of God's Spirit and, second, that individual, natural, authentic expression is important in worship. Individual difference, then, is important to God and, not only that, is a symbol of the creative work of His Spirit. While these qualities serve to specifically differentiate the prayer room, they are rooted in the same underlying rationale that governs the, very different, musical practices within Sunday services. Behind both is a desire for deep engagement in spiritual worship, a quality which, in the context of the prayer room manifests itself in a much more individual and intimate way than in the shared worship of the church on a Sunday. As both arenas share the same underlying basis the way in which this works itself out in music is a matter of appropriate contextualisation within particular spaces and not a core structural concern for those in leadership. For Lauren, the diversity of the prayer room is something that is wonderful, but there is no particular need for it to have anything meaningful to contribute to the life of the main church services other than its potential to deepen the spiritual lives of individuals.

When asked more specifically how the life and qualities of the prayer room fit alongside the church's Sunday services, Lauren isn't quite sure; it's a relationship she is still in the process of figuring out. She believes that separation between the two is something that is 'ok', but she does suggest there might be some influence on Sunday services as those who have spent time in the prayer room lead worship in the church and, as a result of their time spent alone with God, display some of this influence through the way in which they shape Sunday worship. It is the intimate quality of the prayer room that for Lauren seems to characterise both why it is currently a set apart space and why she would like to see some of its spiritual life crossing over to Sunday services. Intimacy with God is an important characteristic for individuals to pursue, but is something that can be hard to engage in on a corporate level if the congregation are not used to that experience. Intimacy and individuality are closely connected: it is in the place of being alone with God that intimacy can be pursued and this, perhaps, is why diversity and creativity are seen as signs of the work of God, because they are the result of individuals devoting time to knowing God intimately and flow out of this time of deep and personal spiritual engagement.

The prayer room, then, fosters a particular relationship between spirituality, individuality and style. Deep spiritual engagement is fostered in the private realm in which personal expressions of style are entirely appropriate as both a natural means of engagement with God and a sign of His diverse creative work. The move from this space to the public space is a carefully controlled one in which it is primarily the fruit of a deep spiritual engagement which is expected to make itself manifest in other settings in ways appropriate to those particular environments. Rich expresses the nature of this dynamic:

> I think there needs to be wisdom in what does come into the public. I think you always have to make a judgment on where something is helpful or distracting, and as I say, because our, the role of the worshipper, the lead worshipper is to fulfil a role of serving and enabling people to worship God, if it draws more attention to themselves than it does to the one they're worshipping, I think then it's not really fulfilling that role very well, so I think there needs to be wisdom.
>
> Rich – interview with the author, 10 May 2012

Because different musical practices are engaged in privately within the prayer room they have no potential, by drawing attention to themselves, to become problematic for other people. Diverse style is, perhaps, allowed in the prayer room because as the 'natural' expression of individual worshippers it is not regarded as something that risks overtaking spirituality as the main focus of attention. Joseph, a prayer room regular, is clearly aware of the set apart nature of the prayer room space. Nevertheless, discussing events in the prayer room beyond the prayer week, he finds the potential for some kind of connection with the regular life of the church to be an exciting one:

> It is interesting, isn't it, that prayer rooms tend to be sort of have that fringe location in the church body, like that's why I find it so exciting that [the rector] Charlie's given us permission to bring the worship and intercession team from the Catacombs up into to lead the Hungry meetings, and things like to sort of enable the wider church body to engage with what this small, small fragment of the church body is actually doing down in the prayer rooms and putting so much effort into.
>
> Joseph – interview with the author, 2 May 2012

For Joseph it is the intense spirituality of the prayer room which seems to provide the major draw of the environment and this, perhaps, is why he finds the prospect of some level of engagement with the broader church life to be something that carries a great deal of potential. It is not seen by him primarily in terms of personal expression but of deep and free engagement with God. The combining of the worship and intercession team and the church's monthly week-night prayer meetings known as Hungry provides a means of contact between the broader life of the prayer room and the church as a whole. Worship and intercession, as a regular group activity within the prayer room offers a space in which there is both an element of individuality in the way that individuals can contribute short sung fragments to a free-flowing improvised musical whole and a lesser degree of individual influence on the musical whole than in the 24-7 prayer week. The Hungry meetings likewise provide an environment in which there is both some expectation that much of the wider church body will be present and in which there is a more intimate dynamic than Sunday meetings. In providing a contact point between the prayer room and wider church the meetings Joseph describes involved a pairing of the most-similar activities of each setting so as to produce a minimum of disruption. They thus very much represent the care that Rich felt the need to exercise in contact between prayer room and church.

The diverse musical life of the prayer week, then, provides a different way in which individuals can mediate the relationship between their broader musical lives and the shared musical life of the church. While allowing diversity, it does so in relation to conceptions of spirituality, individuality and freedom which particular individuals find allows them to find a space for meaningful spiritual expression through musical practices that are significant to them in a way that more-constrained parts of the church's musical scene do not currently give room for. The prayer room thus seems to be an important location for individuals to let off steam that would otherwise not have a particular outlet within the regular life of the church. It is clear that such models are specific to the prayer room setting and do not translate easily into more communal activities. The space, while providing connection between the different individuals making music within it, functions largely on the basis that it is a space for the individual. The kind of interest that Sing O Barren Woman seemed to stir among members of the church suggests that it has the potential to bring particular aspects of individuals' musical lives to a place of broader attention, while the use of a recording device in order for those in leadership to hear the various sessions means that some conversations are, perhaps, likely to revolve more around the musical sounds than their significance for those in the room. This dynamic, in which diverse expressions co-exist without a great deal of analysis or scrutiny, mirrors Guest's understanding of the broader 'alternative' worship scene – from which 24–7 rooms seem to draw much of their inspiration – in which theological questioning takes priority over any desire to come to a sense of reso-lution or agreed truth and in which the 'multi-media technology of services facilitates the simultaneous bombardment of a continuously changing series of sounds, words and images [and in which] little effort is made to offer inter-pretations of the symbolism used ... the juxtaposition of sharply varying images frustrat[ing] the possibility of any unified meaning' (2002, p49). Rather than producing a desire to bring diverse musics into a unified environment,[10] then, the prayer week provides a safe environment in which particular kinds of relation-ships between music and the spirituality, worship and life of the church can be explored and in which individuals are doing precisely that. Nevertheless the space exists in relation to a much more fixed institutional environment in which a sense of shared meaning and purpose is central, relying on the conceptualisa-tions and priorities established in a shared context to establish the background against which other creative practices can take place. Through Rich and Lauren's cautious attitudes to my questioning we can sense the potential that the prayer room has to operate as a more disruptive kind of third space. It has to be kept at some distance from Sunday services in order to avoid upsetting the patterns and models which have been carefully established in this setting. In line with Bhabha's theories of third space, their uncertain attitudes towards the prayer-room/Sunday relationship highlight how it can be hard to understand the space through standard church discourses. The space takes familiar and valued musical symbols and systems and redeploys them such that they invite both affirmation for their familiarity and caution due to their transformation.

Word on the street

Word on the street is a musical and missional project which has a degree of connection with the prayer room. Prior to going out onto Cornmarket,

Oxford's busy pedestrianised shopping street, the prayer room is used as a venue for assembling, planning and praying about the week's outing. The group is made up of whoever is willing to take part – often students – and engages in regular evangelism and outreach excursions, meeting regularly to play music on the streets and to use this as a forum for engaging with the people whom they encounter while musicking. Luke, who until recently took responsibility for leading the group, expresses the connection like this:

> What we said to them was [that] a lot of what WOTS is, is just taking the prayer room and putting it out on the street, because it's pretty much the same thing, you know, just making a, an atmosphere of worship and then praying and prophesying as God leads, it just has the extra element of being out in the public marketplace, so there's an evangelistic aspect to it as well.
>
> Luke – interview with the author, 14 May 2012

Freedom and anarchy

The music of the group clearly exhibits a much greater degree of freedom than would be possible in a worship context. Indeed, in contrast even to the prayer room, it provides a space in which secular music can be re-appropriated not simply stylistically but also in terms of content. An email report on one on of the weekly trips details the range of music used on one particular Saturday:

> Highlights included a learnt-on-the-spot a capella rendition of Psalm 23 interspersed with evangelistic rap, Revelation Song, a song by Amber Brookes, and a worshipful re-appropriation of the secular pop chorus 'You and me always'.
>
> WOTS report email, 7 May 2012

I asked Luke about the contrast between this and the Sunday environment and he expressed an uncertainty about the relationship:

> I could say that there might be a small element of rebelliousness on my part of wanting to make it a bit sort of anything goes and, not anarchic, but you know, no hierarchy, you know anyone can turn up and play anything. But I don't think that's just sort of rebelliousnessness [sic]. I think as a lot of that comes from the fact that not lots of people are willing to go out on the street and worship, and so you almost have to just take what you can get, and especially I've done a little, I've just started a little bit to play a little bit of guitar out there, but especially as being an organiser and being a drummer.
>
> Luke – interview with the author, 14 May 2012

There is a knowledge that this kind of music-making is transgressive of the kinds of boundaries that have been erected within regular church praxis and this leads to an element of self-examination. There is also, however, an awareness that with this kind of musical praxis individuals find a very different kind of relationship to and role within the group and that a different kind of authority structure is almost a necessity when musical resources are limited. Such freedom isn't disconnected from spirituality; rather it seems to embody something of the prayer room ethos of 'just making an atmosphere of worship and then praying and prophesying as God leads'.

Stephen was involved in setting up Word on the street, and its naming and goals resonate closely with the lyrical focus which he finds significant within, and which extends out of, his love for hip-hop:

> It came to be deliberately called Word on the street as opposed to worship on the street because of not wanting just for it to be about worship music on the street, but bringing sort of the presence of the word, the living word, Christ and also bringing his word to people and sharing his message.
> Luke – interview with the author, 14 May 2012

As a project at some distance from both the authority structures and the physical space of the church, Word on the street provides a place of great freedom, to the extent that almost any music and musician is welcome within it whether or not they have any connection with the church or with faith. The element of chance encounters is clearly an important part of WOTS outings, not just in terms of conversations with passers-by but of openness to the same strangers' participation in and contribution to the musicking of the group. The musical practice is shaped by those who are part of it, accompanied by a sense that this also allows freedom to respond to and participate in whatever God is doing in a particular situation. The element of musical style is almost incidental to these factors and clearly emerges out of and in response to them. Luke acknowledges that the patterns of the group often open up the potential for something to go wrong, or simply for everything to sound bad, but this seems to be part of the price that is worth paying for the work that the group is involved in. The musical shape of the group evolves partly out of what is possible – bringing the established patterns of the church's musical worship into the setting of the street is not possible with the musical resources available and would also, perhaps, constrain the kind of engagement which the group is seeking to involve itself in.

Musical significance and group dynamics

While Luke frames much of the group's activity in terms of simply providing an 'atmosphere of worship' on the streets of Oxford, it is clear through his regular email reports that musical style and the manner in which individuals are able to contribute to this does seem to carry some kind of significance. This is evident both through his detailed descriptions of particular weekly happenings and through the way in which he describes the encounters it opens up:

> Last month, the day after the amazing 7:14 prayer event in town, Claire, Mike D, Alex, Joanna and Luke went out onto Cornmarket Street to worship God and invite people to the St Aldates and Emmanuel carol services for a special Christmas edition of WOTS. Here's what happened: God was worshiped; services were advertised; a Turin Breaks comparison was made by a complimentary member of the public; a group of what can only be described as 'heavy-metal-heads' stopped to listen to Mike's jazzed up carols and took fliers; 20p was generously contributed towards post-WOTS refreshments; Claire sang some beautiful renditions of carols to guitar accompaniment; lots more carol service fliers were handed out to enthusiastic listeners; a drummer man dressed as Santa who used to be in the Aldates choir in the 1960s ('then I found jazz') was conversed with; Alex made his brilliant WOTS debut; and, fittingly, Jo prayed for a lady called Carol. It was great!
>
> WOTS report email, 11 January 2012

In this report Luke closely intertwines the narratives of encounters with passers-by and individual musical contributions such that there seems to be a clear connection between the two. Particular musical items which arise out of the creativity and personal musical attachments of the group become points of encounter with particular people around them. The jazzed up carols pique the interest of heavy-metal-heads, the novel rendition of carols is connected to people's willingness to accept carol service fliers, and something about the general musical setup seems to draw in someone who had previously been drawn away from St Aldates through music. In a similar manner to the 24–7 prayer week, there is a sense that the diversity of encounters is a sign of the work of God's Spirit. These are not planned by the group, but seem to occur as different musics emerge and happen to connect with particular people that come along. The theme of money is one that Luke has remarked upon multiple times; the receiving of money seems always to come as something unexpected as WOTS is primarily about spirituality, not about busking, but it nevertheless serves as a sign of the musical and public validity of the activities of the group. The individual musical expressions of those within the group are both closely connected to the work of the Spirit and the activity of worship that they are providing but also, in contrast perhaps to music within the church, they have the possibility of affirmation from the general public and the possibility to become points of significance for that same public.

While this narrative largely emphasises the element of public encounter, the reverse can also be true, with the internal journey of the group coming to the foreground:

Mike's highlights:

'My Only' by John Mark Macmillan; in our hands, a driving kind of English folk samba. Merged into group-sung prophetic heraldings; You are awesome, You are awesome You are welcome! You are welcome!

I see my Sun, I see my Sun Behold He comes, behold He comes!

With healing in His wings!

'You Make me Come Alive' from the Bethel Music team; had a kind of Balkan garage feel (?), merged into a joyous and raucous stomp! People joined in with our clapping, and the gathered crowds were ministered to by HOTS [healing on the streets, a group that offers prayer for healing to passers-by] members. This was actually the kind of worshipful fun I'm unaccustomed to having on Cornmarket. Beaut!

'Amazing Grace' was powerful as ever. It was wonderful to have many saints around me, singing of their cleansing from shame, and their 'life of joy and peace' within the veil.

Also, many of our songs declared the power of the Living God! Which, I think, made a difference in unseen places. It was great to have some U2, Sinead O'Connor, Duke Special & Wannadies all in the musical mix.

WOTS report email, 5 June 2012

In Mike's account the significance of the wide-ranging musical activity is clearly connected to the worshipping journey of the group. Different styles emerge and, as they do, they connect to particular theological acts – English folk samba leads to a prophetic declaration, Balkan garage leads to joyous worship and prayer for healing. Each song acts as a one-off individual occurrence, appearing in a moment and form that is unlikely to ever be repeated. Again, the form of the narrative gives the impression that this is all orchestrated from beyond by God's hand, the passive form of the narrative seeming to imply an unseen divine agency beyond, and yet perhaps incorporating, the agencies of and within the group.

Word on the street, then, while emerging out of the prayer room, has a very different dynamic to that of the 24–7 prayer week. Individuals contribute to the process of group musicking as the Spirit orchestrates and in so doing form significant connections both with God and with the world around them. Personal musical attachments and contributions are able not just to be expressed as public displays of individuality but to become a means by which others can be engaged and by which the Spirit is able to do particular things within the group as a whole. This process of coming together as a group is a crucial one as it is something that does not always seem to be guaranteed from the start:

Next in Cornmarket, we had a pleasant surprise. Having found our groove a bit more we moved into a time of free improvisation and inviting the presence of God, with a sung emphasis on the power of the blood of Jesus and the 'strong love' of God which became freshly tangible to us as we declared it.

WOTS report email, 15 November 2012

Last Saturday's WOTS session started out slow and in some respects a bit tricky. However, we persevered, and to our delight we found by the end that we had been joined on the spot by a community chorus of friends old and new who turned up and joined in with the singing, proclaiming God's praises in unison in the street, drawing a big crowd ... This Saturday, our musical duo of Luke and Mike grew organically into an 8-piece band (hastily christened 'Joy Central'). Members of St Aldates and OCC rocked up and helped sing, be percussive, and praise Him on some instruments – so three congregations represented (including Emmanuel). The Lord did some holy action while we sang about ... um, His holy action ... That's His kind of coincidence, I suppose.

WOTS report email, 5 June 2012

On the first occasion the group seems to already be in place, but only after a process of searching do they come together into a groove and a flow that works for this particular selection of people in this place and time. They can't rely on any existing dynamics but need to keep going and exploring until they discover something appropriate for the occasion. On the second occasion it is only over the course of the session that the group comes together at all, a process which is not primarily seen as the assemblage of a diverse group of individual lives, but as an ever-expanding group of those being drawn to what God is doing in a particular location. God's activity in incorporating people into his ongoing work among the group, a work of which they are an essential part, is the underlying dynamic behind individual–group negotiations. Meaning-making is the result of this coming together and something that emerges spontaneously within the group dynamic rather than out of individual impositions. Individuals are able to make different musical contributions, but meaning is made through the process of public encounter and interaction, a process which is enabled by the open environment of the group and would be less possible either within the individual-centred environment of the 24–7 week or the front-led group engagement of a Sunday service.

Word on the street thus provides a very different dynamic to that of the prayer room and, again, a differently nuanced musical ontology. While both affirm individuals' diverse musical abilities and attachments, Word on the street allows these attachments to take on a degree of significance that is much more centred around the group, and in which they find a place of public, shared value as they are mixed in an event co-ordinated not by the individuals themselves but by the unseen hand of God's Spirit. While the space of the prayer room represented a relatively controlled and contained dynamic, WOTS, by contrast is an environment where many normal attempts at control are abandoned to the winds of chance and the divine hand. Meaning, here, spills over between individual, group and public in a dynamic and chaotic interplay. Luke's awareness of this as a rebellious space is partly a symptom of the fact that a much greater structural re-ordering goes on here than in the prayer room. This space, therefore, moves us further away from Moje et al's

(2004) understandings of third spaces as navigational in nature and leads us much more directly to Bhabha's ideas of third spaces as disruptive, unpredictable and unrecognisable in relation to the spaces which they mediate. The juxtaposition of individual, church and world leaves none unaffected or completely in control and we are presented with a situation which is both closely related to the church and self-consciously disruptive of church norms.

Disruptive and productive spaces

In contrast to the espoused Sunday ideal[11] that worshippers set aside their own musical tastes and preferences when entering the doors of the church, the environments provided during Sing O barren woman and Word on the street offer the complete opposite. Each provides a way for worshippers to transform the music of the church in a way that is suited to their particular skills, enthusiasms and offerings. In the case of the prayer room this consisted of the provision of a space that was highly valued and appreciated by many of those who came to make music (and others who didn't), while in the case of Word on the street the activity of the group opened up a range of ways for music to contribute in a significant manner to events, journeys and encounters. The musical choices possible in each context clearly relate to the situation in which they are embedded. The freedom of the prayer room stems from its tendency to be a more private and individual space in which personal authenticity is appropriate, while the range of musics found in Word on the street is a result of a desire to engage with a secular public through the medium of busking culture and the freedom of an ad-hoc space in which the expectations surrounding Sunday services are less imposing.

Each space occupies an implicit relationship with the broader worshipping culture of the church. There is an understanding that each is in some way an expression of the same basic act of Spirit-led worship while also allowing the opportunity to engage in musical acts which would not be permitted in other settings. These two settings offer worshippers a place in which they can find different answers to the question of how they relate their existing musical attachments to those of the church environment not just internally through the way they process shared experiences but through acts of musicking. In achieving a different balance of individual and communal relationships from that of the Sunday services they reflect a different set of trade-offs and balances. Each is reflective of broader trends displayed most prominently within movements such as the emerging church[12] in which traditional models of church are challenged and re-thought within a post-modern context. They thus allow multiple voices to be put in dialogue (Hunt 2008, pp290–291), offer a renewed appreciation of the aesthetic (Bader-Saye 2006, p19), affirm individual identity (Guest and Taylor 2006, p52), offer transformed authority structures (Guest 2002, p48), and experiment with new possibilities of meaning with a certain degree of reflexivity. Consonant with the multiple functions of third space described in the literature, both spaces have the potential both to reinforce and to challenge predominant musical models, carrying both productive and disruptive potential: in successfully relegating personal style to a semi-private realm, the prayer room provides the potential to reinforce a strong separation between public and private. In providing a rich and fruitful range of musical expressions that come out of the encounter between individuals and the worshipping life of the church it has the potential to draw attention to the (currently unacknowledged) ways in which the encounter between individuals' musical lives and the worshipping life of the church might potentially be productive. Likewise, WOTS serves to position communal musical engagement with different musics firmly outside the walls of the church building while also providing a space in which the spiritually meaningful nature of different musical encounters is grappled with and celebrated. As such they occupy an ambiguous position in relation to the broader life of the church, one that both enables and challenges, reinforces and disrupts.

Notes

1 This chapter is derived in part from an article published in Journal of Contemporary Religion, 2016, copyright Taylor & Francis, available online: http://www.tandfonline.com/doi/full/10.1080/13537903.2016.1152680

2 See Elisha (2013) for a discussion of the reimagining of city space that can take place as part of city-wide prayer events.

3 See Greig and Roberts (2003) for a good introduction to the story of 24–7 and its growth from a single prayer room in Reading to a worldwide movement.

4 These happen at a frequency of roughly one per university term.

5 'Die Gebetskette selbst symbolisiert und erzeugt eine soziale Dynamik, an der die einzelnen Individuen selbst teilhaben können – und dies nicht nur als Konsumenten, sondern als Produzenten religiöser Sinnstiftung. Entsprechend wird in dieser Bewegung auch der Einzelne immer wieder als "history maker" dargestellt, als jemand, der die große Geschichte Gottes mit den Menschen aktiv mitgestalten kann. Zugleich begreift sich die Bewegung selbst als ein Glied in einer Kette von christlichen "history makers", die quer durch die Geschichte wichtige spirituelle Anstöße gegeben haben' (Schüler 2013, p256). [The prayer chain symbolises and generates a social dynamic in which individuals can participate not only as consumers but as producers of religious sense-making. Accordingly in this movement the individual is again and again (re)presented as 'history maker' as someone who can play an active role with people in shaping the big story of God. At the same time the movement conceptualises itself as a part of a chain of Christian 'history makers', who right across history, have given important spiritual impetus.] (My translation.)

6 Eavesdropping on what often seemed to be particularly intimate expressions of individual worship and expression felt somewhat voyeuristic, particularly when combined with face-to-face interviews with the musicians involved at a later stage.

7 'Alternative worship (or alt.worship in the preferred web-speak) ... was originally inspired by the now infamous [due to scandal] ... Nine O'Clock Service (NOS) in Sheffield, England. From the late 1980s onwards, groups of young, technologically minded Christians began to establish creative, multimedia services in response to

the liturgical experimentation and cutting edge cultural engagement pioneered at NOS' (Guest and Taylor 2006, p50). Guest traces the history of the alternative worship movement from its origins to more recent expressions. He suggests two means for classifying different alternative worship groups 'Firstly, there are services which adopt multi-media technology primarily in order to attract young people into a church environment in which they feel more comfortable ... Secondly, there are groups which incorporate experimental [in the sense of trying out new things] worship into a broader shared project of rethinking the notions of church, cultural identity and Christian faith' (2002, pp37–38).

8 Schüler follows Charles Lindholm in placing the desire for authentic lifestyle as a defining characteristic of modern society.

9 'Harp and Bowl' is a name given to a model of prayer and worship involving a continuous flow of intercession, scripture-reading and improvised singing (followed by corporate repetition) of short musical phrases. Its name is derived from passages in the book of Revelation. It originated at IHOP but has subsequently spread further afield.

10 Although insofar as this all takes place under the umbrella of the same extended event there is some element of this.

11 See interviews in Chapter 1.

12 The boundaries between 'alternative worship' and 'emerging church' are somewhat slippery and difficult to define and both are, in many ways, part of the same broader trends. While the former, as a term, focuses largely on rethinking the aesthetic and presentational element of worship, the latter points more strongly to the rethinking of models of community. I point the reader to Spinks (2010) for one attempt at bringing some order to the tangle of terminological confusion.

Conclusion

A close study of St Aldates reveals a series of gaps between church discourse around music and lived experience. These gaps surround the significance attributed to music, musical attachments and the manner in which these are negotiated by individuals. The detailed descriptions of the ways in which individuals experience music and negotiate the movement between musical environments have on the one hand served to repeatedly bring into question existing pictures of the church's musical community while also beginning to piece together the foundations for an alternative understanding.[1] I suggest the importance of grounding such an understanding in the articulations of musical experience which individuals are already able to offer, as it is these that both allow a basis in lived reality and which provide the tools that others might be able to use in navigating musical value.

In Chapter 2 I suggested that a question posed by Nancy Ammerman formed a key part of this book:

> Given that members participate in multiple public narratives, from both religious and secular institutional sources, we can ask which religious institutions supply the most robust and portable plot lines. The narratives supplied by religious organizations may be more or less richly nuanced, allowing them to address wider or narrower ranges of human existence. They may also be more or less able to incorporate counter-narratives, making sense of the very events that would seem to challenge their plausibility. Part of the analyst's job is to assess the degree to which any given religious organization is generating, nurturing, and extending the language, grammar, gestures, and stories that are capable of surviving in the everyday practical competition among modern identity narratives.
>
> Ammerman (2003, p218)

It is clear, from the experiences outlined in earlier chapters, that many worshippers are adept at navigating precisely these challenges, using a variety of idiosyncratic strategies which piece together different aspects of their lives in a range of different ways. In doing so they exhibit varying degrees of individual agency in relation to the broader organisation of which they are a part. I have yet to discuss the source of these strategies. On the one hand, some worshippers clearly seem to find theological and conceptual resources available to them within the church and elsewhere which help them to navigate these areas of intersection; some of these provide a more satisfactory result for the worshipper than others. On the other hand, there often also seems to be a large conceptual gap between the kinds of experiences and strategies that I have been describing and the pastoral strategies suggested by those in a position of worship leadership. Indeed, the place where these strategies come most into play is precisely the place where worshippers are encountering the most problematic or dissonant experiences.

Most of the negotiation of these questions takes place under the radar, in realms set aside from public discourse and from the public gaze. As has been highlighted, this enables a great deal of freedom; however, it also divorces experience from communal practice, negotiation and assistance. The framework of discourse ethics discussed in Chapter 2 suggests the potentially problematic nature of such a community dynamic as it draws attention to this individual-community nexus as a site of ethical significance. Musical experiences do not have a method of being acknowledged or fed back into shaping the ongoing life of the church community, nor do strategies for negotiating them have an established means of being nurtured within it. My work suggests, however, that these are not futile areas of investigation. By paying attention to the ways in which worshippers negotiate the intersection of their everyday musical lives with their musical worship in church we have seen that lived musical experience reflects neither straightforward ideas of representation within nor of assimilation to church music culture. Successful negotiation of questions of musical style encompasses a far more wide-ranging and complex state of affairs. This research suggests that the challenges of discourse ethics are approachable within a worshipping community and that the realm of musical experience is full of precisely the kinds of significance that both by going unacknowledged impoverish the community's musical and ethical life together and that by making their way into discourse have the potential to significantly enrich these same areas of activity and experience. By illustrating some of the ways in which worshippers hold together potentially dissonant aspects of their varied musical lives, the possibility is opened up that some of those experiencing these tensions as problematic might be able to find tools for navigating dissonance. Rather than desiring direct stylistic representation of their own musical interests within the church community, more often worshippers found meaningful aspects of their broader musical lives that were lacking within the church context; likewise, those who adapted in some way to the music of the church did so in a way that was laden with a range of significances beyond a simple acceptance of any qualities and meanings that were presented or given. My work therefore highlights the dynamic and active nature of this relationship and the importance of individual agency in negotiating this relationship.

St Aldates as a cosmopolitan musical community

In bringing this work to a close I want to return to the framework of cosmopolitanism introduced in Chapter 2. The various chapters of this book suggest a multi-faceted conception of musical identity that is far from straightforward. It is the result of an interplay of boundaries and connections, individuals and institutions, freedom and constraint such that these elements and a host of others are in a constant process of negotiation and contestation. Different individuals balance different factors in a variety of ways such that one person rarely seems to provide a completely predictable model for another. As I suggested earlier, there seems to be a close parallel between such descriptions of St Aldates and theoretical descriptions of what it is like to live in a cosmopolitan society.

To invoke cosmopolitanism here is primarily a descriptive move, but it nonetheless has the ability to imply prescriptive connotations as a guide to real-world thought and practice. It is noteworthy that a number of theorists have sought to develop accounts of cosmopolitan ethics that suggest a close connection between social descriptions and their normative implications. Included among lists of suggested cosmopolitan virtues are tolerance, curiosity about and empathy with others, epistemic humility and generosity (Van Hooft 2007), irony, reflexivity, scepticism towards grand narratives, care for other cultures, commitment to dialogue and a nomadism that is never entirely at home in any one set of boundaries (Delanty 2006) and self-reflexivity, heightened care for the world and skill in self-disclosure (Smith 2007). Greg Noble, on a social level, suggests the need for 'protocols for negotiating differences, developing obligations and reciprocities that facilitate an ongoing intercultural interaction' with consideration being given to 'the complicated entanglements of togetherness-in difference' (2009, p63); and Carol Gould in a similar way suggests that cosmopolitan ethics 'calls for a concrete recognition of people's differentiated needs and interests' including 'a mutual recognition of others as equally agential in possessing capacities for self-transformation' in ways that are 'differentiated, both individually and culturally' (2010, pp156–157). Bettina Scholz, from the opposite direction, draws attention to the possible ethical pitfalls of neglecting the cosmopolitan elements of social groups, suggesting that 'a non-cosmopolitan identity is one that hinders liberty by prohibiting individuals from participating in other associations' while 'cosmopolitanism prohibits "presenting oneself and one's cultural preferences non-negotiably to others"' (Scholz 2011). Finally, Delanty, focusing on the level of description, suggests that cosmopolitanism is inescapable, and that part of the point of cosmopolitan theory is 'that the diversity of cultures should be seen in terms of cultures being related rather than different' (2006, p39). This relation is clearly already in place, but is rarely subjected to significant examination within the life of the church. Following this model the appropriate way to conceive of the diversity of musical lives present at St Aldates would be to acknowledge the inescapability of the web of relationships that they are caught up in and, perhaps, to allow this to underpin negotiation of musical questions.[2]

In order to untangle the varying descriptive and presecriptive dimensions of cosmopolitan theory as it relates to St Aldates, we can usefully employ a taxonomy of cosmopolitan theories sketched out by Steven Vertovec and Robin Cohen. Vertovec and Cohen suggest six principal ways of imagining cosmopolitanism; they 'argue that cosmpolitanism can be viewed or invoked as: (a) a socio-cultural condition; (b) a kind of philosophy or world-view; (c) a political project towards building transnational institutions; (d) a political project for recognizing multiple identities; (e) an attitudinal or dispositional orientation; and/or (f) a mode of practice or competence' (Vertovec and Cohen 2002, pp8–9). In describing St Aldates in this manner, then, I am suggesting that the church exemplifies a particular socio-cultural condition (a), within which some members have developed particular modes of practice and competence (f), which are largely developed away from institutional support or acknowledgment and might therefore suggest the appropriateness of recognition (d), and possible related alterations in institutional orientation (e).

Hannerz suggests that the kinds of competence involved (f) are of 'both a generalized and a more specialized kind. There is the aspect of a state of readiness, a personal ability to make one's way into other cultures, through listening, looking, intuiting, and reflecting. And there is cultural competence in the stricter sense of the term, a built-up skill in manoeuvring more or less expertly with a particular system of meanings' (Hannerz 1990, p239). While this description foregrounds the role of the individual, Anthony Appiah instead foregrounds social, shared conversations as the primary mechanisms of a cosmopolitan environment, suggesting that:

> Cosmopolitanism can work because there can be common conversations about these shared ideas and objects. But what makes the conversations possible is not always shared "culture"; not even, as the older humanists imagined, universal principles or values (though, as I say, people from far away can discover that their principles meet); nor yet shared understanding (though people with very different experiences can end up agreeing about the darnedest things). What works in encounters with other human beings across gaps of space, time, and experience is enormously various.
>
> Appiah (2005, p258)

The difference between Hannerz and Appiah's foci mirrors, perhaps, the difference between the kinds of strategies that individuals at St Aldates are able to put in place when navigating these transitions largely on their own and those that might be possible were these to break beyond such private spaces into the realm of public conversation. Appiah thus brings us neatly back to the question of discourse. For Appiah it is the possibility of common conversations that makes this kind of community able to flourish and come together. In a similar way to Marti in Chapter 4, he guides our attention back towards the social processes which enable diverse individuals to come together into a common project. Unlike Marti, however, he focuses us on a process in which it is precisely conversations about the significance of cultural products and shared ideas which become the focal point of human interactions. These conversations are able to provide a binding force which neither an expectation of uniformity nor a reification of individual difference are able to provide. Appiah raises a theoretical challenge to views which place the burden of negotiation squarely on the individual. Individual agency, while powerful, clearly has limited scope and within a cosmopolitan formation it therefore might be fruitful to explore possible means of bringing individual agency into closer contact with the social structures and arrangements of which it is a part.

If cosmopolitanism has now become an appropriate model for the current reality of everyday interactions with Contemporary Worship Music then it represents a significant movement beyond the societal models and concerns that led to the music's initial emergence. This should not be an unexpected finding – both the church and society as a whole have evolved a great deal since the music's origins in the 1960s. Popular music has now found its place in the church and, as such, the marginalisation of popular culture is no longer a concern that will drive change in the same way. Likewise, music cultures have become increasingly diversified such that a unified movement for change centred around one specific music would likely have less appeal now than it may, at one stage, have done. It is, then, almost to be expected that new models of the church's music should emerge. Whether these concerns will be the drivers of future change is a harder question to answer; they certainly have a potential ability to do so and, as existing patterns begin to age and mature it is likely that there will be some degree of introspection and opportunity for critical reflection within the wider church. The course of this research has demonstrated the presence both of reflective and creative engagement on the part of a great many individuals and a degree of institutional stability and inertia. While I was nervous at points that my work had the potential to function disruptively within the community, it is clear that, at least within St Aldates, it has achieved relatively little disruption. Interviews themselves, while they did provide a space for individuals to articulate thoughts and feelings that were sometimes dissonant with church discourses and practices, seemed largely to function as a therapeutic outlet, processing existing experiences and thus providing a space of consolidation rather than disruption. In a similar manner, feeding my research and conclusions back to those in leadership resulted in affirmations of interest and enjoyment from those who read it rather than any sense of challenge or intrigue. Change and evolution may, indeed, happen in response to new patterns of interacting with music, but equally there may be sufficient in-built resilience for existing patterns to continue relatively undisrupted.

Notes

1 I am very aware in writing these conclusions that there are a variety of other priorities to be balanced within a church community, not least theological priorities, which serve to provide an ultimate ground for the life of the Christian

community. The task of piecing these all together is beyond the scope of my work here. In suggesting that ethnographic work has the potential to contribute in a sphere often governed by theological priorities I point the reader to recent work that suggests various ways in which ethnography and ecclesiology may be complementary (Scharen and Vigen 2011a; Scharen 2012; Ward 2012). In particular, James Nieman and Roger Haight (2012) set out a number of theses as a grounding for how the flow between normative and descriptive accounts of churches should function. From the perspective of ecclesiology they suggest that:

1 The study of the church must attend simultaneously to the historical and theological character of the church.
2 Congregational studies [ethnography] ultimately specifies the object specified by ecclesiology.
3 General ecclesiology, rather than field studies, determines the formal nature and mission of the church.
4 Congregational studies determines the credibility of the formal theological account of the church.

   It is, perhaps, to the last of these suggestions to which my work can claim to make the greatest contribution.

2 It might be objected that a cosmopolitan model fails to do complete justice to the particular loyalties that a church like St Aldates endeavours to establish as a community and that modelling the community in this way, in attending closely to the particularities of individuals, neglects the particular tasks that the church is called to. Cosmopolitan theory, in other words, whilst perhaps accurate as a description of reality, is an unfruitful route for church communities to pursue. A number of theorists have sought to articulate nuances to cosmopolitan theories that ensure a place for specific particularities and loyalties of community: Appiah (1997) argues for the possibility and value of institutional allegiance whilst nevertheless relating to it in different ways that carry different meanings. Writing on the level of national allegiance, Appiah suggests that: 'what I think we really need is not citizens centred on a common culture but citizens committed to common institutions, to the conditions necessary for a common life. What is required to live together in a nation is a mutual commitment to the organization of the state the institutions that provide the overarching order of our common life. But this does not require that we have the same commitment to those institutions, in the sense that the institutions must carry the same meaning for all of us' (1997, p629). Likewise, Stuart Hall articulates the need for balance and for a middle view, suggesting that 'We are in that open space that requires a kind of vernacular cosmopolitanism, that is to say a cosmopolitanism that is aware of the limitations of any one culture or any one identity and that is radically aware of its insufficiency in governing a wider society, but which nevertheless is not prepared to rescind its claim to the traces of difference, which make its life important' (2002, p30). Bettina Scholz goes further, arguing for the importance of indirect and partial forms of cosmopolitanism, placing it in ongoing tension with more universal forms of association (Scholz 2011). Cosmopolitan theory, then, does not in and of itself rule out such specifics of community, rather it places them in relation to other layers and aspects of existence. It adds a layer of understanding to our interpretation of the world, one that can be held together in appropriate ways with other theoretical priorities just as cosmopolitanism itself holds together varying identities and associations.

Appendix A

Morning service repertoire list – January 2012

This is the list of repertoire to be used in St Aldates morning services as of January 2012. Dates, authors and publishers have been added to the information provided by St Aldates worship department by the author.

Main repertoire

- A thousand times I've failed (Inside out)
  Joel Houston; Hillsong Music Publishing (2005)
- Alleluia (Agnus Dei)
  Michael W. Smith; Sony/ATV Milene Music (1990)
- Amazing grace (My chains are gone)
  Chris Tomlin, John Newton, Louie Giglio; sixstepsrecords, Vamos Publishing, worshiptogether.com songs (2006)
- Behold the Lamb
  Lauren Keenan; Thankyou Music (2010)
- Build Your Kingdom Here
  Rend Collective; Thankyou Music (2011)
- Defender of this heart (Remain)
  Ben Cantelon; Thankyou Music (2007)
- Even though I walk (Never let go)
  Beth Redman, Matt Redman; Thankyou Music (2005)
- Everlasting God (Yesterday, today and forever)
  Vicky Beeching; Thankyou Music (2002)
- Everyone needs compassion (Mighty to save)
  Ben Fielding, Reuben Morgan; Hillsong Music Publishing (2006)
- Everything within me
  Jamie Thomson (2009)
- Father of everlasting grace (My soul is complete)
  Phil Shaw; Thankyou Music (2008)
- Fire fall down (chorus/tag)
  Matt Crocker; Hillsong Music Publishing (2005)

- God in my living (Be my everything)
  Tim Hughes; Thankyou Music (2005)
- Great are You Lord (Awesome is the Lord most high)
  Cary Pierce, Chris Tomlin, Jesse Reeves, Jon Abel; 45 Degrees Music, Bridge Building Music, Inc., Popular Purple Publishing, sixstepsrecords, Vamos Publishing, worshiptogether.com songs (2006)
- Great is Your faithfulness (Holy hands)
  Chris Tomlin; sixstepsrecords, worshiptogether.com songs (2002)
- Hallelujah (Be high and lifted up)
  Ben Cantelon; Thankyou Music (2007)
- He came so we could know the Father's love
  Eoghan Heaslip, Neil Bennetts; Thankyou Music, Trinity Publishing (2008)
- He who appoints
  Rich White, Ben Judson, Lauren Keenan (2010)
- Holy, holy (Lift up His Name)
  Nathan Fellingham; Thankyou Music (1995)
- Hungry (Falling on my knees)
  Kathryn Scott; Vineyard Songs (1999)
- In every circumstance (You reign)
  Jamie Thomson; Thankyou Music (2010)
- I'm forgiven (Amazing love)
  Billy J. Foote; worshiptogether.com songs (1996)
- I'm giving You my heart (Surrender)
  Marc James; Vineyard Songs (2000)
- I lift my eyes up
  Brian Doerksen; Mercy /Vineyard Publishing, Vineyard Songs Canada (1990)
- In the name of the Father (Our God saves)
  Brenton Brown, Paul Baloche; Integrity's Hosanna! Music, Leadworship Songs, Thankyou Music (2007)
- Into Your hands (Jesus I believe)
  Reuben Morgan; Hillsong Music Publishing (2003)
- I see the King of glory (Hosanna)
  Brooke Ligertwood; Hillsong Music Publishing (2006)
- I will exalt You
  Brooke Ligertwood; Hillsong Music Publishing (2009)
- O come let us adore Him
  C. Frederick Oakeley, John Francis Wade, Matt Redman, Terl Bryant; Public Domain, Thankyou Music (2003)
- One thing
  Lauren Keenan (2010)
- Our Father in heaven (We pray)
  Eoghan Heaslip, Neil Bennetts; Thankyou Music, Trinity Publishing (2010)

- Our God is a consuming fire (A mighty fortress)
  Christy Nockels, Nathan Nockels; Christy Nockels Publishing Designee, sixstepsrecords, worshiptogether.com songs (2009)
- Our God is an awesome God
  Rich Mullins; Universal Music – Brentwood Benson Publishing (1988)
- Our God He lives forever (Yahweh)
  Reuben Morgan; Hillsong Music Publishing (2009)
- Praise awaits You
  Matt Redman; Thankyou Music (2004)
- Praise Him you heavens
  Russell Fragar; Hillsong Music Publishing (1998)
- Praise is rising (Hosanna)
  Brenton Brown, Paul Baloche; Integrity's Hosanna! Music, Thankyou Music (2005)
- Precious cornerstone (All to us)
  Chris Tomlin, Jesse Reeves, Matt Maher, Matt Redman; Said And Done Music, sixstepsrecords, Thankyou Music, Valley of Songs Music, Vamos Publishing, worshiptogether.com songs (2010)
- Strength will rise (Everlasting God)
  Brenton Brown, Ken Riley; Thankyou Music (2005)
- Thank You for the cross Lord
  Darlene Zschech; Wondrous Worship (2000)
- The eyes of the King
  Rich White (2009)
- The heavens (Far greater)
  Rich White; Thankyou Music (2010)
- The sun comes up (Bless the Lord)
  Jonas Myrin, Matt Redman; Atlas Mountain Songs, Said And Done Music, sixstepsrecords; Thankyou Music, worshiptogether.com songs (2011)
- There is a God (He lives)
  Rich White (2009)
- There is a love that I know (The same power)
  Dave George, Grant Pankratz; HarvestOKC Music Publishing, Hillsong Music Publishing (2007)
- There is a welcome
  Rich White (2012)
- There is love (Stronger)
  Ben Fielding, Reuben Morgan; Hillsong Music Publishing (2007)
- There must be more than this (Consuming fire)
  Tim Hughes; Thankyou Music (2002)
- Turn your ear to heaven (O praise Him)
  David Crowder; sixstepsrecords, worshiptogether.com songs (2003)
- Wake every heart (Highest and greatest)
  Nick Herbert, Tim Hughes; Thankyou Music (2006)

- Water You turned into wine (Our God)

  Chris Tomlin, Jesse Reeves, Jonas Myrin, Matt Redman; Atlas Mountain Songs, sixstepsrecords, Thankyou Music, Vamos Publishing, worshiptogether.com songs (2010)

- We bow our hearts (Adoration)

  Brenton Brown; Thankyou Music (2008)

- We fall down (We cry holy)

  Chris Tomlin; worshiptogether.com songs (1998)

- We lift our hands in praise to You (Glorious)

  Chris Tomlin, Jesse Reeves; sixstepsrecords, Vamos Publishing, worshiptogether.com songs (2006)

- We stand and lift up our hands (Holy is the Lord)

  Chris Tomlin, Louie Giglio; sixstepsrecords, worshiptogether.com songs (2003)

- What good is it (Living for Your glory)

  Rachel Hughes, Tim Hughes; Thankyou Music (2007)

- When I call on Your Name (Love Came Down)

  Ben Cantelon; Thankyou Music (2006)

- Who O Lord (You alone can rescue)

  Jonas Myrin, Matt Redman; Atlas Mountain Songs, Said and Done Music, sixstepsrecords, Thankyou Music (2008)

- Wonderful so wonderful (Beautiful One)

  Tim Hughes; Thankyou Music (2002)

- You're the God of this city (Greater things)

  Aaron Boyd, Andrew McCann, Ian Jordan, Peter Comfort, Peter Kernoghan, Richard Bleakley; Thankyou Music (2006)

- You alone are worthy (Glory in the highest)

  Al Gordon, Hanif Williams, Luke Hellebronth; Thankyou Music (2009)

- You are good (Forever reign)

  Jason Ingram, Reuben Morgan; Hillsong Music Publishing, Sony/ATV Timber Publishing, Spirit Nashville Three, West Main Music (2009)

- You are mighty and strong to save (Rescuer)

  Cathy Parks, Johnny Parks, Nick Herbert; Thankyou Music (2007)

- You are my light (Believe)

  Darlene Zschech, Reuben Morgan; Hillsong Music Publishing, Wondrous Worship (2009)

- You inhabit the praises of Your people (The wonder of Your love)

  Jack Mooring, Leeland Mooring, Marty Sampson; Hillsong Music Publishing, Jack Mooring Music, Meaux Jeaux Music, Meaux Mercy, The Devil Is A Liar! Publishing (2008)

- You reach beyond imagination (The way that You Father me)

  David Gate, Eoghan Heaslip; Thankyou Music, Trinity Publishing (2008)

- Your grace is enough (This is our God)

  Reuben Morgan; Hillsong Music Publishing (2008)

- You won't relent
  Cassandra Campbell, David Brymer, Misty Edwards; Forerunner Worship (2007)

Hymns

- All creatures of our God and King
  St Francis of Assisi, William Draper; Public Domain (1225)
- Amazing grace
  John Newton; Public Domain (1779)
- And can it be
  Charles Wesley, Thomas Campbell; Public Domain (1738)
- Before the throne of God above
  Charitie Lees Bancroft, Vikki Cook; Sovereign Grace Worship (1997)
- Be Thou my vision
  Eleanor Henrietta Hull, Mary Elizabeth Byrne; Public Domain
- Come thou fount of every blessing
  Robert Robinson; Public Domain (1758)
- Crown Him with many crowns
  Matthew Bridges, George Elvey; Public Domain (1851)
- Great is Thy faithfulness
  Thomas Chilsholm, William Runyan; Hope Publishing Company (1923)
- Hallelujah sing to Jesus
  William Chatterton Dix; Public Domain (1866)
- Here is love vast as the ocean
  William Rees, William Edwards; Public Domain
- Holy, holy, holy, Lord God Almighty
  John Bacchus Dykes, Reginald Heber; Public Domain (1826)
- How deep the Father's love for us
  Stuart Townend; Thankyou Music (1995)
- How great Thou art
  Carl Gustav Boberg, Stuart Hine; Stuart K Hine Trust (1949)
- I cannot tell
  William Fullerton; Public Domain (1920)
- In Christ alone
  Keith Getty, Stuart Townend; Thankyou Music (2001)
- I stand amazed
  Charles Hutchinson Gabriel; Public Domain (1905)
- I will sing the wondrous story
  Francis Rowley, Rowland Pritchard; HarperCollins Religious, Public Domain (1886)
- Joyful, Joyful we adore Thee
  Edward Hodges, Henry Van Dyke, Ludwig van Beethoven; Public Domain (1907)

- Love divine all loves excelling
  Charles Wedley, William Rowlands (1747)
- My hope is built on nothing less
  Edward Mote, Nicky Chiswell; Nicky Chiswell, Public Domain (1992)
- O to see the dawn
  Keith Getty, Stuart Townend; Thankyou Music (2005)
- Praise my soul the King of heaven
  Henry Francis Lyte, John Goss; Public Domain (1834)
- Praise to the Lord the almighty
  Catherine Winkworth, Joachim Neander; Public Domain (1863)
- See what a morning
  Keith Getty, Stuart Townend; Thankyou Music (2003)
- Thine be the glory
  Edmond Louis Burdry, George Frideric Handel, Richard Birch Hoyle; Public Domain (1904)
- What a fellowship (Leaning on the everlasting)
  Elisha Albright Hoffman; Public Domain (1887)
- When I survey the wondrous cross
  Isaac Watts; Public Domain (1707)

Kids' songs

- Blessed be the Name of the Lord
  Clinton Utterbach; Polygram, Utterbach Music (1989)
- God made me who I'm meant to be (Royalty)
  Beci Wakerley, David Wakerley; Hillsong Music Publishing (2005)
- God who made the universe (God's love is big)
  Simon Parry; Vineyard Songs (2005)
- God You're so cool
  Simon Parry; Vineyard Songs (2003)
- I lay my life down (One way)
  Joel Houston, Jonathon Douglass; Hillsong Music Publishing (2003)
- I'm gonna jump up and down
  Doug Horley; Thankyou Music (2001)
- King of love
  Doug Horley; Thankyou Music (1999)
- Our God is alive
  Becky Drake; Song Solutions Daybreak (2007)
- Our God is a great big god
  Jo Hemming, Nigel Hemming; Vineyard Songs (2001)
- Standing here in your presence (For who You are)
  Marty Sampson; Hillsong Music Publishing (2006)
- God You're amazing (Super strong God)
  David Wakerley, Julia A'Bell; Hillsong Music Publishing (2005)

- Who would I really be (GOD)
  Doug Horley; Thankyou Music (2005)
- You know that I love You (King of majesty)
  Marty Sampson; Hillsong Music Publishing (2001)
- You put the stars in outer space (Creator God)
  Becky Drake, Nick J. Drake; Song Solutions Daybreak (2007)

Archived

- All to Jesus I surrender
  Judson Wheeler Van DeVenter, Winfield Scott Weeden; Public Domain (1896)
- Be still for the presence of the Lord
  David J. Evans; Thankyou Music (1986)
- Blessed be Your name
  Beth Redman, Matt Redman; Thankyou Music (2002)
- Come let us worship the King of kings
  Nathan Fellingham; Thankyou Music (2001)
- Come now is the time to worship
  Brian Doerksen; Vineyard Songs (1998)
- Faithful One
  Brian Doerksen; Mercy/Vineyard Publishing, Vineyard Songs Canada (1989)
- Father let me dedicate
  Chris Tomlin, Jesse Reeves, Lawrence Tuttiett, Louie Giglio, Matt Redman; Thankyou Music, worshiptogether.com songs (2003)
- God of justice (We must go)
  Tim Hughes; Thankyou Music (2004)
- Holy, Holy I will bow before (Emmanuel)
  Reuben Morgan; Hillsong Music Publishing (2005)
- Holy, Holy (Holy is Your name)
  Brenton Brown; Vineyard Songs (UK/Eire) (2001)
- How lovely is Your dwelling place
  Matt Redman; Thankyou Music (1995)
- I will worship
  David Ruis; Shade Tree Music, Universal Music – Brentwood Benson Publishing (1991)
- Jesus lover of my soul
  Paul Oakley; Thankyou Music (1995)
- Light of the world (Here I am to worship)
  Tim Hughes; Thankyou Music (2000)
- Lord let Your glory fall (You are good)
  Matt Redman; Thankyou Music (1998)
- Lord You have my heart
  Martin Smith; Thankyou Music (1992)

- Open the eyes of my heart Lord
  Paul Baloche; Integrity's Hosanna! Music (1997)
- Over all the earth (Lord reign in me)
  Brenton Brown; Vineyard Songs (1998)
- Over the mountains and the sea
  Martin Smith; Curious? Music UK (1994)
- Purify my heart
  Brian Doerksen; Mercy/Vineyard Publishing, Vineyard Songs Canada (1990)
- Take my life and let it be (Tomlin)
  Chris Tomlin, Frances Ridley Havergal, Henri Abraham Cesa Malan, Louie Giglio; sixstepsrecords, worshiptogether.com songs (2003)
- Thank You for saving me
  Martin Smith; Curious? Music UK (1993)
- The Lord is gracious and compassionate
  Graham Ord; Vineyard Songs (UK/Eire) (1998)
- There is a redeemer
  Melody Green; Birdwing Music, Ears to Hear, Universal Music – Brentwood Benson Publishing (1982)
- The splendour of the King
  Chris Tomlin, Ed Cash, Jesse Reeves; sixstepsrecords, Wondrously Made Songs, worshiptogether.com songs (2004)
- This is my desire
  Reuben Morgan; Hillsong Music Publishing (1995)
- This is the air I breathe
  Marie Barnett; Mercy/Vineyard Publishing (1995)
- To be in Your presence
  Noel Richards; Thankyou Music (1991)
- Turn my face again towards the cross
  Martyn Layzell; Thankyou Music (2005)
- We're looking to Your promise of old
  Matt Redman; Thankyou Music (1996)
- What a friend I've found
  Martin Smith; Curious? Music UK (1996)
- We lift our hands in praise to You (Glorious)
  Chris Tomlin, Jesse Reeves; sixstepsrecords, Vamos Publishing, worshiptogether.com songs (2006)
- When I survey
  Chris Tomlin, Isaac Watts, J. D. Walt, Jesse Reeves, Lowell Mason; sixstepsrecords, worshiptogether.com songs (2000)
- When the suns brightly shining
  David Ruis; Mercy/Vineyard Publishing, Vineyard Songs Canada (2003)
- Who can know (Stand in awe)
  Martyn Layzell; Thankyou Music (2005)

- Worship the Lord in the beauty (Living for Your glory)
  Al Gordon; Thankyou Music (2006)
- Worthy You are worthy
  Matt Redman; Thankyou Music (1999)
- You chose the cross (Lost in wonder)
  Martyn Layzell; Thankyou Music (2002)
- Your blood (Nothing but the blood)
  Matt Redman; Thankyou Music (2004)
- Your love is amazing
  Brenton Brown, Brian Doerksen; Vineyard Songs (UK/Eire) (2000)
- Your love O Lord (Glory to God)
  Reuben Morgan; Hillsong Music Publishing (2002)

Appendix B

Worship team agreement 2013/2014

Our heart as a Worship Team is to be authentic in our worship to God. Our aim is to respond with praise and worship to who God is, and to gather people in our pursuit of experiencing the presence of the Holy Spirit in our times of musical worship. We are committed to this vision whole heartedly and to serving one another in our community of St Aldates and beyond. Our heart as a team is to be inspired by spending time in worship to God and to be empowered to become disciples of Jesus Christ.

As a member of this team I commit myself to the following values and expectations:

I am committed to St Aldates, its vision, its community and its leaders.

I commit myself to attending a regular St Aldates Pastorate and to spiritual growth, maturity and accountability within this group.

I am committed to attending the Fuel for the Fire Gathering once a term.

I am a lead worshipper regardless of what my involvement in the team is, and am dedicated to leading people to Jesus in every circumstance of life.

I will commit to attend church services, even when I'm not serving publicly; being intentional about getting to know the congregations I lead.

I am committed to musical and technical growth, e.g., I will invest time in developing skills through training and practice.

I am committed to preparing for and being punctual to relevant rehearsals.

I will seek to serve behind the scenes wherever possible, e.g., setting up, tidying up, helping those in need, etc.

I will communicate directly with the band leader if for some reason I cannot serve.

As a Worship Leadership Team, we commit to providing the following:

We will personally commit to all the values above as a member of the worship team.

We will provide spiritual direction and vision for the worship as a whole and for the individuals involved within it.

We will give time to supporting you as a worshipper (note: Pastoral support will be mainly provided within your Pastorate).

We will provide training and forums for spiritual and practical growth.

We will provide relevant resources and means to help you to serve effectively.

We will uphold you in prayer.

Bibliography

Adnams, Gordon (2008). *The experience of congregational singing: An ethno-phenomenological approach*. PhD thesis. Edmonton, Alberta: University of Alberta.

Alexander, Claire, Rosalind Edwards and Bogusia Temple (2007). 'Contesting cultural communities: Language, ethnicity and citizenship in Britain'. In: *Journal of Ethnic and Migration Studies* 33 (5), pp 783–800.

Allison, Gregg (2011). *Historical theology: An introduction to Christian doctrine*. Grand Rapids, MI: Zondervan.

Amin, Ash (2002). *Ethnicity and the multicultural city: Living with diversity (report for the Department of Transport, Local Government and the Regions and the ESRC cities initiative)*. London, UK: Sage.

Amit, Vered (2000). *Constructing the field: Ethnographic fieldwork in the contemporary world*. London, UK: Routledge.

Ammerman, Nancy Tatom (1998). *Studying congregations: A new handbook*. Nashville, TN: Abingdon Press.

—— (2003). 'Religious identities and religious institutions'. In: *Handbook of the Sociology of Religion*. Ed. by Michele Dillon. Cambridge, UK: Cambridge University Press.

Anderson, Abbie M. (1991). *An approach to music in community rhetoric of identity and belonging: Church music and church identity*, http://www.billabbie.com/abracap okey/folklore/dorson.htm.

Anderson, Benedict (1983). *Imagined communities: Reflections on the origin and spread of nationalism*. London, UK: Verso.

Anton, Corey (1998). *Selfhood and authenticity*. PhD thesis. West Lafayette, IN: Purdue University.

Appiah, Kwame Anthony (1997). 'Cosmopolitan patriots'. In: *Critical Inquiry* 23 (3), pp 617–639.

—— (2005). *The ethics of identity*. Princeton, NJ: Princeton University Press.

Araujo, Samuel (2009). 'Ethnomusicologists researching towns they live in: Theoretical and methodological queries for a renewed discipline'. In: *Музикологија* 9, pp 33–50.

Atkinson, Will (2011). 'The context and genesis of musical tastes: Omnivorousness debunked, Bourdieu buttressed'. In: *Poetics* 39 (3), pp 169–186.

Auslander, Philip (2004). 'Performance analysis and popular music: A manifesto'. In: *Contemporary Theatre Review* 14 (1), pp 1–13.

—— (2006). 'Music as performance: Living in the immaterial world'. In: *Theatre Survey* 47 (02), pp 261–269.

Averill, Gage (2003). 'Ethnomusicologists as public intellectuals: Engaged ethnomusicology in the university'. In: *Folklore Forum* 34 (1/2).

Bader-Saye, Scott (2006). 'Improvising church: An introduction to the emerging church conversation'. In: *International Journal for the Study of the Christian Church* 6 (1), pp 12–23.

Bahram, M. (2013). 'Habermas, religion, and public life'. In: *Journal of Contemporary Religion* 28 (3), pp 353–353.

Bailey, Michael and Guy Redden (2011). *Mediating faiths: Religion and socio-cultural change in the twenty-first century*. Aldershot, UK: Ashgate.

Baily, John (2006). '"Music is in our blood": Gujarati Muslim musicians in the UK'. In: *Journal of Ethnic and Migration Studies* 32 (2), pp 257–270.

Baily, John and Michael Collyer (2006). 'Introduction: Music and migration'. In: *Journal of Ethnic and Migration Studies* 32 (2), pp 167–182.

Baker, Geoff (2006). '"La habana que no conoces": Cuban rap and the social construction of urban space'. In: *Ethnomusicology Forum* 15 (2), pp 215–246.

Bakhtin, Mikhail, Michael Holquist Mikhailovich and Caryl Emerson (1981). *The dialogic imagination: Four essays*. Austin, TX: University of Texas Press.

Barz, Gregory Frederick (1997). The performance of religious and social identity: An ethnography of post-mission Kwaya music in Tanzania (East Africa). PhD thesis. Rhode Island, NY: Brown University.

Barz, Gregory Frederick and Timothy J. Cooley (2008). *Shadows in the field: New perspectives for fieldwork in ethnomusicology*. New York; NY: Oxford University Press.

Bauböck, Rainer (2002). 'Farewell to multiculturalism? Sharing values and identities in societies of immigration'. In: *Journal of International Migration and Integration/ Revue de l'integration et de la migration internationale* 3 (1), pp 1–16.

Baumann, Gerd (1996). *Contesting culture: Discourses of identity in multi-ethnic London*. Cambridge, UK: Cambridge University Press.

Baumeister, Andrea T. (2003). 'Habermas: Discourse and cultural diversity'. In: *Political Studies* 51 (4), pp 740–758.

Bayley, Amanda (2012). 'Ethnographic research into contemporary string quartet rehearsal'. In: *Ethnomusicology Forum* 20 (3), pp 385–412.

Beard, David and Kenneth Gloag (2005). *Musicology: The key concepts*. London, UK: Routledge.

Beaudoin, Tom (2013). *Secular music and sacred theology*. Collegeville, MN: Liturgical Press.

Beck, Ulrich (2002). 'The cosmopolitan society and its enemies'. In: *Theory, Culture & Society* 19 (1–2), pp 17–44.

Beck, Ulrich and Natan Sznaider (2006). 'Unpacking cosmopolitanism for the social sciences: A research agenda'. In: *The British Journal of Sociology* 57 (1), pp 1–23.

Becker, Judith O. (2004). *Deep listeners: Music, emotion, and trancing.* Bloomington, IN: Indiana University Press.

Becker, Penny Edgell (1998). 'Making inclusive communities: Congregations and the "problem" of race'. In: *Social Problems*, pp 451–472.

—— (1999). *Congregations in conflict: Cultural models of local religious life.* Cambridge, UK: Cambridge University Press.

Becker, Penny Edgell et al (1993). 'Straining at the tie that binds: Congregational conflict in the 1980s'. In: *Review of Religious Research*, pp 193–209.

Beckford, Robert (2006). *Jesus dub: Theology, music, and social change.* London, UK: Routledge.

Begbie, Jeremy (2000). *Theology, music and time.* Cambridge, UK: Cambridge University Press.

—— (2005). 'Theology and music'. In: *The Modern Theologians: An Introduction to Christian Theology since 1918.* Ed. by David F. Ford and Rachel Muers. Oxford, UK: Blackwell.

Bell, Catherine M. (2006). 'Paradigms behind (and before) the modern concept of religion'. In: *History and Theory* 45 (4), pp 27–46.

—— (2009). *Ritual: Perspectives and dimensions.* New York, NY: Oxford University Press.

Benedict, Cathy (2007). 'Naming our reality: Negotiating and creating meaning in the margin'. In: *Philosophy of Music Education Review* 15 (1), pp 23–35.

Bennett, Andy (1999). 'Subcultures or neo-tribes? Rethinking the relationship between youth, style and musical taste'. In: *Sociology* 33 (3), pp 599–617.

Bennett, Andy (2000). *Popular music and youth culture: Music, identity and place.* Basingstoke, UK: Macmillan.

—— (2009). '"Heritage rock": Rock music, representation and heritage discourse'. In: *Poetics* 37 (5–6), pp 474–489.

Bennett, Tony et al (2008). *Culture, class, distinction.* London, UK: Routledge.

Bentley, Jane (2007). 'Community; authenticity; growth: The role of musical participation in the Iona community's island centres'. In: *International Journal of Community Music* 2 (1), pp 71–78.

Berger, Harris M. (1999). *Metal, rock, and jazz: Perception and the phenomenology of musical experience.* Hanover, NH: University Press of New England [for] Wesleyan University Press.

—— (2009). *Stance: Ideas about emotion, style, and meaning for the study of expressive culture.* Middletown, CT: Wesleyan University Press.

Bergeron, Katherine and Philip Vilas Bohlman (1992). *Disciplining music: Musicology and its canons.* Chicago, IL: University of Chicago Press.

Bhabha, Homi (1994). *The location of culture.* London, UK: Routledge.

Bigenho, Michelle (2008). 'Why I'm not an ethnomusicologist: A view from anthropology'. In: *The new (ethno)musicologies.* Ed. by Henry Stobart. Lanham, MD: Scarecrow Press.

—— (2011). 'Outside the music box: A manifesto'. In: *Anthropology News* 52 (1), p 12.

Biron, Dean (2009). 'Betwixt and between: Musical taste patterns and audience mobility'. In: *Journal of Audience & Reception Studies* 6 (2), pp 320–339.

Bithell, Caroline (2003). 'On the playing fields of the world (and Corsica): Politics, power, passion and polyphony'. In: *British Journal of Ethnomusicology* 12 (1), pp 67–95.

Blacking, John (1976). *How musical is man*. London, UK: Faber and Faber.

Boardman, Richard (2011). *Ethnomusicological theories of 'place' in the context of globalization*, http://musicindevelopment.com/2011/12/11/theories-of-place-in-the-context-of-globalization-towards-a-more-informed-sense-of-place-in-ethnomusicology/.

Bohlman, Philip Vilas (1996). 'Pilgrimage, politics, and the musical remapping of the new Europe'. In: *Ethnomusicology* 40 (3), pp 375–412.

Bohlman, Philip Vilas, Edith Waldvogel Blumhofer and Maria M. Chow (2006). *Music in American religious experience*. New York, NY: Oxford University Press.

Bonzon, Roman (2009). 'Thick aesthetic concepts'. In: *The Journal of Aesthetics and Art Criticism* 67 (2), pp 191–199.

Born, Georgina (2005). 'On musical mediation: Ontology, technology and creativity'. In: *Twentieth-Century Music* 2 (1), pp 7–36.

Born, Georgina and David Hesmondhalgh (2000a). 'Introduction: On difference, representation, and appropriation in music'. In: *Western music and its others: Difference, representation, and appropriation in music*. Ed. by Georgina Born and David Hesmondhalgh. Berkeley, CA: University of California Press, pp 1–56.

—— (2000b). *Western music and its others: Difference, representation, and appropriation in music*. Berkeley, CA: University of California Press.

Bosse, Joanna (2013). 'Salsa dance as cosmopolitan formation: cooperation, conflict and commerce in the Midwest United States'. In: *Ethnomusicology Forum* 22 (2), pp 210–231.

Bossius, Thomas, Andreas Hager and Keith Kahn-Harris (2011). *Religion and popular music in Europe: New expressions of sacred and secular identity*. London, UK: IB Tauris.

Bourdieu, Pierre (1984). *Distinction: A social critique of the judgement of taste*. Boston, MA: Harvard University Press.

Bowman, Wayne (2000). 'A somatic, "here and now" semantic: Music, body, and self'. In: *Bulletin of the Council for Research in Music Education* 144, pp 45–60.

—— (2001). 'Music as ethical encounter'. In: *Bulletin of the Council for Research in Music Education* 151, pp 11–20.

Brăiloiu, Constantin and Albert Lancaster Lloyd (1984). *Problems of ethnomusicology*. Cambridge, CA: Cambridge University Press.

Brettell, Caroline (1993). *When they read what we write: The politics of ethnography*. Westport, CT: Bergin & Garvey.

Brodd, Sven-Erik (2006). 'Ecclesiology and church music: Towards a possible relationship'. In: *International Journal for the Study of the Christian Church* 6 (2), pp 126–143.

Brown, David (2007). *God and grace of body: Sacrament in ordinary*. Oxford, UK: Oxford University Press.

Brown, Frank Burch (2000). *Good taste, bad taste, and Christian taste: Aesthetics in religious life*. Oxford, UK: Oxford University Press.

—— (2009). *Inclusive yet discerning: Navigating worship artfully*. Grand Rapids, MI: William B. Eerdmans Pub. Company.

Bryson, Bethany (1996). "'Anything but heavy metal": Symbolic exclusion and musical dislikes'. In: *American Sociological Review*, pp 884–899.

Bull, Michael (2007). *Sound moves: iPod culture and urban experience*. London, UK: Routledge.

Burnim, Mellonee (1985). 'Culture bearer and tradition bearer: An ethnomusicologist's research on gospel music'. In: *Ethnomusicology* 29 (3), pp 432–447.

Butler, Melvin L. (2000). 'Musical style and experience in a Brooklyn Pentecostal church: An "insider's" perspective'. In: *Current Musicology* 70, pp 33–50.

—— (2002). "'Nou kwe nan sentespri" (we believe in the Holy Spirit): Music, ecstasy, and identity in Haitian Pentecostal worship'. In: *Black Music Research Journal* 22, pp 85–125.

—— (2005). *Songs of Pentecost: Experiencing music, transcendence, and identity in Jamaica and Haiti*. PhD thesis. New York, NY: New York University.

Caccamo, James Frank (2005). *The responsorial self: Christian ethics and ritual song*. PhD thesis. Chicago, IL: Loyola University.

Caldwell, Joyce Arleen (2009). *Living in the intersections: An ethnographic study of an urban Lutheran congregation*. PhD thesis. Fielding Graduate University.

Cameron, Helen (2010). *Talking about God in practice: Theological action research and practical theology*. London, UK: SCM Press.

Carter, Tim (2002). 'The sound of silence: Models for an urban musicology'. In: *Urban History* 29 (01), pp 8–18.

Chamorro-Premuzic, Thomas, Patrick Fagan and Adrian Furnham (2010). 'Personality and uses of music as predictors of preferences for music consensually classified as happy, sad, complex, and social.' In: *Psychology of Aesthetics, Creativity, and the Arts* 4 (4), pp 205–213.

Chang, Paul Y. and Dale J. Lim (2009). 'Renegotiating the sacred-secular binary: IX saves and contemporary Christian music'. In: *Review of Religious Research* 50, pp 392–412.

Chauvet, Louis Marie and François Kabasele Lumbala (1995). *Liturgy and the body*. London, UK: SCM.

Christerson, Brad and Michael Emerson (2003). 'The costs of diversity in religious organizations: An in-depth case study'. In: *Sociology of religion* 64 (2), pp 163–181.

Christiani, Tabita Kartika. *Identity in a multicultural church: An experience of Indonesian Christian church*.

Chua, Daniel K. L. (1999). *Absolute music and the construction of meaning*. Cambridge, UK: Cambridge University Press.

Clark, Lynn Schofield (2007). 'Introduction: Identity, belonging, and religious lifestyle branding (fashion bibles, bhangra parties, and Muslim pop'. In: *Religion, media, and the marketplace*. Ed. by Lynn Schofield Clark. New Brunswick, NJ: Rutgers University Press.

Clarke, Eric F. and Nicholas Cook (2004). *Empirical musicology: Aims, methods, prospects*. Oxford, UK: Oxford University Press.

Clayton, Martin (2001). 'Introduction: Towards a theory of musical meaning (in India and elsewhere)'. In: *British Journal of Ethnomusicology* 10 (1), pp 1–17.

Clayton, Martin, Trevor Herbert and Richard Middleton (2003). *The cultural study of music: A critical introduction.* New York, NY: Routledge.

Cobussen, Marcel and Nanette Nielsen (2012). *Music and ethics.* Aldershot, UK: Ashgate.

Cohen, Anthony P. (1985). *The symbolic construction of community.* Chichester, UK: Ellis Horwood.

Cohen, Sara (1993). 'Ethnography and popular music studies'. In: *Popular Music* 12, pp 123–138.

—— (2007). *Decline, renewal and the city in popular music culture: Beyond the Beatles.* Aldershot, UK: Ashgate.

Cohen, Ted (1998). 'On consistency in one's personal aesthetics'. In: *Aesthetics and ethics: essays at the intersection.* Ed. by Jerrold. Levinson. Cambridge, UK: Cambridge University Press.

Collins, Randall (2004). *Interaction ritual chains.* Princeton, NJ: Princeton University Press.

Conway, Mary L. (2006). 'Worship music: Maintaining dynamic tension'. In: *McMaster Journal of Theology and Ministry* 7, pp 132–159.

Cook, Nicholas (2001). 'Theorizing musical meaning'. In: *Music Theory Spectrum* 23 (2), pp 170–195.

Coplan, David B. (2006). '"I've worked longer than I've lived": Lesotho migrants' songs as maps of experience'. In: *Journal of Ethnic and Migration Studies* 32 (2), pp 223–241.

Corness, Greg (2008). 'The musical experience through the lens of embodiment'. In: *Leonardo Music Journal* 18, pp 21–24.

Cottrell, Stephen (2004). *Professional music-making in London: Ethnography and experience.* Aldershot, UK: Ashgate.

—— (2007). 'Local bimusicality among London's freelance musicians'. In: *Ethnomusicology* 51 (1), pp 85–105.

Coulter, David (2002). 'Creating common and uncommon worlds: Using discourse ethics to decide public and private in classrooms'. In: *Journal of Curriculum Studies* 34 (1), pp 25–42.

Cova, Bernard, Stefano Pace and David J. Park (2007). 'Global brand communities across borders: The Warhammer case'. In: *International Marketing Review* 24 (3), pp 313–329.

Cox, Harvey Gallagher (1996). *Fire from heaven: The rise of Pentecostal spirituality and the reshaping of religion in the twenty-first century.* London, UK: Cassell.

Cross, Ian and Elizabeth Tolbert (2008). 'Music and meaning'. In: *Oxford handbook of music psychology.* Ed. by Susan Hallam, Ian Cross and Michael Thaut. Oxford, UK: Oxford University Press.

Crozier, W. Ray (1997). 'Music and social influence'. In: *The social psychology of music.* Ed. by David J. Hargreaves and Adrian C. North. Oxford, UK: Oxford University Press.

Csordas, Thomas J. (1997). *Language, charisma, and creativity: The ritual life of a religious movement.* Berkeley, CA: University of California Press.

Cusick, Suzanne G. (1994). 'Feminist theory, music theory, and the mind/body problem'. In: *Perspectives of New Music* 32, pp 8–27.

Darnley-Smith, Rachel (2012). 'What is distinctive about improvisation in music therapy?' Unpublished paper given at Perspectives on Musical Improvisation conference. Oxford, UK.

DeHanas, Daniel Nilsson (2010). *Believing citizens: Religion and civic engagement among London's second generation youth*. PhD thesis. University of North Carolina at Chapel Hill.

Delanty, Gerard (2005). 'The idea of a cosmopolitan Europe: On the cultural significance of Europeanization'. In: *International Review of Sociology – Revue Internationale de Sociologie* 15 (3), pp 405–421.

—— (2006). 'The cosmopolitan imagination: Critical cosmopolitanism and social theory'. In: *The British Journal of Sociology* 57 (1), pp 25–47.

DeNora, Tia (1999). 'Music as a technology of the self'. In: *Poetics* 27 (1), pp 31–56.

—— (2000). *Music in everyday life*. Cambridge, UK: Cambridge University Press.

—— (2003). *After Adorno: Rethinking music sociology*. Cambridge, UK: Cambridge University Press.

Devine, Kyle (2011). 'The popularity of religious music and the religiosity of popular music'. In: *Scottish Music Review* 2 (1), pp 1–22.

Dibben, Nicola (2002). 'Gender identity and music'. In: *Musical identities*. Ed. by Raymond A. R. MacDonald, David J. Hargreaves and Dorothy Miell. Oxford, UK: Oxford University Press.

Dickerson, Valerie Anne (2009). *Are those congas in the pulpit? Hymns, alabanza y adoracion (praise and worship) music, and the Evangelical subculture of Western Cuba*. PhD thesis. Los Angeles, CA: University of California.

Dillon, Michele (1999). 'The authority of the holy revisited: Habermas, religion, and emancipatory possibilities'. In: *Sociological theory* 17 (3), pp 290–306.

—— (2003). *Handbook of the sociology of religion*. Cambridge, UK: Cambridge University Press.

Dirksen, Rebecca (2012). 'Reconsidering theory and practice in ethnomusicology: Applying, advocating, and engaging beyond academia'. In: *Ethnomusicology Review* 17.

Dougherty, Kevin D. and Andrew L. Whitehead (2011). 'A place to belong: Small group involvement in religious congregations'. In: *Sociology of Religion* 72 (1), pp 91–111.

Du Gay Paul, and Stuart Hall (1996). *Questions of cultural identity*. London, UK: Sage.

Dueck, Jonathan (2003). *An ethnographic study of the musical practices of three Edmonton Mennonite churches*. PhD thesis. Edmonton, Alberta: University of Alberta.

—— (2005). 'Worship wars, world music, and Mennonots: Recent studies in Mennonite music'. In: *Journal of Mennonite Studies* 23 (1), pp 123–136.

—— (2011). 'Binding and loosing in song: Conflict, identity and Canadian Mennonite music'. In: *Ethnomusicology* 55 (2), pp 229–254.

Ebstyne King, Pamela (2003). 'Religion and identity: The role of ideological, social, and spiritual contexts'. In: *Applied Developmental Science* 7 (3), pp 197–204.

Ecklund, Elaine Howard (2003). 'Catholic women negotiate feminism: A research note'. In: *Sociology of Religion* 64 (4), pp 515–524.

Einstein, Mara (2007). *Brands of faith: Marketing religion in a commercial age.* London, UK: Routledge.

Eisentraus, Jochen (2001). 'Samba in Wales: Making sense of adopted music'. In: *British Journal of Ethnomusicology* 10 (1), pp 85–105.

Elisha, Omri (2013). 'The time and place for prayer: Evangelical urbanism and citywide prayer movements'. In: *Religion* 43 (3), pp 312–330.

Engelhardt, Jeffers (2008). 'Late-and post-Soviet music scholarship and the tenacious ecumenicity of Christian musics in Estonia'. In: *Journal of Baltic Studies* 39 (3), pp 239–262.

Engelhardt, Jeffers (2009). 'Right singing in Estonian Orthodox Christianity: A study of music, theology, and religious ideology'. In: *Ethnomusicology* 53 (1), pp 32–57.

Erel, Umut (2010). 'Migrating cultural capital: Bourdieu in migration studies'. In: *Sociology* 44 (4), pp 642–660.

Erlmann, Veit (1990). 'Migration and performance: Zulu migrant workers' isicathamiya performance in South Africa, 1890-1950'. In: *Ethnomusicology* 34 (2), pp 199–220.

Evans, Mark (2006). *Open up the doors: Music in the modern church.* London, UK: Equinox.

Fagan, Madeleine (2009). 'The inseparability of ethics and politics: Rethinking the third in Emmanuel Levinas'. In: *Contemporary Political Theory* 8 (1), pp 5–22.

Fassler, Margot Elsbeth (2001). *Musicians for the churches: Reflections on vocation and formation.* New Haven, CT: Institute of Sacred Music at Yale University.

Feld, Steven (1995). 'From schizophonia to schismogenesis: The discourses and practices of world music and world beat'. In: *The Traffic in Culture.* Ed. by George Marcus and Fred Myers. Berkeley and Los Angeles, CA: University of California Press, pp 96–126.

—— (2012). *Jazz cosmopolitanism in Accra: Five musical years in Ghana.* Durham, NC: Duke University Press.

Ferm, Cecilia (2008). 'Playing to teach music – embodiment and identity-making in Musikdidaktik'. In: *Music Education Research* 10 (3), pp 361–372.

Finnas, Leif (1989). 'A comparison between young people's privately and publicly expressed musical preferences'. In: *Psychology of Music* 17 (2), pp 132–145.

Finnegan, Ruth H. (1989). *The hidden musicians: Music making in an English town.* Cambridge, UK: Cambridge University Press.

Flyvbjerg, Bent (1998). 'Habermas and Foucault: Thinkers for civil society?' In: *British Journal of Sociology*, pp 210–233.

Ford, David F. and Rachel Muers (2005). *The modern theologians: An introduction to Christian theology since 1918.* Oxford, UK: Blackwell.

France, Alan, Jo Meredith and Adriana Sandu (2007). 'Youth culture and citizenship in multicultural Britain'. In: *Journal of Contemporary European Studies* 15 (3), pp 303–316.

Francis, Mark R. and Kathleen Hughes (1991). *Living no longer for ourselves: Liturgy and justice in the nineties.* Collegeville, MN: Liturgical Press.

Frith, Simon (1996a). 'Music and identity'. In: *Questions of cultural identity.* Ed. by Paul Du Gay and Stuart Hall. London, UK: Sage.

—— (1996b). *Performing rites: On the value of popular music.* Oxford, UK: Oxford University Press.

—— (2002). 'Music and everyday life'. In: *Critical Quarterly* 44 (1), pp 35–48.

—— (2004a). 'What is bad music?' In: *Bad music: the music we love to hate*. Ed. by Christopher Washburne and Maiken Derno. New York, NY: Routledge.

—— (2004b). 'Why does music make people so cross?' In: *Nordic Journal of Music Therapy* 13 (1), pp 64–69.

Fultz, Daniel D. (2010). *Style matters: Worship preferences of university students regarding the use of music and technology*. PhD thesis. Bowling Green, OH: Bowling Green State University.

Garces-Foley, K. (2007). 'New opportunities and new values: The emergence of the multicultural church'. In: *The Annals of the American Academy of Political and Social Science* 612 (1), pp 209–224.

Garces-Foley, Kathleen (2007). *Crossing the ethnic divide: The multi ethnic church on a mission*. Oxford, UK: Oxford Scholarship Online.

Gebesmair, Andreas and Alfred Smudits (2001). *Global repertoires: Popular music within and beyond the transnational music industry*. Aldershot, UK: Ashgate.

Geertz, Clifford (2000). *The interpretation of cultures: Selected essays*. New York, NY: Basic Books.

Gelder, Ken (2005). *The subcultures reader*. London, UK: Routledge.

Gerstin, Julian (1998). 'Reputation in a musical scene: The everyday context of connections between music, identity and politics'. In: *Ethnomusicology* 42, pp 385–414.

Gervais, Christine L. M. (2012). 'Canadian women religious' negotiation of feminism and Catholicism'. In: *Sociology of Religion*.

Giddens, Anthony (1991). *Modernity and self-identity: Self and society in the late modern age*. Cambridge, CA: Polity Press.

Glanzer, Perry (2003). 'Christ and the heavy metal subculture'. In: *Journal of Religion and Society* 5, pp 1–16.

Glasser, Ruth (1990). 'Paradoxical ethnicity: Puerto Rican musicians in post-World War I New York City'. In: *Latin American Music Review/Revista de Música Latinoamericana* 11 (1), pp 63–72.

Glazer, Nathan (1997). *We are all multiculturalists now*. Boston, MA: Harvard University Press.

Godwin, Joscelyn (1996). 'Taste, snobbery and spiritual style in music'. In: *Contemporary Music Review* 14 (3–4), pp 47–53.

Goffman, Erving (1959). *The presentation of self in everyday life*. Garden City, NY: Doubleday.

Gormly, Eric (2003). 'Evangelizing through appropriation: Toward a cultural theory on the growth of contemporary Christian music'. In: *Journal of Media and Religion* 2 (4), pp 251–265.

Gould, Carol (2010). 'Do cosmopolitan ethics and cosmopolitan democracy imply each other?' In: *Questioning cosmopolitanism*. Ed. by Stan van Hooft and Wim. Vandekerckhove. Dordrecht, New York, NY: Springer.

Gracyk, Theodore (1999). 'Valuing and evaluating popular music'. In: *The Journal of Aesthetics and Art Criticism* 57, pp 205–220.

Green, Emily C. (2011). 'Authenticating identity: The quest for personal validation through authenticity in music'. In: *Vanderbilt Undergraduate Research Journal* 7.

Green, Leslie (2003). 'Pluralism, social conflict and tolerance'. In: *Pluralism and law: proceedings of the 20th IVR World Congress, Amsterdam, 2001*. Ed. by Arend. Soeteman. Stuttgart, Germany: Kluwer Academic.

Green, Lucy (2003). 'Music education, cultural capital and social group identity'. In: *The cultural study of music: a critical introduction*. Ed. by Martin Clayton, Trevor Herbert and Richard Middleton. New York, NY: Routledge.

—— (2005). 'Musical meaning and social reproduction: A case for retrieving autonomy'. In: *Educational Philosophy and Theory* 37 (1), pp 77–92.

Greig, Pete and Andy Freeman (2011). *Punk monk: New monasticism and the ancient art of breathing*. Ventura, CA: Gospel Light Publications.

Greig, Pete and Dave Roberts (2003). *Red moon rising*. Lake Mary, FL: Survivor Kingsway.

Grimes, Ronald (1982). *Beginnings in ritual studies*. Washington, DC: University Press of America.

Grimm, Erica (2012). *The aesthetics of attentiveness: A philosophy for artists and educators*. PhD thesis. Burnaby, British Columbia: Simon Fraser University.

Grossman, Alan and Áine O'Brien (2006). 'Kurdish lyrical protest: The terrain of acoustic migration'. In: *Journal of Ethnic and Migration Studies* 32 (2), pp 271–289.

Guarino, Maria (2012). '"So, they aren't always this angelic?" an ethnographic study on being and becoming an All Saints choirboy'. In: *Ethnomusicology Review 16*.

Guest, Mathew (2002). 'Alternative worship: Challenging the boundaries of the Christian faith'. In: *Theorizing faith: The insider/outsider problem in the study of ritual*. Ed. by Elisabeth Arweck and Martin Stringer. Birmingham, UK: University of Birmingham Press, pp 35–56.

—— (2004). '"Friendship, fellowship and acceptance": The public discourse of a thriving Evangelical congregation'. In: *Congregational studies in the UK: Christianity in a post-Christian context*. Ed. by Mathew Guest, Karin Tusting and Linda Woodhead. Aldershot, UK: Ashgate.

—— (2007). 'Reconceiving the congregation as a source of authenticity'. In: *Redefining Christian Britain: post-1945 perspectives*. Ed. by Jane Garnett et al. London, UK: SCM Press.

—— (2010). 'In search of spiritual capital: The spiritual as a cultural resource'. In: *A sociology of spirituality*. Ed. by Kieran Flanagan and Peter C. Jupp. Aldershot, UK: Ashgate.

Guest, Mathew and Steve Taylor (2006). 'The post-Evangelical emerging church: Innovations in New Zealand and the UK'. In: *International Journal for the Study of the Christian Church* 6 (1), pp 49–64.

Guest, Mathew, Karin Tusting and Linda Woodhead (2004). *Congregational studies in the UK: Christianity in a post-Christian context*. Aldershot, UK: Ashgate.

Habermas, Jürgen (1984). 'Habermas: Questions and counterquestions'. In: *Praxis International* 3, pp 229–249.

—— (1989). *The structural transformation of the public sphere: An inquiry into a category of bourgeois society*. Cambridge, MA: MIT Press.

—— (1990a). 'Jürgen Habermas: Morality, society and ethics an interview with Torben Hviid Nielsen'. In: *Acta Sociologica* 33 (2), pp 93–114.

—— (1990b). *Moral consciousness and communicative action*. Cambridge, MA: MIT Press.

—— (1993). *Justification and application: Remarks on discourse ethics*. Cambridge, MA: MIT Press.

—— (1995). 'Reconciliation through the public use of reason: Remarks on John Rawls's political liberalism'. In: *The Journal of Philosophy* 92 (3), pp 109–131.

—— (1996). *Between facts and norms: Contributions to a discourse theory of law and democracy*. Cambridge, MA: MIT Press.

—— (2006). 'Religion in the public sphere'. In: *European Journal of Philosophy* 14 (1), pp 1–25.

Hackley, Chris and Arthur J. Kover (2007). 'The trouble with creatives: Negotiating creative identity in advertising agencies'. In: *International Journal of Advertising* 26 (1), pp 63–78.

Hall, Patrick C. (2012). *The influence of prayer and the IHOP movement on the lives of today's Christian youth: A qualitative investigation*. PhD thesis. Deerfield, CA: San Diego State University.

Hall, Stuart (1996). 'Who needs identity?' In: *Questions of cultural identity*. Ed. by Paul Du Gay and Stuart Hall. London, UK: Sage.

—— (2002). 'Political belonging in a world of multiple identities'. In: *Conceiving cosmopolitanism: theory, context and practice*. Ed. by Steven Vertovec and Robin Cohen. Oxford, UK: Oxford University Press.

Hall, Stuart, David Held and Anthony G. McGrew (1992). *Modernity and its futures*. Cambridge, UK: Polity Press in association with the Open University.

Hannerz, Ulf (1990). 'Cosmopolitans and locals in world culture'. In: *Theory, culture and society* 7 (2), pp 237–251.

—— (1996). *Transnational connections: Culture, people, places*. London, UK: Routledge.

Hargreaves, David J. and Adrian C. North (1997). *The social psychology of music*. Oxford, UK: Oxford University Press.

—— (1999). 'The functions of music in everyday life: Redefining the social in music psychology'. In: *Psychology of Music* 27 (1), pp 71–83.

Harnish, David (2013). 'The hybrid music and cosmopolitan scene of Balinese guitarist I Wayan Balawan'. In: *Ethnomusicology Forum* 22 (2), pp 188–209.

Harrington, Elisabeth Brooke and Gary Alan Fine (2000). 'Opening the "black box": Small groups and 21st century sociology'. In: *Social Psychology Quarterly* 63 (4), pp 312–323.

Harrison, Klisala (2012). 'Epistemologies of applied ethnomusicology'. In: *Ethnomusicology* 56 (3), pp 505–529.

Hartje, Gesa F. (2009). 'Keeping in tune with the times – praise & worship music as today's Evangelical hymnody in North America'. In: *Dialog* 48 (4), pp 364–373.

Hauerwas, Stanley and Samuel Wells (2004). *The Blackwell companion to Christian ethics*. Malden, MA: Blackwell.

Hawn, Michael (2007). 'Christian song in a global church: The role of musical structure in community formation'. In: *International Journal of Community Music* 2 (1), pp 57–70.

Hebdige, Dick (1979). *Subculture: The meaning of style.* London, UK: Methuen.

Heelas, Paul (2005). *The spiritual revolution: Why religion is giving way to spirituality.* Malden, MA: Blackwell Publishing.

Hellberg, Jan (2010). 'To worship God in our way: Disaffection and localisation in the music culture of the Evangelical Lutheran Church in Namibia'. In: *Journal of Musical Arts in Africa* 7 (1), pp 17–50.

Hellier-Tinoco, Ruth (2003). 'Experiencing people: Relationships, responsibility and reciprocity'. In: *British Journal of Ethnomusicology* 12, pp 19–34.

Hemetek, Ursula (2006). 'Applied ethnomusicology in the process of the political recognition of a minority: A case study of the Austrian Roma'. In: *Yearbook for Traditional Music* 38, pp 35–57.

—— (2010a) *Applied ethnomusicology as an intercultural tool: Some experiences from the last 25 years of minority research in Austria.* Proceedings of cAIR10, the first Conference on Applied Interculturality Research, Graz, Austria, 7–10 April 2010.

—— (2010b). 'Unexpected musical worlds of Vienna: Immigration and music'. In: *Migrações Journal* 7, pp 115–138.

Hendershot, Heather (2004). *Shaking the world for Jesus: Media and conservative Evangelical culture.* Chicago, IL: University of Chicago Press.

Hendrickson, Marion Lars (2005). *Musica Christi: A Lutheran aesthetic.* New York, NY: Peter Lang.

Hennion, Antoine (2001). 'Music lovers. Taste as performance'. In: *Theory, Culture & Society* 18 (5), pp 1–22.

—— (2002). 'Music and mediation: Towards a new sociology of music'. In: *The cultural study of music: A critical introduction.* Ed. by Martin Clayton, Trevor Herbert and Richard Middleton. London, UK: Routledge, pp 80–91.

—— (2005). 'Pragmatics of taste'. In: *The Blackwell companion to the sociology of culture.* Ed. by Mark Jacobs and Nancy Hanrahan. Oxford, UK: Wiley-Blackwell, pp 131–144.

Herbert, Ruth (2011). 'Reconsidering music and trance: Cross-cultural differences and cross-disciplinary perspectives'. In: *Ethnomusicology Forum* 20 (2), pp 201–227.

Herl, Joseph (2004). *Worship wars in early Lutheranism: Choir, congregation, and three centuries of conflict.* New York, NY: Oxford University Press.

Hesmondhalgh, David (2005). 'Subculture, scenes or tribes? None of the above'. In: *Journal of Youth Studies*, pp 21–40.

—— (2007). 'Audiences and everyday aesthetics talking about good and bad music'. In: *European Journal of Cultural Studies* 10 (4), pp 507–527.

—— (2008). 'Towards a critical understanding of music, emotion and self-identity'. In: *Consumption, markets and culture* 11 (4), pp 329–343.

—— (2010). 'Normativity and social justice in the analysis of creative labour'. In: *Journal for Cultural Research* 14 (3), pp 231–249.

—— (2013). *Why music matters.* Chichester, UK: Wiley-Blackwell.

Higgins, Kathleen Marie (2011). *The music of our lives.* Lanham, MD: Lexington Books.

Hirabayashi, Eri (2007). 'Identity, roles and practice in ritual music'. In: *International Journal of Community Music* 2 (1), pp 39–56.

Hirschkind, Charles (2006). *The ethical soundscape: Cassette sermons and Islamic counterpublics*. New York, NY: Columbia University Press.

Hollinger, David (2001). 'Not universalists, not pluralists: The new cosmopolitans find their own way'. In: *Constellations* 8 (2), pp 236–248.

Holsinger, Bruce W. (2001). *Music, body and desire in medieval culture: Hildegard of Bingen to Chaucer*. Stanford, CA: Stanford University Press.

Holt, Douglas B. (1997a). 'Distinction in America? Recovering Bourdieu's theory of tastes from its critics'. In: *Poetics* 25 (2), pp 93–120.

—— (1997b). 'Post structuralist lifestyle analysis: Conceptualizing the social patterning of consumption in postmodernity'. In: *Journal of Consumer Research*, pp 326–350.

Holt, Fabian (2013). *Musical performance and the changing city*. London, UK: Routledge.

Hood, Mantle (1982). *The ethnomusicologist*. Kent, OH: Kent State University Press.

Hoover, Stewart M. and Nabil Echchaibi (2013). 'The "third spaces" of digital religion.' In: *Working paper 1.0 'finding religion in the media: work in progress on the third spaces of digital religion'*.

Howard, Jay R. and John M. Streck (1999). *Apostles of rock: The splintered world of contemporary Christian music*. Lexington, KY: University Press of Kentucky.

Hughes, Kathleen (1991). 'Liturgy and justice: An intrinsic relationship'. In: *Living no longer for ourselves: liturgy and justice in the nineties*. Ed. by Mark R Francis and Kathleen Hughes. Collegeville, MN: Liturgical Press.

Hunt, Stephen (1995). 'The Anglican Wimberites'. In: *Pneuma* 17 (1–2), pp 1–2.

—— (2000). 'All things bright and beautiful: The rise of the Anglican Charismatic Church'. In: *Journal of Empirical Theology* 13 (1), pp 16–34.

—— (2003). 'The Alpha programme: Some tentative observations of state of the art evangelism in the UK'. In: *Journal of Contemporary Religion* 18 (1), pp 77–93.

—— (2008). 'The emerging church and its discontents'. In: *Journal of Beliefs & Values* 29 (3), pp 287–296.

Huq, Rupa (2006). *Beyond subculture: Pop, youth and identity in a postcolonial world*. London, UK: Routledge.

Ingalls, Monique M. (2008). *Awesome in this place: Sound, space, and identity in contemporary North American Evangelical worship*. PhD thesis. Philadelphia, PA: University of Pennsylvania.

—— (2011). 'Singing heaven down to earth: Spiritual journeys, eschatological sounds, and community formation in Evangelical conference worship'. In: *Ethnomusicology* 55 (2), pp 255–279.

—— (2012a). 'Contemporary worship music'. In: *Continuum encyclopedia of popular music of the world volume 8: genres: North America*. Ed. by John Shepherd and David Horn. London, UK: Bloomsbury Publishing, pp 147–152.

—— (2012b). 'Singing praise in the streets: Performing Canadian Christianity through public worship in Toronto's Jesus in the city parade'. In: *Culture and Religion* 13 (3), pp 337–359.

—— (2013). 'Transnational connections, musical meaning, and the 1990s "British invasion" of North American Evangelical worship music'. In: *The Oxford Handbook of Music and World Christianities*. Ed. by Suzel Reily and Jonathan Dueck. Oxford, UK: Oxford University Press.

—— (Forthcoming). 'International gospel and christian popular music'. In: *Encyclopedia of popular music of the world, part III: genres, international volume*.

Ingalls, Monique M., Carolyn Landau and Tom Wagner (2013). *Christian congregational music: Performance, identity, and experience*. Aldershot, UK: Ashgate.

Irvin, Dale T. (1994). 'Contextualization and catholicity: Looking anew for the unity of the faith'. In: *Studia Theologica* 48 (2), pp 83–96.

Jay, Gregory (1994). 'Taking multiculturalism personally: Ethnos and ethos in the classroom'. In: *American Literary History*, pp 613–632.

Jenkins, Richard (2008). *Social identity*. London, UK: Routledge.

Jennings, Mark (2008). '"Won't you break free?" an ethnography of music and the divine-human encounter at an Australian Pentecostal church'. In: *Culture and Religion* 9 (2), pp 161–174.

Johnson, Birgitta Joelisa (2008). 'Oh, for a thousand tongues to sing' music and worship in African American megachurches of Los Angeles, California'. PhD thesis. Los Angeles, CA: University of California.

Johnson, SueAnn (2009). 'How is the body of Christ a meaningful symbol for the contemporary Christian community?' In: *Feminist Theology* 17 (2), pp 210–228.

Johnson, Terri Lynne (2006). *Worship styles, music and social identity: A communication study*. PhD thesis. Cleveland, OH: Cleveland State University.

Jones, Ian and Peter Webster (2006). 'The theological problem of popular music for worship in contemporary Christianity'. In: *Crucible*, pp 9 16.

—— (2007). 'Expressions of authenticity: Music for worship'. In: *Redefining Christian Britain. Post 1945 perspectives*. Ed. by Jane Garnett *et al*. London, UK: SCM.

Joppke, Christian (1996). 'Multiculturalism and immigration: A comparison of the United States, Germany, and Great Britain'. In: *Theory and Society* 25(4), pp 449–500.

—— (2004). 'The retreat of multiculturalism in the liberal state: Theory and policy'. In: *The British Journal of Sociology* 55 (2), pp 237–257.

Joseph, Mark (2003). *Faith, God & rock 'n' roll*. London, UK: Sanctuary.

Keil, Charles and Steven Feld (1994). *Music grooves: Essays and dialogues*. Chicago, IL: University of Chicago Press.

Kemp, Anthony E. (1997). 'Individual differences in musical behaviour'. In: *The social psychology of music*. Ed. by David J Hargreaves and Adrian C North. Oxford, UK: Oxford University Press.

Key, Matthew (2012). *Singing [church]*, https://sites.google.com/site/oxfordprayer room/news/singingchurch.

Kirby, Erika L. et al (2006). 'The Jesuit difference (?): Narratives of negotiating spiritual values and secular practices'. In: *Communication Studies* 57 (1), pp 87–105.

Knapp, D. (2004). 'The portrayal of pastoral authority in worship'. In: *Liturgy* 19 (4), pp 45–45.

Komitee, Shana (n.d.) *A student's guide to performance studies*, https://writingproject. fas.harvard.edu/files/hwp/files/peformance_studies.pdf?m=137045427.

Kong, Lily (2001). 'Religion and technology: Refiguring place, space, identity and community'. In: *Area* 33 (4), pp 404–413.

Koopman, Constantijn and Stephen Davies (2001). 'Musical meaning in a broader perspective'. In: *The Journal of Aesthetics and Art Criticism* 59 (3), pp 261–273.

Koskoff, Ellen (1987). *Women and music in cross-cultural perspective*. New York, NY: Greenwood.

Kramer, Lawrence (2003). 'Musicology and meaning'. In: *The Musical Times* 144, pp 6–12.

—— (2004). 'Music, metaphor and metaphysics'. In: *The Musical Times* 145 (1888), pp 5–18.

Kraus, Rachel (2010). 'They danced in the bible: Identity integration among Christian women who belly dance'. In: *Sociology of Religion* 71 (4), pp 457–482.

Krims, Adam (2007). *Music and urban geography*. New York, NY: Routledge.

Kruse, Holly (1993). 'Subcultural identity in alternative music culture'. In: *Popular Music* 12 (1), pp 33–41.

Ku, Agnes S. (2008). 'Revisiting the notion of "public" in Habermas's theory – toward a theory of politics of public credibility'. In: *Sociological Theory* 18 (2), pp 216–240.

Kunst, Jaap (1950). *Musicologica; a study of the nature of ethnomusicology, its problems, methods, and representative personalities*. Amsterdam, Netherlands: Indisch Instituut.

Kwon, Yoo Jin and Kyoung-Nan Kwon (2013). 'Cultural omnivores' consumption: Strategic and inclusively exclusive'. In: *International Journal of Marketing Studies* 5 (1), pp 118–127.

Lahire, Bernard (2008). 'The individual and the mixing of genres: Cultural dissonance and self-distinction'. In: *Poetics* 36 (2), pp 166–188.

Lamont, Michèle and Virag Molnar (2002). 'The study of boundaries in the social sciences'. In: *Annual Review of Sociology* 28, pp 167–195.

Langlois, Tony (1996). 'The local and global in North African popular music'. In: *Popular Music* 15 (3), Middle East Issue, pp 259–273.

Lassiter, Luke Eric (2001). '"From here on, I will be praying to you": Indian churches, Kiowa hymns, and native American Christianity in southwestern Oklahoma'. In: *Ethnomusicology* 45 (2), pp 338–352.

Layzell, Martyn (2006). *Lost in wonder (CD recording)*. Eastbourne, UK: Survivor.

Leaver, Robin A. (2007). *Luther's liturgical music: Principles and implications*. Grand Rapids, MI: WB Eerdmans.

Lee, Sung Ho (2006). *Building bridges through cross-cultural experience*. PhD thesis. Madison, NJ: Drew University.

Lindenbaum, John (2012). 'The pastoral role of contemporary Christian music: The spiritualization of everyday life in a suburban Evangelical megachurch'. In: *Social & Cultural Geography* 13 (1), pp 69–88.

Lizardo, Omar (2004). 'The cognitive origins of Bourdieu's habitus'. In: *Journal for the Theory of Social Behaviour* 34 (4), pp 375–401.

Lizardo, Omar and Sara Skiles (2012). 'Reconceptualizing and theorizing "omnivorousness" genetic and relational mechanisms'. In: *Sociological Theory* 30 (4), pp 263–282.

Looseley, David (2006). 'Antoine Hennion and the sociology of music'. In: *International Journal of Cultural Policy* 12 (3), pp 341–354.

Luhrmann, Tanya M. (2004). 'Metakinesis: How God becomes intimate in contemporary US Christianity'. In: *American Anthropologist* 106 (3), pp 518–528.

—— (2006). *Learning religion at the Vineyard: Prayer, discernment and participation in the divine.*

Lynch, Gordon (2006). 'The role of popular music in the construction of alternative spiritual identities and ideologies'. In: *Journal for the Scientific Study of Religion* 45 (4), pp 481–488.

Lysaught, M. Therese (1998). *Inritualed bodies: Ritual studies and liturgical ethics.* Atlanta, CA: Society of Christian Ethics.

MacDonald, Raymond A. R., David J. Hargreaves and Dorothy Miell (2002). *Musical identities.* Oxford, UK: Oxford University Press.

Manuel, Peter (1988). *Popular musics of the non-western world: An introductory survey.* Oxford, UK: Oxford University Press.

Marti, Gerardo (2005). *A mosaic of believers: Diversity and innovation in a multiethnic church.* Bloomington, IN: Indiana University Press.

—— (2012). *Worship across the racial divide: Religious music and the multiracial congregation.* Oxford, UK: Oxford University Press.

Martin, Nancy J. (2007). Small groups in big churches. PhD thesis. Tucson, AZ: University of Arizona.

Mauthner, Melanie L. (2002). *Ethics in qualitative research.* London, UK: SAGE.

McCarthy, Thomas (1989). 'Introduction'. In: *The structural transformation of the public sphere: an inquiry into a category of bourgeois society.* Cambridge, MA: MIT Press.

McClary, Susan and Robert Walser (1994). 'Theorizing the body in African-American music'. In: *Black Music Research Journal* 14, pp 75–84.

McClendon, David Michael (2007). *Plugging into worship: How contemporary Christian music is impacting church musicians.* PhD thesis. Williamsburg, VA: College of William and Mary.

McCollum, Jonathan Ray (2004). *Music, ritual and diasporic identity: A case study of the Armenian Apostolic Church.* PhD thesis. Baltimore, MD: University of Maryland.

McGann, Mary (2005). *A precious fountain: Music in the worship of an African American Catholic community (Virgil Michel).* Blackrock, Ireland: Columba Press.

—— (2010). 'Liturgical musical ethnography. Challenges and promise'. In: *Jaarboek voor Liturgie-Onderzoek* 26.

McKenna, Bernard (2004). 'Critical discourse studies: Where to from here?' In: *Critical Discourse Studies* 1 (1), pp 9–39.

McKinnon, James W. (1987). *Music in early Christian literature.* Cambridge, UK: Cambridge University Press.

—— (1998). *The temple, the church fathers and early western chant.* Aldershot, UK: Ashgate.

McLean, Janice (2007). 'Make a joyful noise unto the Lord: Music and songs within Pentecostal West Indian immigrant religious communities in diaspora'. In: *Studies in World Christianity* 13(2),pp 127–141.

McLeod, Kembrew (1999). 'Authenticity within hip-hop and other cultures threatened with assimilation'. In: *Journal of Communication* 49 (4), pp 134–150.

Meier, Leslie M. (2008). 'In excess? Body genres, "bad" music, and the judgment of audiences'. In: *Journal of Popular Music Studies* 20 (3), pp 240–260.

Merriam, Alan P. (1964). *The anthropology of music*. Evanston, IL: Northwestern University Press.

Meskell, Lynn and Peter Pels (2005). *Embedding ethics*. Oxford, UK: Berg.

Meyer, Birgit (2009). *Aesthetic formations: Media, religion, and the senses*. Basingstoke, UK: Palgrave Macmillan.

Meyer, Rachel S. (2000). 'Fluid subjectivities: Intertextuality and women's narrative performance in north India'. In: *Journal of American Folklore*, pp 144–163.

Miller, Donald E. (1997). *Reinventing American Protestantism: Christianity in the new millennium*. Berkeley, CA: University of California Press.

Miller-McLemore, Bonnie J. (2012). *The Wiley-Blackwell companion to practical theology*. Malden, MA: Wiley-Blackwell.

Moberg, Marcus (2007). 'The transnational Christian metal scene expressing alternative Christian identity through a form of popular music'. In: *INTER: A European Cultural Studies Conference in Sweden*. Linköping University Electronic Press, pp 423–432.

Moje, Elizabeth Birr, Kathryn Mcintosh Ciechanowski et al (2004). 'Working toward third space in content area literacy: An examination of everyday funds of knowledge and discourse.' In: *Reading Research Quarterly* 39 (1), pp 38–70.

Moore, Bruce (2010). *Metal missionaries*. Gloucester, UK: Wide Margin.

Muggleton, David and Rupert Weinzierl (2003). *The post-subcultures reader*. Oxford, UK: Berg.

Müller, B. A. (2006). 'The role of worship and ethics on the road towards reconciliation'. In: *Verbum et Ecclesia* 27 (2), pp 641–663.

Nekola, Anna E. (2009). *Between this world and the next: The musical "worship wars" and Evangelical ideology in the United States 1960–2005*. PhD thesis. Madison, WI: University of Wisconsin-Madison.

—— (2011). 'US Evangelicals and the redefinition of worship music'. In: *Mediating faiths: religion and socio-cultural change in the twenty-first century*. Ed. by Michael Bailey and Guy Redden. Aldershot, UK: Ashgate.

—— (2013). '"More than just a music": Conservative Christian anti-rock discourse and the US culture wars'. In: *Popular Music*.

Nettl, Bruno (1978). *Eight urban musical cultures: Tradition and change*. Urbana, IL: University of Illinois Press.

—— (2005). *The study of ethnomusicology: Thirty-one issues and concepts*. Urbana, IL: University of Illinois Press.

Niebuhr, H. Richard (1952). *Christ and culture*. London, UK: Faber and Faber.

Nieman, James and Roger Haight (2012). 'On the dynamic relation between ecclesiology and congregational studies'. In: *Explorations in ecclesiology and ethnography*. Ed. by Christian Batalden Scharen. Grand Rapids, MI: W. Eerdmans Pub Co.

Noble, Greg (2009). 'Everyday cosmopolitanism and the labour of intercultural community'. In: *Everyday multiculturalism*. Ed. by Amanda Wise and Selvaraj Velayutham. Palgrave London, pp 46–65.

Nooshin, Laudan (2011). 'Hip-hop Tehran: Migrating styles, musical meanings, marginalized voices'. In: *Migrating music*. Ed. by Jason. Toynbee and Byron. Dueck. London, UK: Routledge.

North, Adrian C., David J. Hargreaves and Jon J. Hargreaves (2004). 'Uses of music in everyday life'. In: *Music Perception* 22 (1), pp 41–77.

Ochs, Elinor and Lisa Capps (1996). 'Narrating the self'. In: *Annual Review of Anthropology*, pp 19–43.

O'Grady, Alice (2012). 'Spaces of play: The spatial dimensions of underground club culture and locating the subjunctive'. In: *Dancecult: Journal of Electronic Dance Music Culture* 4 (1), pp 86–106.

Ollivier, Michèle (2008). 'Revisiting distinction'. In: *Journal of Cultural Economy* 1 (3), pp 263–279.

Onyx, Jenny et al (2011). 'Scaling up connections: Everyday cosmopolitanism, complexity theory & social capital'. In: *Cosmopolitan Civil Societies: An Interdisciplinary Journal* 3 (3), pp 47–67.

Oosterbaan, Martijn (2008). 'Spiritual attunement: Pentecostal radio in the soundscape of a favela in Rio de Janeiro'. In: *Social Text* 26 (3), pp 123–145.

Pachucki, Mark A., Sabrina Pendergrass and Michele Lamont (2007). 'Boundary processes: Recent theoretical developments and new contributions'. In: *Poetics* 35 (6), pp 331–351.

Packard, J. and G. Sanders (2013). 'The emerging church as corporatization's line of flight'. In: *Journal of Contemporary Religion*.

Packard, Joshua Ryan (2008). *Organizational structure, religious belief, and resistance: The emerging church*. PhD thesis. Nashville, TN: Vanderbilt University.

Pecora, Vincent P. (1991). 'Ethics, politics, and the middle voice'. In: *Yale French Studies* 79, pp 203–230.

Peirano, Mariza G. S. (1998). 'When anthropology is at home: The different contexts of a single discipline'. In: *Annual review of anthropology*, pp 105–128.

Pelinski, Ramón (2005). 'Embodiment and musical experience'. In: *Trans. Revista Transcultural de Música* 009.

Pelosi, Francesco (2010). *Plato on music, soul and body*. Cambridge, UK: Cambridge University Press.

Penman, Joshua and Judith Becker (2009). 'Religious ecstatics, "deep listeners," and musical emotion'. In: *Empirical Musicology Review* 4 (2), pp 49–70.

Percy, Martyn (1996). *Words, wonders and power: Understanding contemporary Christian fundamentalism and revivalism*. London, UK: SPCK.

—— (2000). 'All things bright and beautiful: A theological response'. In: *Journal of Empirical Theology* 13 (1), pp 35–41.

—— (2003). 'The future of Charismatic Christianity'. In: *Predicting religion: Christian, secular and alternative futures*. Ed. by Grace Davie, Linda Woodhead and Paul Heelas. Aldershot, UK: Ashgate.

—— (2005). *Engaging with contemporary culture: Christianity, theology, and the concrete church*. Aldershot, UK: Ashgate.

Perman, Tony (2011). 'The ethics of Ndau performance: Questioning ethnomusicology's aesthetics'. In: *Journal of Musicological Research* 30 (3), pp 227–252.

—— (2012). 'Sungura in Zimbabwe and the limits of cosmopolitanism'. In: *Ethnomusicology Forum* 21 (3), pp 374–401.

Peterson, Richard A. (2001). 'Globalization and communalization of music in the production perspective'. In: *Global repertoires: Popular music within and beyond the transnational music industry*. Ed. by Andreas Gebesmair and A. Smudits. Aldershot, UK: Ashgate.

Phillips, Elizabeth (2012). 'Charting the "ethnographic turn": Theologians and the study of Christian congregations'. In: *Perspectives on ecclesiology and ethnography (studies in ecclesiology and ethnography)*. Ed. by Pete Ward. Grand Rapids, MI: William B. Eerdmans Publishing Co, pp 95–106.

Pickstock, Catherine (2000). 'Liturgy, art and politics'. In: *Modern Theology* 16 (2), pp 159–180.

Porter, Mark (2013). 'Moving between musical worlds: Worship music, significance and ethics in the lives of contemporary worshippers'. In: *Christian congregational music: Performance, identity, and experience*. Ed. by Monique M. Ingalls, Carolyn Landau and Tom Wagner. Aldershot, UK: Ashgate.

—— (2014). 'The developing field of Christian congregational music studies'. In: *Ecclesial practices* 1 (2), pp 149–166.

Post, Jennifer C. (2006). *Ethnomusicology: A contemporary reader*. New York, NY: Routledge.

Praßl, Franz Karl and Anthony William Ruff (2011). 'Church music scholarship'. In: *Religion Past and Present*. Ed. by Hans Dieter Betz et al. Leiden, Germany: Brill.

Prior, Nick (2011). 'Critique and renewal in the sociology of music: Bourdieu and beyond'. In: *Cultural Sociology* 5 (1), pp 121–138.

—— (2013). 'Bourdieu and the sociology of music consumption: A critical assessment of recent developments'. In: *Sociology Compass* 7 (3), pp 181–193.

Randall, Annie Janeiro (2005). *Music, power, and politics*. New York, NY: Routledge.

Randel, Dan Michael (1992). 'The canons in the musicology toolbox'. In: *Disciplining music: Musicology and its canons*. Ed. by Katherine Bergeron and Philip Vilas Bohlman. Chicago: University of Chicago Press.

Redfield, Robert and Milton B. Singer (1954). 'The cultural role of cities'. In: *Economic Development and Cultural Change* 3 (1), pp 53–73.

Redman, Robb (2002). *The great worship awakening: Singing a new song in the postmodern church*. San Francisco, CA: Jossey-Bass Wiley.

Rees, Robin L. D. (1993). *Weary & ill at ease: A survey of clergy and organists*. Leominster, UK: Gracewing.

Reid, John Edgar Jr (1993). 'The use of Christian rock music by youth group members'. In: *Popular Music and Society* 17 (2), pp 33–45.

Rentfrow, Peter J., Lewis R. Goldberg and Daniel J. Levitin (2011). 'The structure of musical preferences: A five-factor model'. In: *Journal of Personality and Social Psychology* 100 (6), pp 1139–1157.

Rice, Timothy (1987). 'Toward the remodeling of ethnomusicology'. In: *Ethnomusicology* 31 (3), pp 469–488.

—— (2001). 'Reflections on music and meaning: Metaphor, signification and control in the Bulgarian case'. In: *British Journal of Ethnomusicology* 10 (1), pp 19–38.

—— (2003). 'Time, place, and metaphor in musical experience and ethnography'. In: *Ethnomusicology* 47 (2), pp 151–179.

—— (2007). 'Reflections on music and identity in ethnomusicology'. In: *Journal of the Serbian Academy of Sciences and Arts* 7, pp 17–38.

—— (2010). 'Disciplining ethnomusicology: A call for a new approach'. In: *Ethnomusicology* 54 (2), pp 318–325.

Riches, Tanya and Tom Wagner (2012). 'The evolution of Hillsong music: From Australian Pentecostal congregation into global brand'. In: *Australian Journal of Communication* 39 (1), p17.

Rimmer, Mark (2012). 'Beyond omnivores and univores: The promise of a concept of musical habitus'. In: *Cultural Sociology* 6 (3), pp 299–318.

Robbins, Joel (2003). 'What is a Christian? Notes toward an anthropology of Christianity'. In: *Religion* 33 (3), pp 191–199.

—— (2004). 'The globalization of Pentecostal and Charismatic Christianity'. In: *Annual Review of Anthropology*, pp 117–143.

—— (2006). 'Anthropology and theology: An awkward relationship?' In: *Anthropological Quarterly* 79 (2), pp 285–294.

—— (2007). 'Continuity thinking and the problem of Christian culture'. In: *Current Anthropology* 48 (1), pp 5–38.

Robinson, Oliver C. (2013). 'Sampling in interview-based qualitative research: A theoretical and practical guide'. In: *Qualitative Research in Psychology*.

Rodríguez-García, Dan (2010). 'Beyond assimilation and multiculturalism: A critical review of the debate on managing diversity'. In: *Journal of International Migration and Integration* 11 (3), pp 251–271.

Roeland, Johan (2009). *Selfation: Dutch Evangelical youth between subjectivization and subjection*. Amsterdam, Netherlands: Pallas Publications.

Romanowski, William D. (1992). 'Roll over Beethoven, tell Martin Luther the news: American Evangelicals and rock music'. In: *Journal of American Culture* 15 (3), pp 79–88.

Roman-Velazquez, Patria (1999). 'The embodiment of salsa: Musicians, instruments and the performance of a Latin style and identity'. In: *Popular Music* 18 (1), pp 115–132.

Rommen, Timothy (2002). 'Watch out my children': Gospel music and the ethics of style in Trinidad and Tobago. PhD thesis. Chicago, IL: University of Chicago, Department of Music.

—— (2006). 'Protestant vibrations? Reggae, Rastafari, and conscious Evangelicals'. In: *Popular Music* 25 (2), pp 235–263.

—— (2007a). '"Localize it": Rock, cosmopolitanism, and the nation in Trinidad'. In: *Ethnomusicology* 51 (3), pp 371–401.

—— (2007b). *Mek some noise: Gospel music and the ethics of style in Trinidad*. Berkeley, CA: University of California Press.

Rössel, Jörg (2011). 'Cultural capital and the variety of modes of cultural consumption in the opera audience'. In: *The Sociological Quarterly* 52 (1), pp 83–103.

Rouget, Gilbert (1985). *Music and trance: A theory of the relations between music and possession*. Chicago, IL: University of Chicago Press.

Routledge, Paul (1996). 'The third space as critical engagement'. In: *Antipode* 28 (4), pp 399–419.

Russell, Philip A. (1997). 'Musical tastes and society'. In: *The social psychology of music.* Ed. by David J. Hargreaves and Adrian C. North. Oxford, UK: Oxford University Press.

Ryan, Jennifer (2008). *'Can I get a witness?': Soul and salvation in Memphis music.* PhD thesis. Philadelphia, PA: University of Pennsylvania.

Samanta, Soumyajit (2010). 'Negotiating cultural difference'. In: *IASS 2010 Proceedings.*

Savage, Roger W. H. (2009). *Crossing the disciplinary divide: Hermeneutics, ethnomusicology and musicology.* College Music Symposium, http://symposium.music.org/index.php?option=com_k2&view=item&id=9246:crossing-the-disciplinary-divide-hermeneutics-ethnomusicology-and-musicology.

Schaefer, Nancy A. (2012). '"Oh, you didn't think just the devil writes songs, do ya?" music in American Evangelical culture today'. In: *Popular Music and Society* 35 (1), pp 53–70.

Schäfer, Thomas and Peter Sedlmeier (2010). 'What makes us like music? Determinants of music preference.' In: *Psychology of Aesthetics, Creativity, and the Arts* 4 (4), pp 223–234.

Scharen, Christian Batalden (2012). *Explorations in ecclesiology and ethnography.* Grand Rapids, MI: W. Eerdmans Pub. Co.

Scharen, Christian Batalden and Aana Marie Vigen (2011a). *Ethnography as Christian theology and ethics.* London, UK: Continuum.

—— (2011b). 'The ethnographic turn in theology and ethics' In: *Ethnography as Christian theology and ethics.* Ed. by Christian Batalden Scharen and Aana Marie Vigen. London, UK: Continuum.

Scheer, Greg (2007). 'A musical icthus: Praise & worship and Evangelical identity'. In: *International Journal of Community Music* 2 (1), pp 91–98.

Scherer, Andreas Georg and Moritz Patzer (2010). 'Beyond universalism and relativism: Habermas's contribution to discourse ethics and its implications for intercultural ethics and organization theory'. In: *IOU Working Paper Series* 119.

Schilderman, Hans (2007). *Discourse in ritual studies.* Leiden, Germany: Brill.

Schiller, Nina Glick, Tsypylma Darieva and Sandra Gruner-Domic (2011). 'Defining cosmopolitan sociability in a transnational age. An introduction'. In: *Ethnic and Racial Studies* 34 (3), pp 399–418.

Schoen-Nazzaro, Mary B. (1978). 'Plato and Aristotle on the ends of music'. In: *Laval Théologique et Philosophique* 34 (3).

Scholz, Bettina (2011). *Embracing the tensions in cosmopolitanism,* http://www.interdisciplinary.net/wp-content/uploads/2011/02/scholzppaper.pdf.

Schrag, Brian and Neil Coulter (2003). 'Response to "ethnomusicology as tool for the Christian missionary"'. In: *European Meetings in Ethnomusicology* 10, pp 98–108.

Schramm, Adelaida Reyes (1982). 'Explorations in urban ethnomusicology: Hard lessons from the spectacularly ordinary'. In: *Yearbook for Traditional Music* 14, pp 1–14.

Schüler, Sebastian (2008). 'Unmapped territories: Discursive networks and the making of transnational religious landscapes in global Pentecostalism'. In: *PentecoStudies* 7(1), pp 46–62.

—— (2013). "'Sie beten, als ob alles von Gott abhängt, und sie leben, als ob alles von ihnen abhängt" – posttraditionale vergemeinschaftung und religiöse produktivität in einer evangelikalen gebetsbewegung'. In: *Religionshybride*. Ed. by Peter Berger, Klaus Hock and Thomas Klie, pp 243–266.

Scott, Derek B. (2000). *Music, culture, and society: A reader*. Oxford, UK: Oxford University Press.

Seeger, Charles (1977). *Studies in musicology, 1935–1975*. Berkeley, CA: University of California Press.

Selfhout, Maarten H. W. et al (2009). 'The role of music preferences in early adolescents' friendship formation and stability'. In: *Journal of Adolescence* 32 (1), pp 95–107.

Shelemay, Kay Kaufman (2006). *Soundscapes: Exploring music in a changing world*. London, UK: W. W. Norton.

Sherinian, Zoe C. (2007). 'Musical style and the changing social identity of Tamil Christians'. In: *Ethnomusicology* 51 (2), pp 238–280.

Short, Chadwick L. (2006). *Meeting the challenge of diversity: Ministry and mission in a multicultural milieu*. PhD thesis. Wilmore, KY: Asbury Theological Seminary.

Shusterman, Richard (1992). *Pragmatist aesthetics: Living beauty, rethinking art*. Oxford, UK: Blackwell.

Slobin, Mark (2000). 'Multicultural metamethods: Lessons from Visby'. In: *Yearbook for Traditional Music* 32, pp 166–173.

Small, Christopher (1998). *Musicking: The meanings of performing and listening*. Hanover, NH: Wesleyan/University Press of New England.

Smith Brugh, Lorraine (1998). *Responsive contextualization: A liturgical theology for multicultural congregational worship*. PhD thesis. Evanston, IL: Northwestern University.

Smith, Christy Miranda (2005). *Identifying musical worship at the New Harvest Christian Fellowship*. PhD thesis. Johannesburg, South Africa: University of the Witwatersrand.

Smith, Michael Peter (1992). 'Postmodernism, urban ethnography, and the new social space of ethnic identity'. In: *Theory and Society* 21 (4), pp 493–531.

Smith, William (2007). 'Cosmopolitan citizenship virtue, irony and worldliness'. In: *European Journal of Social Theory* 10 (1), pp 37–52.

Solie, Ruth A. (1993). *Musicology and difference: Gender and sexuality in music scholarship*. Berkeley, CA: University of California Press.

Solis, Gabriel and Bruno Nettl (2009). *Musical improvisation: Art, education, and society*. Urbana, IL: University of Illinois Press.

Solomon, Thomas (2005). '"Listening to Istanbul": Imagining place in Turkish rap music'. In: *Studia Musicologica Norvegica* 31, pp 46–67.

Sonnett, John (2004). 'Musical boundaries: Intersections of form and content'. In: *Poetics* 32 (3), pp 247–264.

Spinks, Bryan D. (2010). *The worship mall: Contemporary responses to contemporary culture*. London, UK: SPCK.

St Aldates Church (2003). *Heaven's door (CD recording)*. Oxford, UK: St Aldate's Church.

St Aldates Church (2006). *Stand in awe (CD recording)*. Eastbourne, UK: Kingsway.

—— (2010). *You (CD recording)*. Oxford, UK: St Aldates Church.

—— (n.d.). *Pastorates*. URL: http://www.staldates.org.uk/content.asp?pageRef=292.

Stapley, Kathryn (2006). 'An urban music with rural roots'. In: *Journal of Ethnic and Migration Studies* 32 (2), pp 243–256.

Stengel, Kathrin (2004). 'Ethics as style: Wittgenstein's aesthetic ethics and ethical aesthetics'. In: *Poetics Today* 25 (4), pp 609–625.

Sterne, Jonathan (1997). 'Sounds like the mall of America: Programmed music and the architectonics of commercial space'. In: *Ethnomusicology* 41 (1), pp 22–50.

Steven, James H. S. (2002). *Worship in the spirit: Charismatic worship in the Church of England*. Milton Keynes, UK: Paternoster Press.

Stillman, Amy Ku'uleialoha (1993). 'Prelude to a comparative investigation of Protestant hymnody in Polynesia'. In: *Yearbook for Traditional Music*, pp 89–99.

Stobart, Henry (2008). *The new (ethno)musicologies*. Lanham, MD: Scarecrow Press.

Stock, Jonathan P. J. and Chou Chiener (2008). 'Fieldwork at home'. In: *Shadows in the field: new perspectives for fieldwork in ethnomusicology*. Ed. by Gregory Frederick Barz and Timothy J. Cooley. Oxford, UK: Oxford University Press.

Stoczkowski, Wiktor (2008). 'The 'fourth aim' of anthropology between knowledge and ethics'. In: *Anthropological Theory* 8 (4), pp 345–356.

Stokes, Martin (1994). *Ethnicity, identity and music: The musical construction of place*. Oxford, UK: Berg.

—— (2000). ''Beloved Istanbul': Realism and the transnational imaginary in Turkish popular culture'. In: *Mass Mediations: New Approaches to Popular Culture in the Middle East and Beyond*, pp 224–242.

—— (2004). 'Music and the global order'. In: *Annual Review of Anthropology*, pp 47–72.

—— (2007). 'On musical cosmopolitanism'. The Macalester International Roundtable.

Stowe, David W. (2004). *How sweet the sound: Music in the spiritual lives of Americans*. Cambridge, MA: Harvard University Press.

Straw, Will (2001). 'Scenes and sensibilities'. In: *Public* 22–23.

Stringer, Martin D. (1999). *On the perception of worship: The ethnography of worship in four Christian congregations in Manchester*. Birmingham, UK: University of Birmingham Press.

—— (2005). *A sociological history of Christian worship*. Cambridge, UK: Cambridge University Press.

Sugarman, Jane C. (1989). 'The nightingale and the partridge: Singing and gender among Prespa Albanians'. In: *Ethnomusicology* 33 (2), pp 191–215.

—— (2010). 'Building and teaching theory in ethnomusicology: A response to Rice'. In: *Ethnomusicology* 54 (2), pp 341–344.

Sullivan, Lawrence Eugene (1997). *Enchanting powers: Music in the world's religions*. Cambridge, MA: Distributed by Harvard University Press for the Harvard University Center for the Study of World Religions.

Summit, Jeffrey A. (1993). ''I'm a yankee doodle dandy?': Identity and melody at an American simḥattorah celebration'. In: *Ethnomusicology* 37, pp 41–62.

—— (2000). *The Lord's song in a strange land: Music and identity in contemporary Jewish worship*. Oxford, UK: Oxford University Press.

Swijghuisen Reigersberg, Muriel E. (2011). 'Research ethics, positive and negative impact, and working in an indigenous Australian context'. In: *Ethnomusicology Forum* 20 (2), pp 255–262.

Sylvan, Robin (2002). *Traces of the spirit: The religious dimensions of popular music*. New York, NY: New York University Press.

Taranger, Angela Marie (1996). *A site of meaning: 'Black gospel' in a multicultural church*. PhD thesis. Edmonton, Alberta: University of Alberta.

Tarrant, Mark, Adrian C. North and David J. Hargreaves (2002). 'Youth identity and music'. In: *Musical identities*. Ed. by Raymond A. R. MacDonald, David J. Hargreaves and Dorothy Miell. Oxford, UK: Oxford University Press.

Taylor, Bruce L. (2005). 'Reflections from Seattle'. In: *Liturgy*.

Taylor, Charles (1991). *The ethics of authenticity*. Cambridge, MA: Harvard University Press.

Thompson, Gordon R. (1991). 'The cāraṇs of Gujarat: Caste identity, music, and cultural change'. In: *Ethnomusicology* 35 (3), pp 381–391.

Thornton, Sarah (1995). *Club cultures: Music, media and subcultural capital*. Cambridge, UK: Polity Press.

Tilley, Liz, and Kate Woodthorpe (2011). 'Is it the end for anonymity as we know it? A critical examination of the ethical principle of anonymity in the context of 21st century demands on the qualitative researcher'. In: *Qualitative Research* 11 (2), pp 197–212.

Titon, Jeff Todd (1985). 'Stance, role, and identity in fieldwork among folk Baptists and Pentecostals'. In: *American Music* 3 (1), pp 16–24.

—— (1992). 'Music, the public interest and the practice of ethnomusicology'. In: *Ethnomusicology* 36 (3), pp 315–322.

—— (2009). 'Ecology, phenomenology, and biocultural thinking: A response to Judith Becker'. In: *Ethnomusicology* 53 (3), pp 502–509.

Tsiouslakis, Ioannis (2011). 'Jazz in Athens: frustrated cosmopolitans in a music subculture'. In: *Ethnomusicology Forum* 20 (2), pp 175–199.

Turino, Thomas (1984). 'The urban-mestizo charango tradition in southern Peru: A statement of shifting identity'. In: *Ethnomusicology* 28 (2), pp 253–270.

—— (1988). 'The music of Andean migrants in Lima, Peru: Demographics, social power, and style'. In: *Latin American Music Review* 9 (2).

—— (1990). 'Structure, context, and strategy in musical ethnography'. In: *Ethnomusicology*, pp 399–412.

—— (2000). *Nationalists, cosmopolitans, and popular music in Zimbabwe*. Chicago, IL: University of Chicago Press.

—— (2003). 'Are we global yet? Globalist discourse, cultural formations and the study of Zimbabwean popular music'. In: *British Journal of Ethnomusicology* 12 (2), pp 51–79.

—— (2004). 'Introduction'. In: *Identity and the arts in diaspora communities*. Ed. by Thomas Turino and James Lea Warren, Sterling Heights, MI: Harmonie Park Press.

—— (2008). *Music as social life: The politics of participation*. Chicago, IL: University of Chicago Press.

Turino, Thomas and James Lea (2004). *Identity and the arts in diaspora communities*. Warren, MI: Harmonie Park Press.

Vallier, John (2003a). 'Ethnomusicology as tool for the Christian missionary'. In: *European Meetings in Ethnomusicology* 10, pp 85–97.

—— (2003b). 'Reply to Schrag-Coulter's response'. In: *European Meetings in Ethnomusicology* 10, pp 109–116.

Van Aken, Mauro (2006). 'Dancing belonging: Contesting in the Jordan valley, Jordan'. In: *Journal of Ethnic and Migration Studies* 32 (2), pp 203–222.

Van Eijck, Koen (2001). 'Social differentiation in musical taste patterns'. In: *Social Forces* 79 (3), pp 1163–1185.

Van Hooft, Stan (2007). 'Cosmopolitanism as virtue'. In: *Journal of Global Ethics* 3 (3), pp 303–315.

Van Hooft, Stan and Wim Vandekerckhove (2010). *Questioning cosmopolitanism*. Dordrecht; NY: Springer.

Varatharajan, Nishan (2010). 'Organic zombie & synthetic soul: The unity between preservation & progress in contemporary church music'. In: *Ideas in History* 2 (1).

Vásquez, Manuel A and Marie Friedmann Marquardt (2003). *Globalizing the sacred: Religion across the Americas*. New Brunswick, NJ: Rutgers University Press.

Vega, April (2013). 'Considering genre in the study of liturgical music'. Unpublished paper.

Vertovec, Steven and Robin Cohen (2002). *Conceiving cosmopolitanism: Theory, context and practice*. Oxford, UK: Oxford University Press.

Volk, Terese M. (1998). *Music, education, and multiculturalism: Foundations and principles*. Oxford, UK: Oxford University Press.

Wagner, Tom (2011). *Hearing the "Hillsong sound": City, scene and branding in the religious experience economy*. London: Royal Holloway University of London.

Ward, Pete (1996). *Growing up Evangelical: Youthwork and the making of a subculture*. London, UK: SPCK.

—— (2005a). 'Affective alliance or circuits of power: The production and consumption of contemporary Charismatic worship in Britain'. In: *International Journal of Practical Theology* 9 (1), pp 25–39.

—— (2005b). *Selling worship: How what we sing has changed the church*. Milton Keynes, UK: Paternoster Press.

—— (2012). *Perspectives on ecclesiology and ethnography (studies in ecclesiology and ethnography)*. Grand Rapids, MI: William B. Eerdmans Publishing Co.

Ward, Pete and Paul S. Fiddes (2012). 'Affirming faith at a service of baptism in St Aldates Church, Oxford'. In: *Explorations in ecclesiology and ethnography*. Ed. by Christian Batalden Scharden. Grand Rapids, MI: WB Eerdmans Pub. Co.

Wardle, Huon (2010). 'A cosmopolitan anthropology?' In: *Social Anthropology* 18 (4), pp 381–388.

Warner, Michael (2002). 'Publics and counterpublics'. In: *Public culture* 14 (1), pp 49–90.

Warner, R. Stephen (1997). 'Religion, boundaries, and bridges'. In: *Sociology of Religion*, pp 217–238.

Washburne, Christopher and Maiken Derno (2004a). *Bad music: The music we love to hate*. New York, NY: Routledge.

—— (2004b). 'Introduction'. In: *Bad music: The music we love to hate*. Ed. by Christopher Washburne and Maiken Derno. New York, NY: Routledge.

Waterman, Christopher A. (1990). '"Our tradition is a very modern tradition": Popular music and the construction of pan-Yoruba identity'. In: *Ethnomusicology* 34 (3), pp 367–379.

Watling, Tony (2005). '"Experiencing" Alpha: Finding and embodying the Spirit and being transformed–empowerment and control in a ("Charismatic") Christian worldview'. In: *Journal of Contemporary Religion* 20 (1), pp 91–108.

Wax, Murray L. (1993). 'How culture misdirects multiculturalism'. In: *Anthropology & Education Quarterly* 24 (2), pp 99–115.

Webb, Michael (2011). 'Palang conformity and fulset freedom: Encountering Pentecostalism's "sensational" liturgical forms in the postmissionary church in Lae, Papua New Guinea'. In: *Ethnomusicology* 55 (3), pp 445–472.

Webster, Peter and Ian Jones (2008). 'New music and the 'Evangelical style' in the Church of England, c. 1958–1991'. In: *British Evangelical identities past and present*. Ed. by Mark Smith. Milton Keynes, UK: Paternoster.

Webster-Kogan, Ilana (2014). 'Song style as strategy: nationalism, cosmopolitanism and citizenship in the Idan Raichel Projec's Ethiopian-influenced songs'. In: *Ethnomusicology Forum* 23 (1), pp 27–48.

Weekes, Melinda E. (2005). 'This house, this music: Exploring the interdependent interpretive relationship between the contemporary black church and contemporary gospel music'. In: *Black Music Research Journal* 25 (1/2), pp 43–72.

Werbner, Pnina (2008). *Anthropology and the new cosmopolitanism: Rooted, feminist and vernacular perspectives*. Oxford, UK: Berg.

Westermeyer, Paul (1998). *Te deum: The church and music, a textbook, a reference, a history, an essay*. Minneapolis, MN: Fortress Press.

White, Bob (2008). 'Nationalists, cosmopolitans, and popular music in Zimbabwe'. In: *American Ethnologist* 29 (2), pp 464–465.

Whitfield, Sarah (2010). 'Music: Its expressive power and moral significance'. In: *Musical Offerings* 1 (1).

Widdowson, Henry G. (1995). 'Discourse analysis: A critical view'. In: *Language and Literature* 4 (3), pp 157–172.

Williams, Rowan (2012). *Faith in the public square*. London: Bloomsbury Continuum.

Willis, Jonathan P. (2010). *Church music and Protestantism in post-reformation England: Discourses, sites and identities*. Burlington, VT: Ashgate.

Witvliet, John (2001). 'Training church musicians as pastoral liturgists'. In: *Musicians for the churches: Reflections on vocation and formation*. Ed. by Margot Elsbeth Fassler. New Haven, CT: Institute of Sacred Music at Yale University, pp 17–22.

Wollman, Elizabeth L. (2004). 'Much too loud and not loud enough: Issues involving the reception of staged rock musicals'. In: *Bad music: The music we love to hate*. Ed. by Christopher Washburne and Maiken Derno. New York, NY: Routledge.

Wood, Nichola, Michelle Duffy and Susan J. Smith (2007). 'The art of doing (geographies of) music'. In: *Environment and Planning D* 25 (5).

Woods, Robert and Brian Walrath (2007). *The message in the music: Studying contemporary praise and worship*. Nashville, TN: Abingdon Press.

Woodward, Ian and Michael Emmison (2001). 'From aesthetic principles to collective sentiments: The logics of everyday judgements of taste'. In: *Poetics* 29 (6), pp 295–316.

Wrazen, Louise (1991). 'Traditional music performance among Górale in Canada'. In: *Ethnomusicology* 35 (2), pp 173–193.

Wuthnow, Robert (2007). *After the baby boomers: How twenty- and thirty-somethings are shaping the future of American religion*. Princeton, NJ: Princeton University Press.

Wuthnow, Robert and Stephen Offutt (2008). 'Transnational religious connections'. In: *Sociology of Religion* 69 (2), pp 209–232.

Zon, Bennett (2011). 'Bedazzled by breakthrough: Music theology and the problem of composing music in words'. In: *Journal of the Royal Musical Association* 136 (2), pp 429–435.

Index

24–7 prayer movement 129–35, 141–2, 145–7, 149n3

absolute music 32, 53n1
acoustic guitar 15–16, 19, 30n12
Adnams, Gordon 12n14, 44–5, 66–7, 81n10
aesthetic experience 34, 42–3, 54n11, 56n24, 56n27, 66, 71–2, 74–5, 90, 103n2, 106, 119, 124–5, 136, 148
agency 5, 43, 47, 56n29, 63, 146, 152, 155
ambiguity 106–10
ambivalence 108–10
Ammerman, Nancy 13n15, 29, 47, 55n16, 78–9, 123, 151
analytical framework 52–3
Appiah, Anthony 51, 154–5, 156n2
assimilation 48–50, 57n37
Atkinson, Will 104n6
auditions 22
Augustine 6–7
authenticity 6, 8, 47, 66, 78, 81n11, 97, 135–6, 139, 148, 150n8

Bach, J. C. 77
bad music see value judgements; individual taste
Baloche, Paul 31n23
bands 12n2, 14, 19, 31n13, 36, 54n12, 73, 88, 110, 116
bass guitar 15, 19, 90, 110, 116
Baumann, Gerd 54n8
Baumeister, Andrea T. 55n14
Beck, Ulrich 51
Becker, Penny Edgell 31n26, 57n36
Beethoven's 9th Symphony 77
Bell, Catherine 82
belly dancing 52–3, 57–8n38, 58n41
Berger, Harris M. 30n8

Bethel/Jesus Culture 31n16
Bezalel 103n4
Bhabha, Homi 128, 148
blogs 20, 129–30, 134
blues music 121
Boethius 6
boredom 25, 122
Born, Georgina 47
boundaries 86–8, 95–6, 98–9, 101–3, 144, 150n12, 153 see also eclecticism
    alternative outlets 92–5
    maintaining 89–92
    significance of 84–6
    worship and ritual separation 82–4
Bourdieu, Pierre 43, 56n24, 56n25, 81n4, 95
Bowman, Wayne 42
brass instruments 19, 64 see also individual instruments
bridging 63–7, 70, 76–7, 86–8, 128
Brookes, Amber 143
Brown, Brenton 31n23, 116–17
Brown, Frank Burch 55n19
Bublé, Michael 68
busking 11, 148 see also Word on the Street
Butler, Melvin 12–13n14

Cameron, Helen 54n8
carol services see Christmas services
Chernoff, John Miller 54n11
children's songs 19–20, 162–3
choirs 76, 99, 108
chordsheets 1, 22
Christmas services 3, 121, 145
Chua, Daniel K. 53n1
Church of England 8
classical music 1–2, 27, 64, 85, 115
Cleverly, Charlie 22
Cobussen, Marcel 36–7, 41–2

Cohen, Anthony 101–2
Cohen, Robin 11, 50–1, 154
Coldplay 120
connection, moments of 76–8
consumerism 72, 107
Contemporary Christian Music 6, 12n8, 112
Contemporary Worship Music, definition of 5–6
Contemporary Worship Music, introduction of 32 *see also* worship wars
corporate worship 27, 69, 102, 112
cosmopolitanism 11, 50–2, 153–4, 156n2
creativity 26, 72, 92–3, 97–8, 110–11, 117, 121–2, 136, 139–40, 145

Darnley-Smit, Rachel 31n25
Delanty, Gerard 50, 153
demographics 118–22
DeNora, Tia 46, 56n29
Dillon, Michele 55n15
disco 113
discrimination 114
disruption 138–42, 148–9, 155
distraction 33–4, 110–11
diversity 4, 10, 19, 26, 34, 36, 48, 50, 69, 83, 95–6, 98, 139–41, 147 *see also* multiculturalism
drums 14–16, 19, 110–11, 116, 143
dubstep 27
Dueck, Jonathan 12n14, 60–1

easy listening 6
Echchaibi, Nabil 128
eclecticism, musical 95–101, 137
Edwards, Misty 75
electric guitar 1, 19, 21, 84, 90, 110, 116
Elisha, Omri 149n2
emo music 17
emotions, expression of 67–8
Enlightenment 42
ethics and music 5, 10, 35–44, 51, 54n11, 55n21, 80, 87, 103, 106–7, 113–14, 122, 124
ethnicity 51, 83–4
ethnomusicology 32, 36–7, 50, 54n6
Eucharist Prayer 20
evangelicalism 6–8, 37, 135
Evans, Mark 30n5
evensong 99

Facebook 77, 109
feminism 58n39
festivals 7, 21–2, 28
folk music 17, 33, 92, 121, 126n12, 133, 146

framing 82, 109
freedom in worship 114–16, 143–4, 152–3
Frith, Simon 54n11, 55n22, 106–7
funk 15, 113

Garces-Foley, Kathleen 57n34
gender 35, 50–1, 120–1, 123
gigs 77, 86, 88, 99, 109, 113, 120
Gilbert and Sullivan 65
gospel music 2, 38–9, 90–1, 132
Gould, Carol 153
Green, Leslie 54n10
Greig, Pete 149n3
Guest, Matthew 37, 79, 135, 142, 149–50n7
guitars 30n7, 74, 125n4, 130, 143, 145
    acoustic 15–16, 19, 30n12
    bass 15, 19, 90, 110, 116
    electric 1, 19, 21, 84, 90, 110, 116

Habermas, Jürgen 40, 54n3, 55n15, 55n21, 124
Haight, Roger 156n1
Hall, Stuart 46, 156n2
Hannerz, Ulf 154
Harp and Bowl 136–7, 150n9
Harrison, Klisala 54n6
Heaven's Door 20
Hennion, Antoine 43–4, 56n24, 56n27
Hesmondhalgh, Desmond 34, 46–7, 120, 123–4, 126n13
Higgins, Kathleen Marie 42
Hillsong 15, 20, 30n5
hip hop 112
Holt, Douglas 56n25
Holy Trinity Church (Brompton) 7, 12n4, 97, 126n11
homosexuality 37, 58n39, 114
Hoover, Stewart M. 128
horns 19, 64
house church movement 7, 12n10
house music 27
Howard, Jay R. 7, 49
Hughes, Ted 112
Hungry meetings 141
Hunt, Stephen 57n33
hymns 6, 20, 137, 161–2

identity 4, 10, 23, 39, 44–9, 51–2, 55n16, 61, 70, 96, 121
immigration 49, 67
indie music 86
individual taste 16, 25, 41, 43–4, 56n24, 56n25, 80, 95, 107 *see also* preferences
Ingalls, Monique 5–6, 32, 35, 80n1

interculturalism 49–50
International House of Prayer 31n16, 129, 136–7, 139, 150n9
internet 129 *see also* blogs
Islam 80–1n3
iTunes 21

jazz 2, 15, 81n3, 111–12, 132, 145
Jenkins, Richard 48
Jesus movement 7
Jones, Ian 8, 30n12, 54n2
Joppke, Christian 57n35
Judaism 81n11

key 16, 30n7
keyboards 19
Kingsway label 21
Kramer, Lawrence 53n1
Kraus, Rachel 52–3, 58n38, 58n41

Lahire, Bernard 96
Layzell, Martyn 22, 77
Lindholm, Charles 150n8
Linkin Park 94
liturgy 2, 19–20, 90–1
Looseley, David 56n27
Lost in Wonder 22
lowest common denominator 116–17
lyrics 15, 23, 31n23, 69, 74, 88, 108, 112

MacDonald, Raymond A. R. 55n23
malleability of music 59–63, 78–80
marginal spaces 127–8, 135, 148–9 *see also* prayer room
marketing 83
Marti, Gerardo 12n14, 57n32, 83–4, 103
McCarthy, Thomas 124
McGavran, Donald 57n34
meaning of music 32–3, 36, 41, 46, 59–63, 67, 70, 90–1, 101–2, 123, 128
metaphor, music as 61–2
Middle Eastern music 119
migration, musical 60, 87
modernity 50, 120, 125n10
Moje, Elizabeth Birr 127–8, 135, 147–8
money 145
multiculturalism 1, 36, 38, 48–50, 57n32, 57n37, 78, 83–4
Mumford and Sons 27, 121, 126n12, 132
musical theatre 65–6, 132
musicology 32, 53n1 *see also* ethnomusicology

Nekola, Anna E. 5–8, 11n1, 31n25, 55n22, 61, 72, 83
neo-tribe 46
neutrality of music 32–6
New Wine 15–16, 20–1, 23, 30n6
Niebuhr, H. Richard 7
Nielsen, Nanette 36–7, 41–2
Nieman, James 156n1
Nine O'Clock Service 149–50n7
Noble, Greg 153
Nooshin, Laudan 60, 80n2
normativity 5, 153, 156n1

O'Connor, Sinead 146
omnivore thesis 95, 104n6
ontologies, musical 11, 31n25, 40–1, 43, 62, 111, 125, 135, 143, 147
Onyx, Jenny 51
orchestras 64–5, 68
organ 1–2, 19, 55n19, 90
Oxford Symphony Orchestra 64

Passion 20
Patzer, Moritz 55n14
personal taste *see* individual taste
piano 30n12
piccolo 20
pipe organ *see* organ
popular culture 31n24, 49, 122, 155
popular music 1, 5, 16, 25, 30n12, 32, 45–6, 64, 83, 89–91, 99, 103n3, 106, 108, 113, 115, 118, 121, 125n1, 155
Porter, Mark 12n6
power balance 40–1, 56n24
prayer 16–17, 20, 23, 40, 55n18, 74, 129, 133 *see also* 24–7 prayer movement
prayer events 11, 127 *see also* Sing O Barren Woman
prayer room 31n16, 93, 103n4, 110, 127–43, 149n3
preferences 10, 43–4, 134 *see also* individual taste
Prior, Nick 56n24
priorities 122–5
professionalization of sound 21–2
public discourse 37, 40, 54n6, 54n7, 79, 105, 160

rap music 69, 111
Redman, Matt 112
Rees, Robin L. D. 55n19
Reformation 6
reggae 113
rehearsals 14–17, 40

responsiveness 114–16
Rice, Timothy 45, 56n28, 61–2, 79, 80–1n2–3
Riches, Tanya 30n5
Rimmer, Mark 104n6
Roberts, Dave 149n3
Robinson, Oliver C. 13n17
rock music 1, 6, 17, 19, 21, 54n12, 66, 73–4, 84–5, 108, 113, 116, 119–20 *see also* soft rock
Rodríguez-García, Dan 49
Rommen, Timothy 13n14, 38–40, 54n9, 54n11, 55n21, 90–1
Routldge, Paul 128
Russian Orthodox music 75

saxophones 14–15, 19–20
scene 46
Scherer, Andreas Georg 55n14
Schola Cantorum 76, 99, 108
Scholz, Bettina 153, 156n2
Schüler, Sebastian 135–6, 150n8
secular music 73–5, 77–8, 88, 90, 94, 99, 108–9 *see also* popular music
secularization 34
selfishness 24–5, 34, 45, 55n20
sermons 19, 40
Shusterman, Richard 42–3
Sing O Barren Woman 11, 127, 129–33, 142, 148
singing, congregational 10, 12n14, 44, 58n41, 60, 66–7
Snow Patrol 116
soft rock 2, 16, 19, 25, 30n12, 83, 98, 116, 120
Sonnett, John 95–6
soul, music coming from the 73–6, 113–14
soul music 113
Soul Survivor 22
soundcheck 15, 17
Special, Duke 146
Spinks, Bryan D. 30n12, 150n12
spiritual engagement 25–8, 33, 70–1, 78, 87, 91, 93, 99, 105, 113, 115, 123, 140–1
St Aldates musical values and conceptions 22–30
St Aldates repertoire 157–65
St Aldates worship staff 21–2, 166–7
St Andrews Church (Chorleywood) 7
St George the Martyr Church (Holborn, London) 1–3, 12n2, 12n4, 48

St Michael-le-Belfrey Church (York) 7, 37
Stand in Awe 20–1
Steven, James 7–8, 11–12n1, 12n12
Streck, John M. 7, 49
subcultures 46, 49
subjectivity 43–4
Summit, Jeffrey 81n11
Sunday services 18–19, 22, 60, 62, 65–6, 70–1, 86, 93–4, 96, 105–6, 109–10, 112, 115–16, 127, 132, 137, 139–42, 147–8
Sznaider, Natan 51

taste *see* individual taste
Taylor, Charles 44
third spaces 127–8, 135, 148–9 *see also* prayer room
Trinidadian Full Gospel 38–9, 90–1
trumpets 19
Turin Brakes 145
Turino, Thomas 46, 56–7n30, 61, 65, 81n6, 117

U2 116, 146

value judgements 105–8, 110–14, 116, 122–4
values 10, 36, 41, 75–6, 78–80, 89–91, 120, 122, 148
Vertovec, Steven 11, 50–1, 154
visibility of musicians 66

Wagner, Peter 48
Wagner, Tom 30n5
Wannadies 146
Ward, Pete 7–8, 11n1, 30n12
Warner, R. Stephen 57n37
websites 129
Webster, Peter 8, 30n12, 54n2
weeksweeksweeks 21
Wigley, Pete 14
Williams, Rowan 34
Wollman, Elizabeth 66
Wood, Nichola 30n9
Wooden Chairs 103n4
Word on the Street 11, 127, 142–9
Worship Central 20, 120, 126n11
worship wars 6, 32, 34
written music 22 *see also* chordsheets

You 21
youth culture 7, 46